SHEET PAN SUPPERS*

120 RECIPES FOR SIMPLE, SURPRISING, HANDS-OFF MEALS STRAIGHT FROM THE OVEN

*Plus Breakfasts. Desserts. And Snacks, too!

Molly Gilbert

WORKMAN PUBLISHING · NEW YORK

Library of Congress Cataloging-in-Publication Data is available.

ISBN 978-0-7611-7842-2

Design by Becky Terhune
Photographs on front cover and page 89 by Jim Franco
Front cover food stylist: Suzanne Lenzer
Author photograph (page 296) © Emily Zulauf

Workman books are available at special discounts when purchased in bulk for
premiums and sales promotions as well as for fund-raising or educational use.
Special editions or book excerpts also can be created to specification. For details,
contact the Special Sales Director at the address below, or send an email to
specialmarkets@workman.com.

Workman Publishing Company, Inc.
225 Varick Street
New York, NY 10014-4381
workman.com

WORKMAN is a registered trademark of the Workman Publishing Co., Inc.

Printed in the United States of America

First printing November 2014

10 9 8 7 6 5 4 3 2 1

*For Andi and Bruce, the best parents I know,
with all my love and gratitude.*

Acknowledgments

If you're reading this, then it must be true: I wrote a cookbook. My first cookbook! Hooray! But it wasn't without help (and lots of it). I've got a few people to thank for this thing.

Thank you, thank you:

To you! For reading this book. For cooking from it. For bringing it to life.

To Alyssa (best agent), Kylie (best editor), and the Workman crew: for taking a chance on me, and turning my drawn-out ramblings into . . . shorter ramblings. Because of you, I'm an author.

To my Dunk & Crumble readers: for stopping by every week, and creating a community that I feel so grateful to be a part of.

To Liz and Jen at Liddabit: for giving me my first job in food (and as many candy scraps as I could eat), and for cheering me on from afar.

To my army of fabulous recipe testers: Maggie, Jane, Emily and John, Jenny and Steve, Laura and Peter, Lissie, Katie, Lauren, Casey, Mom and Dad: Without you, this book wouldn't work.

To Mom, Dad, Emily, Casey, and the rest of my (amazing) family: Thanks for being my biggest supporters and best friends, always. Because of you, I'm the luckiest.

To Ben: my favorite dinner date. I love you so much. Thanks for the pep talks, long walks, and big hugs. Without you, life is flavorless.

Contents

Introduction

I love a good one-pot meal. Really, who doesn't? Maximum ease, minimal cleanup, and boom: dinner. But beyond soup, chili, and stew, the one-pot meal quickly loses its legs. It's pretty much all soupy stuff, all the time. And do you really want to eat Dad's "famous" beef chili again? (Sorry, Dad.)

I want the simplicity and ease of a one-pot meal, but I want more. I want the flexibility to get creative. I want an elegant, satisfying, complete meal. And most of all, I want amazing, intense flavor.

Enter the sheet pan. Also known as a "half sheet" or "rimmed baking sheet," the sheet pan is one seriously underrated kitchen tool. Sheet pans combine pure ease (easy prep, easy process, easy cleanup) and interesting, sophisticated flavor. Beef stew? Try rack of lamb with herby breadcrumbs and buttered carrots. All on one pan, in the oven. No mess, no fuss. Boom! Dinner.

"Sheet pan cooking" means roasting, baking, and broiling, three methods that concentrate and intensify flavor. That's just science talking, not me. If you too tune out when science starts to talk, take courage—it's actually pretty simple: The shallow sides of a sheet pan allow your oven's dry, even heat to fully surround that chicken breast (or stuffed eggplant or shrimp or cherry tomato) and draw out its natural sugars, producing a crisp brown exterior and an amazingly tender and juicy interior. So you get succulent chicken, syrupy fruit, crisp potatoes, and tomatoes that taste like dinnertime candy, all by tossing a few fresh things on a pan and then simply shutting your oven door. Constant stirring? Nope. Chance of hot oil jumping up and viciously splattering your wall/stovetop/new silk shirt? No, thanks. Browning meat "in batches"? Who's got time for that when there are guests to entertain, kids to play with, episodes of the latest cable drama to binge-watch?

This book is a roadmap for getting impressively flavorful food on the table simply and enjoyably. Does it use a few shortcuts, like frozen rice and packaged polenta? You bet it does. Do I care about taking time in the kitchen to cook entirely, 100 percent from scratch? Of course I do . . . sometimes.

Other times it's seven o'clock and I've just come home from work and care about nothing but getting a passable meal near my face quickly, instead of throwing my hands up and eating cheese and crackers for dinner.

The truth is, we don't always have time to stand over a pot of polenta for an hour to get it perfectly, authentically smooth. That's okay. I've developed these recipes for real people, taking care to focus on fresh and simple ingredients and the occasional shortcut (see: packaged polenta in a tube), in the hopes of making it easy to pull mouthwatering, sophisticated *full* meals from your oven.

Sound like a plan? Great. Let's get cooking.

A SHEET PAN PRIMER

Why a sheet pan? Good question—one that was never addressed in *Are You There God? It's Me, Margaret.* Which means I had to figure it out on my own. But before we get into the meat of the matter, let's start simpler: What is a sheet pan?

ON SHEET PANS, FOIL & PARCHMENT

A sheet pan, also known as a "rimmed baking sheet," is a flat, rectangular metal pan with a 1-inch lip around the sides. It is often used to bake things like cookies, sheet cakes, scones, or dinner rolls, to name just a few. Sheet pans are usually made out of aluminum or stainless steel, and in a professional kitchen can be as large as 26 by 18 inches, or approximately enormous. For us home cooks, the more readily available 18-by-13-inch variety (professionally called a "half sheet") does perfectly well. Note: Jelly roll pans are the same shape as sheet pans, but smaller and less sturdy; they have a tendency to warp at

high heat, so be sure to use a half sheet for the recipes listed here.

You probably own at least one sheet pan already, perhaps passed down from your mom and a bit brown in the corners, or gleaming and pristine, a gift straight off your wedding registry. Should you be in need, however, rest assured that sheet pans are easy to come by. All kitchen supply stores worth their salt should have them in stock, including places like Bed Bath & Beyond, Williams-Sonoma, and Sur la Table. If you're looking to buy your pans on the cheap, check out online retailers like Overstock. I suggest owning at least two. Probably four. Once you've discovered their magic, you'll find yourself reaching for sheet pans all the time. I've got six (potential overkill), but then, I wrote a book on sheet pan cooking.

Though you can buy sheet pans that have a nonstick coating, I prefer to use ones made from regular aluminum or stainless steel, since nonstick surfaces often don't hold up to daily wear and tear, and can erode and chip off with time, potentially contaminating your food. I assume you'll take your roasted chicken without a side of nonstick coating, thank you. If you're concerned about food sticking to the pan, however—particularly an issue with lean meats, sugary fruit, and baked goods—you can line your pans with aluminum foil or parchment paper. Both are cheap, simple tools that help prevent food from sticking to the pan and also, incidentally, make cleanup an absolute breeze. Both can be found at your local grocery store. I'm also big on olive oil cooking spray; I'll often use it in conjunction with aluminum foil, since roasted meats and vegetables sometimes like to stick to foil.

For fancier nonstickiness, you could think about investing in a Silpat, which is a nonstick silicone baking mat popular with professional bakers (available at most kitchen supply stores). Silpats certainly look cool and can make you feel like a badass baker, but unlike cheaper and easier-to-find parchment and foil, they're not disposable and need to be cleaned after each use. And you can't cut on them—a potential issue if you're making, say, a pizza. We can do without them.

BUT WHAT'S IN IT FOR ME?

Okay. Now we know what we're dealing with. Still, the question remains: Why? Well, aside from all of the science and general geekery that tells us that sheet pan cooking produces flavorful browning and maximum juiciness (both good things, I think you will agree), it's the clean and easy hands-off method that firmly endears the humble sheet pan to my heartstrings. Take, for example, that time I cooked dinner for a new boy (we'll call him Ben). I fancy myself a bit of a chef, so I wanted to make something stunning and delicious to impress him. I also didn't want to spend the whole evening tending to dinner and sweating off my mascara in the process. Sheet pan to the rescue! I put on my cutest yet totally casual and "oh-this-old-thing?" dress and decided on classic roast chicken and mustardy potatoes, simply arranging everything on the pan and sliding it gracefully into the oven. One quick peek inside and a fair amount of wine-induced flirting later, we had ourselves a dinner date. The chicken was moist and crisp-skinned, the potatoes beautifully browned and creamy-centered, the whole thing unfussy yet elegantly impressive. Second date: secured.

I'm not saying that sheet pan cooking can help you get a date, just that it might help you actually enjoy one. Or a dinner party with friends, a weeknight with your kids, a visit with your grandma. Cooking on a sheet pan, letting your oven do most of the work, will put a great meal on the table and give you time to enjoy your life. And isn't that pretty much what it's all about?

SO HOW DO WE DO THIS?

Here's how it works. This book is full of recipes, many of which are complete meals in and of themselves. With these recipes, all you'll need to round out your time at the table is a good loaf of crusty bread or a simple green salad or, if you're positively ravenous, both. Some recipes, like the broiled fajitas, call for a few store-bought add-ons like tortillas, salsa, and sour cream. Others are great paired with a simple starchy side; the Serve-Withs chapter has you covered with a few fast, flavorful recipes for sheet pan rice pilaf, warm garlic bread, herbed polenta, golden drop biscuits, crispy roasted potatoes, and more.

Some recipes in this book are *not* complete meals; rather, they are appetizers or desserts. (No judgment if you want to eat an entire pan of prosciutto-wrapped pears or peach slab pie and call it dinner. I'm just saying.) Though these particular recipes won't yield you an entire meal on their own, they do take advantage of the oven

to maximize simplicity, efficiency, and flavor, all in the name of spending less time fussing about the kitchen and more time with your family and friends. Priorities.

Though all of the recipes here are designed to make the most of the all-mighty sheet pan, you will notice a few minor cheats here and there, like using a ramekin or other small vessel to contain any runny ingredients, or topping a roasted dish with a hard-boiled egg or quickly-whisked yogurt sauce. Not *everything* can be made on a sheet pan, and that's okay. The point is to highlight the sheet pan and end up with a fantastic meal, and if that means topping a dish with some store-bought pesto or cracking open a jar of high-quality tuna or stirring up a fabulous vinaigrette on the side, then that's what we'll do.

LET'S CHAT INGREDIENTS

Before you start cooking, it's important to make sure we're on the same page, ingredient-wise. Because if you use medium-size eggs and I use extra large, someone's going to end up with a weird-looking cake. With that in mind, here's the deal.

Eggs: I always use large eggs. Whenever I call for eggs in a recipe, I'm talking about large ones. It's important to follow suit, especially when we'll be making a dough or batter. In recipes like baked French toast or shakshuka, though, extra large or medium eggs can be substituted without much impact on the final product. The color of the eggs is irrelevant—brown or white, it's all the same, flavor- and nutrition-wise. In fact, the color of an egg corresponds only to the color of the earlobes of the chicken who laid it: white earlobes, white eggs; red earlobes, brown eggs. True story.

Salt: I like to cook with kosher salt, which is flakier and less dense than either plain table salt or fine sea salt. It has a fresh, clean flavor and is free of any added anticaking agents. Since 1 teaspoon of kosher salt weighs less than 1 teaspoon of table salt or fine sea salt, using kosher salt will make your finished dish taste less "salty" in general. Coarse sea salt is a fine substitute, but anytime I call for salt in a recipe, I'm talking about kosher salt (I'm fond of Diamond Crystal brand). If you use a different kind, you'll want to reduce the amount of salt called for to avoid a too-salty finished dish.

Flour: I'll always specify what kind of flour is best for a recipe; usually, it's all-purpose flour. I like to keep it simple when I can, mostly to avoid having to buy and keep five different kinds of flour in the pantry. Still, I'll occasionally call for whole wheat pastry flour, bread flour, or cake flour, which can be crucial to making light, crunchy pizza dough, tender cinnamon rolls, or bouncy, tight-crumbed cakes, respectively. In general, all-purpose flour can be used as a substitute for the others without disastrous effect, though if you don't mind seeking out a few other kinds, I do think it's worth it.

Butter: First, don't be afraid of butter. It's what your great-grandmother ate, and she was fine. Margarine is gross—get rid of that stuff. *Use butter.* To cook and bake, unsalted butter is best. We don't know how much salt is actually in salted butter and it varies from brand to brand anyway, so using unsalted butter takes the unknown out of the equation and lets us control the amount of salt we add to our recipes. Salted butter is good on toast, though. I'll give you that.

Oil: I love olive oil, and use it whenever possible. It's healthy, versatile, and full of flavor. I always use extra virgin olive oil, which is less refined than other kinds, and of a higher quality. There's a range of different extra virgin olive oils out there, though, and I always have two kinds on hand—a relatively cheap bottle for cooking, and a fancier, more expensive bottle (usually one with a really smooth, fruity flavor) for doing things like drizzling on salads and whisking into sauces. The heat of the oven will ruin the nuanced, delicate flavor of the really good stuff, so it's best to save that for uncooked finishing touches. The olive oil I call for here is regular, inexpensive extra virgin, unless otherwise noted.

Besides my beloved olive oil, I'll occasionally call for unfiltered coconut oil (which is healthy and deliciously sweet, and is currently having a moment in the sun) or canola oil, which I use because of its neutral flavor and widespread availability.

YOUR OVEN IS A SNEAK

A quick word on your oven: It's one of a kind. All ovens are different, you see, depending on make, model, vintage, and general oven quirkiness. (That's a real thing.) My advice is: Get to know yours. Does it take extra long to preheat? Is it lying about how hot it's getting in there? Sneaky. What about hot spots, where certain parts of the oven get hotter than others? For instance, the front of my oven gets hotter than the back, so I have to make sure to rotate whatever's cooking in there every so often, so I don't end up burning half a pan of, say, roasted asparagus. Just a hypothetical example that definitely didn't happen to me last week.

The best way to get to know your oven's little quirks is to buy an oven thermometer; these are small, usually stainless-steel, thermometers that sit or hang inside your oven. Then you can see for yourself just how hot your oven gets when you set it to 350°F. You may be surprised to see that your oven runs hot or cold—if this is the case, simply adjust your settings to compensate. For example, if you've set your oven to 350°F but your oven thermometer reads only 300°F, your oven runs cold by 50°F; you can compensate for this by setting it to 400°F when a recipe calls for 350°F.

So the bad news is your oven may be weird. The good news is that yours is not the only one, and the solution is quite cheap—I've seen oven thermometers on sale for as little as three dollars. How's that for sneaky?

Chapter 2

APPETIZERS & SMALL BITES

Sitting down to snack on appetizers with friends is one of life's happiest occurrences—especially if a glass of crisp white wine is involved, at least in my case. Still, I'm not one to spend much time fussing over anything particularly time- or labor-intensive on the appetizer front. My strategy is usually to buy a few good cheeses to set out with some fruit and crackers, maybe some special olives or hummus. If I'm feeling fancy or want to switch things up, or if I've been asked to bring a small bite to a dinner party, I'll put some extra effort into my appetizer routine and whip up a batch of Baked Crab & Corn Cakes with Tangy Aioli (page 20), or maybe a pan of Roasted Figs with Gorgonzola & Honey (page 12). You'll find those foolproof recipes and many more simple, quick, and flavorful apps in this chapter.

So can I come over now? I'll bring kettle kale chips. Just save me a glass of wine, okay?

BAKED BRIE & STRAWBERRIES

SERVES 4 TO 6

Here's an easy one. A quick toss of fresh fruit with flavor-enhancing salt and olive oil, some strategic (or rather, mindless) unwrapping of cheese and crackers, and you're pretty much there, appetizer-wise. A brief jaunt in the oven coaxes the Brie to soften inside and lets our strawberries really shine—they'll hold their shape but yield when eaten, bursting softly with jammy sweetness. Grab a cracker! This one is best served warm.

Feel free to substitute Camembert for the Brie, grapes or pieces of stone fruit for the strawberries.

---

1 wheel (8 ounces) Brie cheese
2 cups (about 1 pint) fresh
    strawberries, hulled and cut in
    half lengthwise

1 tablespoon extra virgin olive oil
¼ teaspoon kosher salt
Crackers and/or crusty bread,
    for serving

LET'S COOK:

1. Preheat the oven to 350°F with a rack in the center position. Line a sheet pan with aluminum foil or parchment paper.

2. Place the Brie in the center of the prepared pan. Place the strawberries in a medium-size bowl, add the olive oil and salt, and toss to combine. Arrange the strawberries around the cheese.

3. Bake until the cheese has softened but not melted through the rind and the strawberries have puckered and released some of their juice, about 20 minutes.

4. Carefully transfer the cheese and fruit to a serving tray, or serve it right on the pan. Enjoy immediately, while everything is still warm, with plenty of crackers and bread alongside.

BAKED FETA & CHUNKY MANGO CHUTNEY

SERVES 8

You can't go wrong with baked cheese appetizers, and warm feta is unexpectedly delicious. It's rich, tangy, and smooth like butter when spread on seeded crackers. Homemade mango chutney is a sweet and hot complement, both bright and warm with roasted fruit, jalapeño pepper, fresh ginger, and plenty of spices. You can serve this marvel straight from the oven, and if the feta cools and starts to firm up during cocktail hour, simply pop the whole pan back into the oven and rewarm the cheese into soft submission.

1 cup finely chopped shallots
1 small jalapeño pepper, stemmed, seeded, and diced
1 red bell pepper, stemmed, seeded, and finely chopped
1 cup finely chopped green apple (skin on is fine)
1 cup golden raisins
¼ cup finely chopped peeled fresh ginger (a 3- to 4-inch piece)
3 large mangoes, peeled, pitted, and cut into ½-inch cubes (4 cups)

½ cup white vinegar
Juice of 1 lime
2½ teaspoons curry powder
½ teaspoon ground cinnamon
⅔ cup sugar
½ teaspoon kosher salt
1 teaspoon garlic powder
1 block (8 ounces) feta cheese
Seeded crackers and/or pita chips, for serving

LET'S COOK:

1. Preheat the oven to 375°F with a rack in the center position.

2. Toss the shallots, jalapeño, bell pepper, apple, raisins, ginger, and mangoes together on a sheet pan to combine. Drizzle with the vinegar and lime juice and sprinkle with the curry powder, cinnamon, sugar, salt, and garlic powder; toss again to coat. Spread out the mixture evenly in a single layer.

3. Cover the pan with foil and bake until the mangoes are quite soft but not turning to mush, about 30 minutes.

4. Remove the pan from the oven and center the block of feta on top of the chutney, spooning a bit of it over the cheese. Bake, uncovered, until most of the liquid has evaporated from the chutney and the feta is soft and tender (it will not melt), an additional 15 minutes.

5. Serve the baked feta and chutney warm, with plenty of crackers and/or pita chips alongside.

DIY OR BUY?
MANGO CHUTNEY
There are some really wonderful condiments out there, especially in the realm of small-batch chutneys and jams. If you find a brand of chutney that you happen to love, by all means, use it here! Just spread 2 to 3 cups on a sheet pan, top with the feta, and bake as directed in Step 4.

ROASTED FIGS WITH GORGONZOLA & HONEY

MAKES 24 PIECES

This is one of those back-pocket recipes, one you'll probably remember even when you've forgotten your grocery list at home, so simple and sweet-salty-satisfying you'll want to make it over and over again. My Grandma Inez tells me she's made it five times in one month, so there you go. She's a grandma! She knows everything.

Depending on where you live, figs will be in season during summer and early fall months. They don't stick around the markets long, though, so grab 'em if you see 'em.

---

12 fresh figs (any color), sliced in
　　half lengthwise
¼ cup extra virgin olive oil
1 teaspoon fresh thyme leaves,
　　chopped

Kosher salt and freshly ground
　　black pepper
¼ cup crumbled Gorgonzola cheese
　　(about 1 ounce)
¼ cup honey

LET'S COOK:

1. Preheat the oven to 375°F with a rack in the center position. Line a sheet pan with parchment paper or aluminum foil.

2. Lay the figs on the pan in a single layer, cut side up. Drizzle the olive oil over the figs, lightly coating each one. Sprinkle each fig with a pinch each of thyme, salt, and pepper.

3. Bake the figs until they look slightly puckery and are beginning to leak their juice, about 15 minutes. Remove the figs from the oven.

4. While the figs are still warm, place a few crumbles of Gorgonzola atop each one and drizzle the honey over the fruit and cheese. Place the figs on a serving platter and enjoy warm or at room temperature.

PEARS IN PROSCIUTTO

MAKES 16 PIECES

"Why do all the figs in Appetizerland get wrapped in prosciutto?" said a lonely pear to himself one day. Luckily for him (and also for me), I'm big into eavesdropping—and decided to champion his cause. After all, pears deserve some prosciutto love, too!

In this showstopping appetizer, warm and yielding pears peek out from inside gorgeously crisped prosciutto, just as lovely and flavorful as their figgy counterparts. And since pears are easier to find (not to mention more affordable) than the elusive fresh fig, you can make these practically any time of year.

---

8 slices (about ¼ pound) prosciutto, cut or ripped in half lengthwise to make 16 strips

2 Bosc pears, unpeeled, cored and cut into 8 wedges each
Freshly ground black pepper

LET'S COOK:

1. Preheat the oven to 400°F with a rack in the upper third. Line a sheet pan with parchment paper.

2. Wrap a strip of prosciutto tightly around each pear wedge, placing the pears skin side down on the prepared pan as you go. Make sure to leave some room between pears on the pan. Sprinkle plenty of ground black pepper atop the prosciutto-wrapped pears.

3. Bake until the prosciutto is firm and crisp and the pears are tender, their tips nicely charred, 15 to 18 minutes.

4. Serve warm, while the pears are meltingly tender inside their crisp shells.

TEACH ME HOW

TO CHOOSE A PEAR

It can be hard to tell if a pear is ripe for eating—especially Bosc pears, which are generally quite firm. Here's the trick: Gently touch the flesh at the pear's neck, just under the stem. If it's rock hard, move on—it's not ready. If it yields slightly, it's ripe and good to eat.

HERBED GOAT CHEESE & ZUCCHINI TART

SERVES 8 TO 10

This is one of my favorite recipes because it lets me get fancy without really getting fancy at all, if you know what I mean. It's a beautiful tart of soft goat cheese and fresh summer zucchini. So elegant! So French! So . . . elegant! Except it takes about three steps to pull together. Using store-bought puff pastry and goat cheese with herbs already mixed in, this impressively gorgeous and wonderfully savory tart is a snap to make. Don't tell anyone, though—this is fancy, remember?

---

1 sheet frozen puff pastry, thawed according to package directions (see Note)
All-purpose flour, for rolling out the dough
½ cup ricotta cheese

1 roll (4 ounces) herbed goat cheese, at room temperature, crumbled
4 or 5 medium-size zucchini
Kosher salt and freshly ground black pepper
1 tablespoon extra virgin olive oil

LET'S COOK:

1. Preheat the oven to 375°F with a rack in the center position. Line a sheet pan with parchment paper.

2. Carefully unfold the puff pastry sheet on a lightly floured work surface. Use a flour-dusted rolling pin to gently roll the puff pastry into a large rectangle roughly 12 by 16 inches; it should be just smaller than your sheet pan.

3. Carefully transfer the puff pastry to the prepared pan. Use a sharp knife to score a ¾-inch–wide border around the puff pastry; do not cut all the way through. Use a fork to prick holes inside the border of the rectangle, poking the dough every inch or so. Place the sheet pan in the fridge or freezer to harden the pastry dough, about 20 minutes.

4. Meanwhile, stir-mash together the ricotta and goat cheeses in a small bowl until fully combined. Set aside.

5. Trim the ends off the zucchini and, using a vegetable peeler, cut them lengthwise into long, thin strips. (Alternatively, you could use a sharp chef's knife to cut them into ¼-inch rounds.) Place the zucchini in a large bowl and sprinkle with a pinch each of salt and pepper. Toss to distribute the seasoning.

6. When the dough is good and chilly, place the pan back on your work surface. Spread the cheese mixture evenly on the pastry, leaving the border bare. Arrange or pile the zucchini atop the cheese, either haphazardly or in your favorite pattern, until the cheese is completely covered. Drizzle the olive oil over the zucchini.

7. Bake the tart until the crust is puffed and deeply browned and the zucchini has softened and browned at the edges, 45 to 50 minutes.

8. Allow the tart to cool slightly before cutting into squares. Serve warm or at room temperature.

NOTE: To thaw puff pastry, remove it from the package, keeping it wrapped in plastic, and leave it in the refrigerator overnight or on your work surface for about 30 minutes. Pastry sheets come folded up like a letter—don't try to unfold them when they're frozen or they'll tear! After the pastry has thawed, you'll be able to easily unfold it. Wrapped well in plastic, thawed pastry will keep for about 2 days in the fridge.

COCONUT SHRIMP WITH SPICY ORANGE DIPPING SAUCE

MAKES ABOUT 25 SHRIMP

This is not the same as that deep-fried coconut shrimp you get on a seaside boardwalk. It's just not. For one thing, it doesn't come with an unavoidable tiny-Speedo sighting (thank goodness). Also, we're taking a walk on the lighter side and baking our shrimp instead of frying them. We still get crisp, juicy coconut-covered shrimp, just without all the grease stains and guilt. Served with a bright, spicy orange dipping sauce, we won't even miss the ocean breeze much.

¼ cup panko breadcrumbs
½ cup unsweetened shredded coconut
Olive oil cooking spray
Grated zest of 1 orange
¼ cup freshly squeezed orange juice
1 teaspoon curry powder
Pinch of crushed red pepper flakes
½ teaspoon garlic powder
1 tablespoon rice vinegar

1 tablespoon honey
2 large egg whites
2 tablespoons all-purpose flour
½ teaspoon kosher salt
½ teaspoon freshly ground
   black pepper
1 pound 21/25 count shrimp, peeled
   and deveined, tails on

LET'S COOK:

1. Preheat the oven to 425°F with a rack in the center position. Line a sheet pan with parchment paper or aluminum foil.

2. Spread the breadcrumbs and coconut evenly on the prepared pan (it's fine if they mix), mist them lightly with cooking spray, and toast in the oven, stirring occasionally, until lightly golden brown, about 5 minutes. Remove the pan from the oven and let the breadcrumb

mixture cool. Transfer the mixture to a medium-size bowl and set it aside. Leave the parchment or foil liner on the sheet pan.

3. To make the dipping sauce, whisk together the orange zest, orange juice, curry powder, red pepper flakes, garlic powder, vinegar, and honey in a small bowl. Pour the sauce into an ovenproof ramekin and place the ramekin on the prepared pan. Set aside.

4. Gently whisk the egg whites in another small bowl until frothy. Set them aside.

5. Add the flour, salt, and pepper to the breadcrumb mixture and whisk gently until evenly combined.

6. Pat the shrimp dry with paper towels. Dip each one first in the egg whites, shaking off any excess, then in the breadcrumb mixture, pressing to coat all over. Place the shrimp on the prepared pan. Repeat with the remaining shrimp, arranging them around the sauce.

7. Mist the shrimp generously with cooking spray. Bake until the coating on the shrimp is deeply golden and the shrimp are cooked through (they'll feel firm when pressed), about 10 minutes.

8. Serve the shrimp hot, with the warm dipping sauce on the side.

LET'S TALK TOOLS

CITRUS ZESTER

To easily remove the zest from citrus fruit, I like to use a rasp grater (Microplane makes a few great ones). I find a paring knife or box grater too clumsy; both require lots of work for very little reward. A rasp grater has teeny blades that produce very finely grated citrus zest—perfect for the majority of recipes, whether sweet or savory. I love to use my rasp grater for non-zesting activities as well, like procuring freshly grated nutmeg, smooth garlic paste, and finely grated Parmesan cheese. A nice one with an easy-to-grasp, plastic handle will set you back about fifteen bucks, but I think you'll find it a worthwhile investment in the useful-kitchen-tool department.

BBQ CHICKEN NACHOS

SERVES 6 TO 8

L eftover rotisserie chicken, meet nachos. You guys are going to get along swimmingly.

As you'll see here, I like to slather my shredded chicken with barbecue sauce—you could use your favorite enchilada sauce, tomato sauce, or even pesto, if you'd rather—and pile it up high with my favorite fixings. I actually had this recipe filed under the dinner section of this book for a while—is that weird? I seriously doubt I'm the only person in the world who views a pan of nachos as a perfectly acceptable meal, but I suppose this one would also be fun to share with friends at a party, predinner, surrounded by salt-rimmed drinks and extra guacamole.

---

2 cups shredded cooked chicken

¼ cup plus 2 tablespoons barbecue sauce (I like Stubb's or Sweet Baby Ray's)

1 can (15 ounces) black beans, rinsed and drained

Juice of ½ lime

1 bag (13 ounces) tortilla chips

½ cup chopped scallions (white and light green parts from about 3 scallions)

1 cup chopped tomato

1 small jalapeño pepper, stemmed and thinly sliced

2 cups shredded Monterey Jack, sharp Cheddar, or Mexican Blend cheese (about 8 ounces)

¼ cup crumbled Cotija cheese (see Note) or feta cheese

¼ cup loosely packed fresh cilantro leaves

1 avocado, pitted, peeled, and chopped

Salsa, hot sauce, and/or sour cream, for serving

LET'S COOK:

1. Preheat the oven to 350°F with a rack in the upper third. Line a sheet pan with aluminum foil or parchment paper.

2. Mix the chicken with the barbecue sauce in a small bowl. In another small bowl, toss together the black beans and lime juice.

3. Spread out the tortilla chips on the prepared baking sheet in a single layer. Layer the chicken, black beans, scallions, tomato, jalapeño, and Monterey Jack on the chips, spreading the toppings around evenly.

4. Bake until the chicken is hot and the cheese is fully melted, about 20 minutes.

5. Remove the nachos from the oven and sprinkle them with the Cotija, cilantro, and avocado. Serve immediately with salsa, hot sauce, and/or sour cream on the side.

NOTE: Cotija is a hard Mexican cow's milk cheese. It's sharp and tangy, and can be found at many grocery stores or your local cheese shop.

JALAPEÑO

AVOCADO + cilantro

TOMATO

MEXICAN BLEND

BBQ CHICKEN!

BLACK BEANS + LIME

SCALLION

COTIJA

BAKED CRAB & CORN CAKES WITH TANGY AIOLI

MAKES ABOUT 25 MINI CAKES

Crab and corn: as happy together as ham and cheese. Bert and Ernie. Bruce Springsteen and The E Street Band. My analogies are subpar, but I think you get the point—fresh crabmeat and sweet corn are a match made in heaven. Paired with cool and tangy aioli, these healthful little baked cakes make for one fantastic appetizer.

Make these in the summertime, when fresh corn is crisp and sweet. And if you can't get your hands on any fresh ears, an equal amount of unthawed frozen corn kernels will do.

FOR THE CRAB & CORN CAKES
1½ cups fresh corn kernels
  (cut from 2 to 3 ears)
1 pound lump crabmeat, picked over
  for pieces of shell and cartilage
½ cup chopped scallions (white and
  light green parts)
1 tablespoon Dijon mustard
2 tablespoons freshly squeezed
  lemon juice
2 large eggs
1 tablespoon Old Bay seasoning
⅛ teaspoon kosher salt
¼ cup panko breadcrumbs

FOR THE TANGY AIOLI
1 cup plain Greek yogurt
½ cup mayonnaise
1½ teaspoons Dijon mustard
1 clove garlic, minced
¼ cup capers, drained
½ teaspoon kosher salt
½ teaspoon freshly ground
  black pepper
½ teaspoon Old Bay seasoning

LET'S COOK:

1. Preheat the oven to 350°F with a rack in the center position. Line a sheet pan with aluminum foil or parchment paper.

2. Make the cakes: Mix together the corn, crabmeat, and scallions in a large bowl. Add the mustard, lemon juice, eggs, Old Bay, salt, and breadcrumbs, and stir well until fully combined.

3. Scoop the crab mixture by the tablespoonful and use your hands to form it into patties roughly ¾ inch thick. The mixture will be pretty loose, but do your best to pack each cake tightly. Place the shaped cakes on the prepared pan, taking care to space them evenly apart. You should get 25 to 28 cakes.

4. Bake the cakes, flipping them halfway through, until firm and golden brown on both sides, 20 to 25 minutes.

5. Meanwhile, make the aioli: Whisk together all the ingredients in a small bowl until smooth.

6. Serve the crab cakes warm, with the aioli alongside for dipping.

FALAFEL BITES

MAKES ABOUT 25 FALAFEL BITES

The first time I had falafel—little fried chickpea patties—was in Israel. I was in fifth grade, on a big family trip, and I took home two distinct lessons from that country: One, you can't order a cheeseburger in a kosher restaurant, and two, falafel is the way to go.

My version is baked instead of fried, full of fresh herbs, and melt-in-your-mouth tender. Topped with an easy, bright-with-tangy-flavor yogurt sauce, these little guys make for a perfectly elegant appetizer. They also do well inside a pita sandwich, or atop a simple arugula salad.

---

1 can (15 ounces) chickpeas, rinsed and drained
½ cup roughly chopped fresh chives, plus extra for garnish
¼ cup tahini (see Notes)
3 cloves garlic, roughly chopped
½ cup packed fresh parsley leaves
½ cup packed fresh cilantro leaves
3 tablespoons extra virgin olive oil
½ cup almond flour (see Notes)

⅛ teaspoon ground cinnamon
½ teaspoon ground cumin
Kosher salt and freshly ground black pepper
1 cup plain Greek yogurt
1 tablespoon freshly squeezed lemon juice
1 cup cherry tomatoes, sliced into ½-inch-thick rounds

LET'S COOK:

1. Preheat the oven to 375°F with a rack in the center position. Line a sheet pan with aluminum foil or parchment paper.

2. In a food processor or blender, combine the chickpeas, chives, tahini, garlic, parsley, cilantro, olive oil, almond flour, cinnamon, ¼ teaspoon of the cumin, 1 teaspoon salt, and ½ teaspoon pepper, and puree until well combined and smooth. The mixture should have a thick but slightly wet consistency.

3. Using a 1-inch scoop or a large spoon dipped in some water (it helps if your hands are damp, too), shape the falafel mixture into small patties, each about ¾ inch thick, and space them evenly apart on the prepared baking sheet.

4. Bake the falafel, flipping them halfway through, until both sides are golden brown and firm, 25 minutes.

5. Meanwhile, in a small bowl whisk together the yogurt, lemon juice, the remaining ¼ teaspoon cumin, and

a pinch each of salt and pepper. Set aside.

6. Remove the falafel from the oven and let them cool slightly, then top each with a slice of tomato, a scant teaspoon of yogurt sauce, and a sprinkling of fresh chives. Serve immediately.

NOTES: Tahini (sesame paste) has a tendency to separate, so stir it well to incorporate the oil before measuring.

Almond flour, also called almond meal, is made from raw blanched almonds that have been ground very finely. You can find it in the baking aisle of many supermarkets.

SPANAKOPITA WITH YOGURT SAUCE

MAKES 20 TO 24 TRIANGLES

Crisp golden triangles filled with warm spinach and cheese do well as a party appetizer, though they're also quite happy playing the part of a simple and satisfying main course—I like to serve them alongside a bright salad studded with cucumber, tomato, and feta.

Both the yogurt sauce and spanakopita are easily prepared a few hours ahead (just remember to thaw the phyllo the night before): Store the sauce in the refrigerator. Cover the cooled triangles and store at room temperature, then uncover and rewarm in a 325°F oven for about 15 minutes before serving.

FOR THE SPANAKOPITA
1 box (16 ounces) frozen phyllo dough (look for a package with 2 rolls of 9-by-14-inch sheets; see box, page 25)
Olive oil cooking spray (optional)
1 box (9 to 10 ounces) frozen chopped spinach, thawed
¼ cup finely chopped fresh parsley leaves
Grated zest of 1 lemon
4 ounces feta cheese, crumbled (about 1 cup)
¼ cup shredded Parmesan cheese
2 large eggs, beaten
¼ teaspoon kosher salt
¼ teaspoon freshly ground black pepper, plus extra for sprinkling
Pinch of freshly grated nutmeg
8 tablespoons (1 stick) unsalted butter, melted

FOR THE YOGURT SAUCE
1 cup plain Greek yogurt
1 tablespoon freshly squeezed lemon juice
1 clove garlic, crushed
2 tablespoons finely chopped fresh parsley leaves
¼ teaspoon kosher salt
¼ teaspoon freshly ground black pepper

LET'S COOK:

1. Remove one roll of phyllo dough from the package and place it in the refrigerator to thaw overnight. Place the opened box in a zip-top freezer bag and return to the freezer for another use.

2. Preheat the oven to 350°F with racks in the upper and lower thirds. Lightly mist two sheet pans with cooking spray or line them with parchment paper.

3. Squeeze the spinach in your hands to press out as much excess water as you can. Place the spinach in a medium-size bowl. Add the parsley, lemon zest, feta and Parmesan cheeses, eggs, salt, pepper, and nutmeg and stir to combine. Set the filling aside.

4. Unroll the phyllo dough and place it on a work surface. Carefully cut it into six 4½-inch squares. (Each of these squares will consist of about 20 paper-thin layers of dough, which you'll pull apart in batches to make the triangles.) Cover the phyllo with a sheet of parchment paper, then a clean, damp kitchen towel.

5. Remove five layers of dough from one square and stack them on top of one another (re-cover the rest with the parchment and towel). Brush the top layer with some melted butter. Place a scant tablespoon of the filling in the center of the dough, then fold the square in half diagonally to form a thick triangle, pressing the edges together gently with your fingers to seal. (You can brush the edges with more butter if needed.) Transfer the finished triangle to a prepared pan and cover the pan with another sheet of parchment and damp towel to prevent drying.

6. Repeat Step 5 with the remaining dough and filling, dividing the triangles equally between the pans.

7. Remove the parchment and towels from the triangles and brush them with melted butter. Sprinkle with some extra black pepper. Bake, rotating the pans and switching between racks halfway through, until the pastry is golden brown and crisp, 25 to 30 minutes.

8. Meanwhile, whisk together all of the ingredients for the yogurt sauce in a small bowl until smooth.

9. Serve the spanakopita warm, with the cool yogurt sauce on the side.

WAIT, WHAT?

PHYLLO DOUGH

Phyllo (FEE-low) dough! It's a kind of dough made in paper-thin layers, popular in the Middle East. It's quite a process to make phyllo from scratch, so store-bought is your best bet. It's typically sold frozen, and thaws easily in its box overnight in the refrigerator.

Note that phyllo comes in two types of 16-ounce packages: one type contains a single roll of 14-by-18-inch phyllo sheets, the other comes with two rolls of 9-by-14-inch sheets. The latter is best for the Spanakopita recipe, though if you can only find the kind with a single roll of dough, you can still get in on this. Just use a sharp knife to cut the large sheet in half widthwise. Cover one half of the phyllo with parchment and a clean, damp kitchen towel to prevent it from drying out on the work surface (you'll want to do this whenever you work with phyllo to keep it supple and prevent it from cracking and tearing). Then re-roll the second half of phyllo, wrap it tightly, first in parchment and then in plastic wrap, and place it back in the freezer for another use (it will keep for a couple of weeks).

TEACH ME HOW

TO CUT CHIFFONADE

What the heck is "chiffonade"? ("You keep saying this word. I do not think it means what you think it means . . . ." Anyone? Okay.) Chiffonade comes from the French, and it's a fancy way to describe the result of slicing leaves, usually fresh herbs like basil or mint, into fine, delicate shreds. Here's how you do it: Stack your herb leaves on top of each other. Roll them into a long, tight cigar-like log. Use a sharp knife to slice across the log, super thinly. When you fluff up the sliced leaves with your fingers, you'll see beautiful ribbons of fresh herb. Voilà! Chiffonade.

FRESH TOMATO BRUSCHETTA

MAKES 25 TO 30 PIECES

If you can find me something that tastes better than toasted bread rubbed with garlic and piled high with summer's best tomatoes, well then you, madam or sir, are a wizard. There are a few things that ensure the superiority of this bright, warm weather–friendly dish: in-season tomatoes, good-quality olive oil, and bread that is well on its way to burned. The crisp garlicky toast will soften once topped with the juicy tomatoes, sharp onion, and sweet basil, and one bite will likely convince you—in the heat of summer, there's honestly just nothing better.

Bruschetta is best enjoyed freshly made, but feel free to combine the tomato mixture a few hours ahead of time and assemble the toasts at the last minute.

---

2 pounds tomatoes, finely chopped
(about 5 medium-size tomatoes)
½ cup good-quality extra virgin
olive oil
¾ cup finely diced shallot or
red onion (from 1 large shallot
or 1 small onion)

Kosher salt and freshly ground black
pepper
1 baguette, sliced horizontally in half
lengthwise, both halves cut into
6 pieces, each about 4 inches long
1 clove garlic, peeled
¼ cup chopped or chiffonade
(see box, page 26) fresh basil leaves

LET'S COOK:

1. Preheat the oven to broil with a rack about 4 inches from the heat.

2. Combine the tomatoes, olive oil, shallot, and salt and pepper to taste in a medium-size bowl, folding gently to combine. Set aside.

3. Place the baguette slices on a sheet pan, cut side up. Broil them until charred and toasty, about 1 minute. Keep an eye on them while they broil—the whole thing happens quickly.

4. While the bread is still hot, rub the cut sides with the garlic. Spoon the tomato topping generously atop the bread, dividing it evenly, and sprinkle with the basil.

5. Serve the bruschetta warm or at room temperature.

CRISPY MUSHROOM & BURRATA CROSTINI

MAKES 25 TO 30 CROSTINI

Everyone needs a good recipe for crostini. It's some kind of rule, I think. I bet Oprah invented it. It's true, though—when party inspiration lacks, you can always count on crostini. A simple stack of good toasted bread, luxurious cheese, and herby roasted vegetables never fails to win hearts and minds, from your book club potluck to your aunt's good-china dinner party. Extra bonus: It's vegetarian friendly.

I love the earthy mix of roasted mushrooms and thyme, but you can switch it up and use whatever deeply roasted vegetables suit your fancy— cubes of butternut squash or even small florets of broccoli would be divine (see Variations). Burrata, if you haven't yet been lucky enough to encounter it, is a particularly fantastic fresh cheese, similar to mozzarella but softer, richer, and gooeyer on the inside. In a really, really good way. You can probably pick it up at your local cheese shop or Italian market, but if you can't find burrata, fresh mozzarella is a good substitute.

5½ cups roughly chopped mixed
  mushrooms (about 1 pound; I like
  cremini, shiitake, and king trumpet)
½ cup extra virgin olive oil
Kosher salt
½ teaspoon freshly ground black
  pepper

1 teaspoon fresh thyme leaves,
  plus extra for garnish
1 baguette, cut on a diagonal into
  ¼- to ½-inch-thick slices
1 clove garlic, cut in half
2 balls (8 ounces each) burrata cheese

LET'S COOK:

1. Preheat the oven to 450°F with racks in the upper and lower thirds.

2. Place the mushrooms on a sheet pan and drizzle with ¼ cup of the olive oil. Sprinkle with ½ teaspoon of the salt, and the pepper and thyme leaves, and toss to coat. Spread the mushrooms in a single layer and roast on the upper rack for 15 minutes while you prepare the baguette.

3. Meanwhile, arrange the baguette slices on another sheet pan, brush the tops with the remaining ¼ cup olive oil, and sprinkle with a pinch of salt.

4. After 15 minutes, lower the oven to 400°F, and slide the pan with the baguette slices onto the lower rack. Roast, flipping the baguette slices halfway through, until the bread is golden and the mushrooms are browned and crisp, an additional 10 minutes. Remove both pans from the oven.

5. While the bread slices are still hot, rub the cut sides with the garlic. Cut the balls of burrata in half. Use a butter knife or spoon to portion out the cheese (a spoon may help wrangle the runny middle) and spread a liberal amount on each slice of baguette. Spoon the mushrooms on top, and finish with an extra sprinkling of fresh thyme leaves.

6. Serve warm or at room temperature.

VARIATIONS
ROASTED BUTTERNUT SQUASH OR BROCCOLI CROSTINI

Replace the mushrooms with 5½ cups peeled, roughly chopped butternut squash or broccoli cut into 1-inch florets.

NANA'S SPICY CHEESE BISCUITS

MAKES ABOUT 60 BISCUITS

These are more like cheese crackers than biscuits, but Nana called them biscuits so I'm going with that. A true Southern lady, Nana (my husband Ben's grandmother) could always be counted on for a warm smile and a home-baked (and always butter-forward) treat. A tin of freshly made cheese biscuits was her calling card, especially around the holidays, when she'd package them up and dole them out to pretty much everyone, ever. Nana's cheese biscuits are spicy (in a slow-burn sort of way) from a generous glug of Tabasco, and a healthy amount of butter (duh) and sharp cheese give them a flaky, tender crumb. They're great on their own or as part of a larger cracker/cheese/fruit spread—try one with a smear of apple butter for an unexpected treat.

One of my favorite things about this recipe is that it's super easy to make the dough ahead of time: You can store the unbaked dough logs, tightly wrapped, in the freezer for up to 3 months before slicing off and baking the biscuit-crackers (no need to thaw them first).

½ pound (2 sticks) unsalted butter, at room temperature

2 cups shredded sharp Cheddar cheese (about 8 ounces)

1 cup shredded Parmesan cheese (about 4 ounces)

2½ teaspoons hot sauce (such as Tabasco)

2 cups all-purpose flour, plus extra for working the dough

LET'S COOK:

1. In a food processor, blend the butter, Cheddar, and Parmesan until smooth and creamy. Add the hot sauce and pulse to combine. Add the flour and pulse just until the dough comes together; you don't want to overwork the dough.

2. Turn the dough out onto a floured surface and with floured hands, divide it and shape it into logs roughly 1 inch in diameter and 12 to 18 inches long (you should get 2 or 3 logs of dough). Wrap the logs tightly in plastic wrap and chill in the refrigerator until firm, about 1 hour, or in the freezer for 30 minutes.

3. While the dough is chilling, preheat the oven to 300°F with racks in the upper and lower thirds. Line two sheet pans with parchment paper.

4. After the dough has firmed up, use a sharp knife to slice the logs into ½-inch-thick rounds. Place the rounds on the prepared pans and prick them gently with a fork (if you're baking them from frozen, don't prick them, since they'll crack apart). Bake until they're just firm and darkened at the edges, about 30 minutes.

5. Let the biscuits cool on the pans. Serve generously during cocktail hour. Cheese biscuits will keep well for a few days in an airtight container at room temperature.

ROASTED SALSA & PITA CHIPS

MAKES 1½ CUPS SALSA AND 25 TO 30 CHIPS

A fresh and elevated version of an old entertaining standby. Who doesn't love chips and salsa? I like how fresh and comforting this salsa and pita chip combo tastes warm from the oven, but it's also wonderful when left to sit at room temperature. If you want to make an extra pan of pita chips, I don't blame you; if you're anything like me, you can polish off a whole pan in one sitting. Oops.

Both the salsa and chips can be made a day or two in advance. Store the salsa, covered, in the refrigerator and the chips in an airtight container at room temperature.

---

1 cup quartered cherry tomatoes
1 cup finely chopped red onion
1 jalapeño pepper, stemmed, seeded, and finely diced
1 cup plus 1 tablespoon extra virgin olive oil

Kosher salt and freshly ground black pepper
1 teaspoon freshly squeezed lime juice
3 or 4 whole wheat pita breads (6-inch diameter)
½ teaspoon garlic powder

LET'S COOK:

1. Preheat the oven to 375°F with a rack in the center position. Line a sheet pan with parchment paper.

2. Combine the tomatoes, onion, and jalapeño on the sheet pan. Drizzle with 1 tablespoon of the olive oil, a pinch each of salt and pepper, and the lime juice. Spread the vegetables in a single layer. Roast until they have softened and are lightly browned in spots, about 15 minutes.

3. Meanwhile, use a sharp knife to cut each pita bread into eight equal wedges.

4. When the salsa is done, remove the pan from the oven, transfer the salsa to a 1- or 2-cup ramekin or other ovenproof dish and set the sheet pan aside. Remove and discard the parchment. Turn up the oven to 400°F.

5. Place the salsa, in its ramekin, in the center of the sheet pan. Pour the remaining olive oil into a shallow bowl and dunk each pita wedge into it to lightly coat both sides. Arrange the wedges around the ramekin in a single layer. Sprinkle ½ teaspoon salt, ½ teaspoon pepper, and the garlic powder over both sides of the wedges to season.

6. Return the pan to the oven. Bake, flipping the pita chips halfway

through, until they are fragrant, browned, and crisp, about 20 minutes. If the salsa starts to look dry, cover the ramekin with a small piece of parchment paper or aluminum foil.

7. Serve the chips and salsa right from the sheet pan, either warm or at room temperature.

ROASTED RADISHES WITH CHIVE BUTTER

SERVES 4

A roasted radish is one I want to eat. Roasting softens the raw bitterness of these little roots and brings out their depth and sweetness. And radishes with salty butter? A pair as famous as peanut butter and jelly! At least, it is for dapper French children.

A few thin slices of baguette would be a nice accompaniment to this simple, elegant, and totally chic appetizer.

---

2 bunches radishes (about 1½ pounds total), stems trimmed to 1 inch, cut in half lengthwise

1½ tablespoons extra virgin olive oil

½ teaspoon kosher salt

4 tablespoons (½ stick) salted butter

2 tablespoons chopped fresh chives

LET'S COOK:

1. Preheat the oven to 450°F with a rack in the center position. Line a sheet pan with aluminum foil or parchment paper.

2. Place the radishes in a large bowl and toss together with the olive oil and salt. Arrange them in a single layer on the prepared pan. Place the butter and chives in a 4-ounce ramekin, and place the ramekin on the pan, too.

3. Roast until the radishes are spotted brown and tender and the butter is quite bubbly, 15 to 18 minutes.

4. Serve the radishes warm, dipped in the melted chive butter.

KETTLE KALE CHIPS

MAKES 1 CUP CHIPS

This is my absolute new favorite snack. A cross between kettle corn and kale chips, these hit the salty, sweet, crisp, crunchy notes that are essential to all great snack foods. The fact that they're made of the nation's new favorite *Brassica* means we can eat as many as we like and still feel good about wearing non–elastic-waist pants. Which, I think you'll agree, is a win for everyone.

I like to use dinosaur kale (also called lacinato kale) for these, because I like its nubbly texture (and the name is fun to say), but any kind will do.

---

3 packed cups stemmed whole kale leaves (from about 1 bunch), washed

1 tablespoon extra virgin olive oil
½ teaspoon kosher salt
½ teaspoon sugar

LET'S COOK:

1. Preheat the oven to 300°F with a rack in the center position. Line a sheet pan with parchment paper.

2. First, you'll want to get your kale really, *really* dry. I like to spin the washed kale in a salad spinner, then thoroughly dry it between clean kitchen towels. Rip the kale into large bite-size pieces, keeping in mind that the pieces will shrink as they cook. Place them on the prepared sheet pan.

3. Drizzle the olive oil evenly over the kale, sprinkle with the salt and sugar, then use your fingers to massage the oil into each piece of kale, ensuring an even coating (and thus even chip crispness). Arrange the pieces in a single layer.

4. Bake the kale until rigid, crisp, and chip-like, 15 to 20 minutes.

5. Let the chips cool before serving (I dare you *not* to eat the entire batch right off of the baking sheet). Kale chips are best eaten the day they're made.

SPICY BROWN SUGAR–ROSEMARY CASHEWS

MAKES 2 CUPS NUTS

Caution: addicting snack ahead. Raw cashews take a tumble with salt, brown sugar, spicy red pepper flakes, and fresh rosemary (plus some egg whites to bind them all together). The result is deeply nutty, spiced, and practically caramelized. Proceed at your own risk.

These are a shoo-in for a fabulous make-ahead party snack. The nuts will keep for over a week (if they last that long!).

---

1 large egg white
½ teaspoon kosher salt
2 cups raw unsalted cashews
   (see box, page 39)

¼ cup packed light or dark
   brown sugar
1½ teaspoons finely chopped fresh
   rosemary leaves
¼ teaspoon crushed red pepper flakes

LET'S COOK:

1. Preheat the oven to 325°F with a rack in the center position. Line a sheet pan with parchment paper.

2. In a medium-size bowl, whisk together the egg white and salt with 1 tablespoon water until just frothy. Add the cashews and toss to coat. Transfer the nuts to a colander and allow them to drain over a bowl or the sink until they are just wet but not goopy, 10 to 15 minutes.

3. Meanwhile, whisk together the brown sugar, rosemary, and red pepper flakes in a medium-size bowl until thoroughly combined.

After the cashews have drained, toss them with the brown sugar mixture to coat.

4. Arrange the cashews in a single layer on the prepared sheetpan. Bake, rotating the pan halfway through, until evenly browned and bubbly, about 35 minutes.

5. Allow the cashews to cool to room temperature. Break them apart with your hands before serving.

6. The cashews will keep in an airtight container at room temperature for 7 to 10 days.

MAKE IT MINE

GO NUTS
Cashews not your thing? I love their rich butteriness, but you could easily swap out. Try it with whole raw almonds, pecans, or another favorite nut instead. Choose your own (nut) adventure.

CRISPY ZA'ATAR CHICKPEAS

MAKES 3 CUPS CHICKPEAS

I've seen different versions of these crisp baked chickpeas all over the place; they seem to be the hipster community's new favorite bar snack (that's totally a compliment, by the way). They're satisfyingly crunchy, surprisingly healthful, and will take on most any herb or spice combination you can think up. I like mine sprinkled with the savory Middle Eastern spice blend called za'atar, plus some smoked paprika (see box, page 55) and salt. I had trouble photographing these because they just wouldn't sit *still* for a picture; they kept jumping from the hot pan into my mouth before I could snap a good one.

If you can't find za'atar at your local market or specialty food shop, you can make a batch of your own by combining ¼ cup dried thyme with 2 teaspoons dried sumac or dried oregano, ½ teaspoon kosher salt, and 1 tablespoon sesame seeds. Store the mixture, airtight, in your spice drawer, where it'll last for months.

---

2 cans (15 ounces each) chickpeas, rinsed, well drained, and patted mostly dry with paper towels

2 teaspoons za'atar
1 teaspoon smoked paprika
1 teaspoon kosher salt

LET'S COOK:

1. Preheat the oven to 450°F with a rack in the center position. Line a sheet pan with aluminum foil or parchment paper.

2. Combine the chickpeas, za'atar, paprika, and salt in a medium-size bowl and toss until the chickpeas are evenly coated. Transfer the chickpeas to the prepared pan and arrange them in a single layer.

3. Bake, shaking the pan periodically to mix up the chickpeas and rotating the pan halfway through cooking, until the chickpeas are browned in spots, completely dry, and crisp, 25 to 30 minutes. (Taste one to check for doneness—the chickpeas should not be soft inside.)

4. Let the chickpeas cool completely before serving. They are best (and crispest!) on the day they're made.

Chapter 3

BIRD'S THE WORD

C hicken and turkey are hard hitters come dinnertime; easy to find, simple to prep, quick to cook (not to mention affordable and pretty healthy, too)—they're my go-to proteins, especially on weeknights. Both birds lend themselves well to all kinds of flavor profiles, whether slathered with spicy Asian-inspired peanut sauce or transformed into Italian-style meatballs (see pages 52 and 48, respectively).

This chapter highlights the versatility of poultry to give you quick and tasty weeknight meals like Chicken Legs with Fennel & Orange (page 60), as well as elegant dinner party fare—Classic Roast Chicken with Mustardy Potatoes (page 67) for the win!

CAPRESE TURKEY BURGERS & SWEET POTATO WEDGE FRIES

SERVES 4

I wanted to know what happens when you smash a caprese salad with a burger. Not on the floor, I mean, but on your plate. This is what happens! With fries. The burgers cook on a wire rack propped over a sheet pan—this setup allows for more even airflow around the burgers as they cook, and also prevents the burgers from steaming in their own fat. The result is a perfectly tender turkey burger, infused with balsamic vinegar and topped with fresh tomato, mozzarella, and homemade pesto. With fries! Of course.

The pesto sauce comes together quickly in a food processor. It's easy to mix it up while the burgers and fries bake, or you can make it a day ahead and store it in an airtight container in the refrigerator until ready to serve.

---

2 sweet potatoes (about 1½ pounds total), peeled and cut lengthwise into 1-inch wedges
2 tablespoons canola oil
1 teaspoon kosher salt
1 teaspoon freshly ground black pepper
1 pound ground turkey (dark meat is best for the juiciest burgers)

¼ cup diced shallot (about 1 small shallot)
¼ cup chopped fresh basil leaves
2 tablespoons balsamic vinegar
1 tablespoon extra virgin olive oil
4 slices fresh mozzarella cheese
1 small tomato, sliced into ½-inch-thick rounds, for serving
Pesto Sauce (recipe follows), for serving

LET'S COOK:

1. Preheat the oven to 450°F with racks in the upper and lower thirds. Line two sheet pans with aluminum foil or parchment paper. Place a wire rack on one of the prepared pans.

2. Place the sweet potatoes on the rackless sheet pan, drizzle with the canola oil, sprinkle with ½ teaspoon of the salt and ½ teaspoon of the pepper, and toss to coat evenly. Spread the potatoes into a single layer and roast on the upper rack until softened and starting to brown, about 15 minutes.

3. Meanwhile, combine the turkey with the shallot, basil, vinegar, olive oil, and the remaining salt and pepper in a medium-size bowl. Gently mix with your fingers just until the ingredients are combined—overmixing the meat will lead to tough, chewy burgers. Divide the turkey mixture into four mounds and shape each into a patty roughly ¾ inch thick. Place the turkey burgers on top of the wire rack on the sheet pan and set aside.

4. After the potatoes have been roasting for 15 minutes, lower the oven temperature to 400°F. Flip the potatoes with a small offset spatula, move them to the lower rack, and place the pan with the turkey burgers on the upper rack. Roast, rotating the pans halfway through, until the turkey burgers are nearly cooked through (an instant-read thermometer inserted into the center of the burgers should register almost 165°F) and the fries are charred and crisp, 25 to 30 minutes.

5. Remove both pans from the oven and set the fries aside. Top each of the burgers with a slice of cheese and return them to the oven. Roast the burgers until they are fully cooked through (the thermometer should register at least 165°F) and the cheese is good and melty, an additional 5 minutes.

6. Serve the turkey burgers topped with tomato slices and generous spoonfuls of bright pesto, the hot sweet potato fries alongside.

PESTO SAUCE

MAKES ABOUT 1½ CUPS PESTO

---

1 cup packed fresh basil leaves
1 heaping cup shredded Parmesan
    cheese
¼ cup extra virgin olive oil

1 teaspoon freshly squeezed lemon
    juice
Kosher salt and freshly ground black
    pepper

Place the basil, Parmesan, olive oil, and lemon juice in a food processor and process until smooth. Add salt and pepper to taste. Pesto sauce can be made a day in advance and stored in the refrigerator in an airtight container.

TURKEY ROULADE WITH AUTUMN HASH

SERVES 6 TO 8

Thanksgiving is my absolute favorite holiday, so I often wonder: Why limit that kind of feast to just once a year? Making a stuffed turkey breast roulade limits the work and time thrown into the real thing, but still gives us juicy breast meat, herby stuffing, and rich roasted autumnal vegetables. Throw in a glass of wine and a slice of pie for dessert and we've pretty much re-created the best dinner of the year, at least in my opinion.

It's definitely possible to debone your own turkey breast, but it's a pretty time-consuming effort, so if you can, have your butcher do the dirty work and buy a boneless breast with the skin still on.

---

3 cups diced white or wheat sandwich bread (3 to 5 slices)

4 cups ½-inch-cubed peeled butternut squash

1 large leek (white and light green parts only), sliced into ½-inch-thick half-moons, washed well, and dried (see box, page 116)

2 medium-size Yukon gold potatoes, cut into ½-inch cubes

About ½ cup extra virgin olive oil

Kosher salt and freshly ground black pepper

4 scallions (whites and light green parts only), finely chopped

½ cup dried cranberries

1 cup diced unpeeled green apple (about ½ apple)

1 teaspoon chopped fresh sage leaves

1 teaspoon chopped fresh thyme leaves

1 cup chicken broth

¼ cup milk

1 large egg yolk

1 teaspoon garlic powder

1 boneless, skin-on turkey breast (about 5 pounds)

LET'S COOK:

1. Preheat the oven to 400°F with a rack in the center position. Line a sheet pan with aluminum foil.

2. Arrange the cubed bread in an even layer on the pan, and toast in the oven until very brown and dry, about 8 minutes. Remove the bread, on the foil, and set aside to cool. Leave the oven on.

3. Toss together the squash, leek, potatoes, ¼ cup olive oil, ½ teaspoon salt, and ½ teaspoon pepper in a large bowl. Arrange the

hash in a single layer on the sheet pan and set it aside.

4. Transfer the bread cubes to the (unwashed) large bowl, add the scallions, cranberries, apple, sage, thyme, broth, milk, egg yolk, garlic powder, 2 tablespoons olive oil, ½ teaspoon salt, and ½ teaspoon pepper, and stir to combine. Set the stuffing aside.

5. Set the turkey breast skin side down on a cutting board and lay a big piece of plastic wrap on top of the meat. Use a heavy pan or flat-sided meat tenderizer to pound the turkey breast to an even thickness, about 1 inch. Remove the plastic and spread the stuffing evenly over the meat, leaving a ½-inch border on

all sides. Starting with one of the long sides, roll up the turkey breast, fairly tightly, like a jelly roll. Use some butcher's twine to tie up the roulade at 1-inch intervals (see box, below).

6. Place the turkey roulade, seam side down, on top of the hash on the sheet pan. Sprinkle the roulade with ¼ teaspoon salt and ¼ teaspoon pepper, and rub a bit of extra olive oil over the skin.

7. Roast until an instant-read thermometer inserted into the thickest part of the roulade registers 165°F, about 1½ hours.

8. Allow the roulade to rest for 15 minutes before cutting it into 1-inch-thick slices. Serve with the autumn hash.

TEACH ME HOW

TO TIE MY ROULADE

Tying the roulade will keep it from unrolling and help it cook more evenly throughout. It's a step that sounds more intimidating than it actually is: All you'll need are four or five foot-long pieces of butcher's twine and the ability to tie a knot. After you've rolled up the turkey breast, place it seam side down and slide a piece of twine under the roll and up to the center, where the roulade is probably thickest. Tie a fairly tight knot around the center of the roulade to secure it, then trim off any excess twine. Repeat this process, climbing up and down the roulade from the center knot, until the roulade is secure and looks somewhat even in thickness (it's tough to get it perfectly even, so just do your best).

BAKED TURKEY MEATBALLS & SLOW-ROASTED TOMATOES

SERVES 4

Yes, these meatballs are made with turkey, and yes, they are baked and not fried in oil. You worried? Afraid they'll be dry and bland and unworthy of your discerning Italian nonna? Come on now—would we do Nonna like that? No, we wouldn't.

Though perhaps a far cry from traditional Italian meatballs, these little guys are equally moist and full-flavored, thanks to the addition of good olive oil, Parmesan cheese, fresh basil, and a smattering of dried herbs. Paired with warm cherry tomatoes—turned plump and astonishingly sweet by slow-roasting—and plenty of ricotta cheese, you've got yourself a full meal worthy of praise, from Nonna and everyone else, too.

It's best to use dark meat for these, since white meat tends to dry out quickly and get tough; dark meat ensures a juicy, tender meatball.

FOR THE TOMATOES
2 pints (4 cups) cherry tomatoes, halved
3 cloves garlic, skins on
¼ cup extra virgin olive oil
Pinch of fine sea salt
Pinch of dried oregano

FOR THE MEATBALLS
1 small yellow onion, peeled
1½ pounds ground turkey (dark meat is best)
1 cup grated Parmesan cheese

¼ cup Italian-style breadcrumbs
½ teaspoon herbes de Provence
1 teaspoon kosher salt
½ teaspoon freshly ground black pepper
¼ teaspoon ground mustard (such as Colman's)
2 tablespoons extra virgin olive oil, plus extra for serving
2 tablespoons chopped fresh basil leaves, plus extra for serving

Ricotta cheese, for serving

LET'S COOK:
1. Preheat the oven to 300°F with racks in the upper and lower thirds. Line two sheet pans with aluminum foil or parchment paper.

2. On one of the pans, arrange the tomatoes in a single layer with the garlic cloves. Evenly drizzle everything with the olive oil and sprinkle with the sea salt and oregano. Toss to coat, then turn the tomatoes cut side up. Bake the tomatoes on the lower rack, rotating the pan halfway through, until they are puckered, crinkly, and sweet, 30 minutes to 1 hour (the longer the tomatoes roast at a low temperature, the sweeter they'll get).

3. Meanwhile, make the meatballs: Use the large holes of a box grater to grate the onion into a large bowl; you will get some onion juice in the bowl as well—this is good. Add the turkey, Parmesan, breadcrumbs, herbes de Provence, kosher salt, pepper, mustard, olive oil, and basil, and use your hands to gently mix everything together until combined. Do not over-squish the meat, as this will lead to tough, dense meatballs.

4. Divide and shape the meat mixture into 24 golf ball–size balls (a cookie scoop is a great tool for this), and place them on the other sheet pan, leaving just a bit of space between the meatballs. Once the tomatoes have been cooking for at least 30 minutes (or a few minutes longer if you want them extra sweet), turn up the oven to 375°F. Slide the meatballs into the oven on the upper rack, above the pan of tomatoes.

5. Bake the tomatoes and meatballs until the tomatoes are puckered and sizzling, about 15 minutes. Remove the tomatoes from the oven and set them aside. (Either discard the garlic cloves or peel them for serving with the tomatoes.) Flip the meatballs, rotate the pan, and continue to bake on the upper rack until they are no longer raw inside (check one with a knife), an additional 20 to 25 minutes.

6. Serve the meatballs warm, on a bed of the slow-roasted tomatoes, with dollops of ricotta on top. Drizzle with extra virgin olive oil and garnish with some extra basil, as much as you like.

WAIT, WHAT?

HERBES DE PROVENCE

What is herbes de Provence? Glad you asked. It's a mixture of dried herbs and spices traditionally found in the Provençal region of France, including thyme, savory, basil, fennel seed, and lavender, among others. Small jars of the blend can usually be found in the spice aisle at the grocery store, though if necessary you can mix up your own using equal parts dried savory, rosemary, thyme, basil, marjoram, and fennel seed—or some other combination thereof—and if you can find culinary lavender, use that, too.

CHICKEN JEROME

SERVES 4

This dish of chicken with mushrooms and artichokes is an old family classic, named after a dear family friend, Elaine Jerome. Elaine's husband, Jerry, was some kind of deal on the jazz saxophone back in the day (he played with Benny Goodman—NO BIG), and her tiny dog, Jazzy, once ate half a bar of good dark chocolate and lived to tell the tale. A great family, clearly.

Chicken Jerome is simple, healthy, feel-good food, easily thrown together and fantastic with a side of rice (see page 191). Like a good friend, this one is a keeper.

---

4 boneless, skinless thin-cut
    chicken breasts or cutlets
    (about 1 pound total)
½ teaspoon kosher salt
2 jars (6 ounces each) marinated
    artichoke hearts, drained and
    quartered, ½ cup marinade reserved
3 cups sliced cremini mushrooms
    (roughly ¾-inch-thick slices)

3 scallions (whites and light green
    parts only), sliced into ½-inch-thick
    rounds
½ cup white wine
¼ cup heavy cream
Grated zest of 1 lemon
½ teaspoon herbes de Provence
¼ teaspoon freshly ground black
    pepper

LET'S COOK:

1. Preheat the oven to broil, with a rack 4 inches from the heat. Line a sheet pan with aluminum foil.

2. Place the chicken pieces on the prepared pan, spaced evenly apart, and sprinkle them with ¼ teaspoon of the salt. Arrange the artichoke hearts and mushrooms around the chicken, filling in the empty spaces and overlapping them occasionally. Sprinkle the sliced scallions atop it all.

3. In a small bowl or 2-cup measuring cup, whisk together the reserved artichoke marinade, wine, cream, lemon zest, herbes de Provence, the remaining ¼ teaspoon salt, and the pepper. Carefully pour this sauce over the chicken and vegetables, making sure the entire pan is covered with liquid.

4. Broil the chicken, rotating the pan once during cooking, until the chicken is cooked through and lightly browned on top, 10 to 15 minutes.

5. Serve hot.

QUICK CHICKEN & BABY BROCCOLI WITH SPICY PEANUT SAUCE

SERVES 4

Peanut sauce is like the chocolate sauce of dinnertime. I'm pretty sure I'd eat my shoe if it were covered in enough of it. This satay-inspired dish pairs my beloved peanut sauce with thinly sliced chicken and baby broccoli charred under the broiler. The whole dish cooks in only about 10 minutes but results in juicy chicken, tender broccolini, and thick, bubbly sauce. It's addicting. Keep it away from your shoes.

I've seen packaged thin-cut chicken breasts or cutlets at some grocery stores, but you can easily make your own by slicing a regular chicken breast in half horizontally to create two thin-cut pieces.

Olive oil cooking spray (optional)
1 tablespoon packed dark brown sugar
¼ cup plus 2 tablespoons creamy peanut butter (commercial or natural)
1 tablespoon toasted sesame oil
¼ cup low-sodium soy sauce
1 tablespoon sriracha sauce

1 tablespoon rice vinegar
¼ cup warm water
1 tablespoon freshly squeezed lime juice
2 bunches broccolini (1 pound total)
4 to 6 thin-cut boneless, skinless chicken breasts or cutlets (1 to 1½ pounds total)

LET'S COOK:

1. Preheat the oven to broil, with a rack 4 inches from the heat. Line a sheet pan with aluminum foil or mist it with cooking spray.

2. Whisk together the brown sugar, peanut butter, sesame oil, soy sauce, sriracha, vinegar, water, and lime juice in a medium-size bowl until smooth. Set aside ¼ cup of the peanut sauce for serving.

3. Rub the broccolini and chicken with the remaining peanut sauce to thickly coat, and arrange them in a tight single layer on the prepared pan. Broil, keeping a close eye on the pan to prevent burning, and

flipping the chicken halfway through, until the chicken is just cooked through, the broccolini is well charred, and the sauce is bubbly and deeply browned, 10 to 12 minutes.

4. Serve the chicken and broccolini hot from the oven with the reserved dipping sauce alongside.

WAIT, WHAT?

SRIRACHA

Have you heard of this stuff? People are obsessed with it. Sriracha is a Thai-style hot sauce, made from chiles, garlic, vinegar, sugar, and salt. It's proven itself a versatile ingredient, adding spice and depth to all kinds of dishes and sauces (like, say, peanut sauce). Sometimes called "rooster sauce" (the Huy Fong company that manufactures the sauce touts the rooster as its official mascot, and its likeness decorates their bottles), sriracha is also used as a condiment to top soup, noodles, eggs, burgers, and anything else that needs a little kick. If you're into spice, do yourself a favor and buy a bottle—it'll keep for 2 years in the refrigerator.

CURRIED CHICKEN WITH CAULIFLOWER, APRICOTS & OLIVES

SERVES 4 TO 6

When I was growing up, my mother (and probably all baby boomer mothers) often made a dish called Chicken Marbella, which included roasted prunes and olives. I loved the mixture of sweet fruit and briny olives next to the deeply roasted chicken. In my version made with chicken thighs and cauliflower, the original seasonings get replaced with Moroccan-inspired spices and dried apricots sub in for the prunes. It's a mother-approved(!) fresh take on an old family favorite.

---

8 boneless, skinless chicken thighs
   (about 2 pounds total)
4 tablespoons extra virgin olive oil
4 teaspoons curry powder
¼ teaspoon cayenne pepper
1 teaspoon smoked paprika
½ teaspoon ground cinnamon

1 tablespoon apple cider vinegar
1 teaspoon kosher salt
1 head cauliflower, cut into florets
¾ cup chopped dried apricots,
   soaked in hot water for 5 minutes
   and drained
1 cup pitted green olives, halved

LET'S COOK:

1. Combine the chicken thighs with 2 tablespoons of the olive oil, 2 teaspoons of the curry powder, the cayenne, ½ teaspoon of the paprika, the cinnamon, vinegar, and ½ teaspoon of the salt in a large zip-top bag. Seal the bag and mush gently to coat the chicken. Let the chicken marinate in the fridge for at least 45 minutes and up to overnight.

2. When you're ready to cook, preheat the oven to 425°F with a rack in the center position. Line a sheet pan with parchment paper.

3. Place the cauliflower on the sheet pan. Add the remaining 2 tablespoons olive oil, 2 teaspoons curry powder, ½ teaspoon paprika, and ½ teaspoon salt and toss to coat. Scatter the apricots and olives over the cauliflower, and toss to combine. Spread into a single layer.

4. Remove the chicken thighs from the marinade and place them atop the cauliflower, spacing them evenly apart. Discard the bag with any remaining marinade. Roast, rotating the pan halfway through, until the cauliflower is slightly charred and the chicken is cooked through (an instant-read thermometer inserted into the thickest part of the meat will register 165°F), about 45 minutes.

5. Enjoy the chicken warm, piled with cauliflower, apricots, and olives.

WAIT, WHAT?

SMOKED PAPRIKA

Unlike the more commonly used sweet Hungarian paprika (which is made from sweet peppers) or hot paprika (made from chiles), smoked paprika comes from Spain and is made from smoked dried pimiento peppers. Sometimes labeled *pimentón* or Spanish paprika, this version brings a warm, sweet, smoky flavor and aroma to all kinds of dishes. Add some to a barbecue dry rub or try a pinch in your next batch of tomato soup. If you can't find smoked paprika, sweet or hot can be substituted here; note that either will subtly change the flavor of the finished dish.

SUN-DRIED TOMATO-STUFFED CHICKEN & CHARD

SERVES 4

When you start assembling this recipe, you'll think you made a mistake—*why* is there so much chard everywhere? It's too much! It's going to swallow me up!!

It won't. Yes, 10 cups is a *lot* of chard. You'll definitely need to wrangle it a bit to get it to fit on the pan and yes, it will look kind of nuts, but not to worry. The chard cooks down significantly in the oven, and comes out looking perfectly respectable—soft and wilted in the middle and brown and crisp at the edges. A perfect bed for a bunch of juicy ricotta, herb, and sun-dried tomato–stuffed chicken breasts.

Make sure you use boneless chicken breasts with the skin still on—otherwise the meat will dry out in the cooking process. The poultry counter at your grocery store should have these on hand, or will be able to remove the bones for you from their bone-in breasts.

---

2 bunches fresh chard (any color), roughly chopped (about 10 packed cups)

3 cloves garlic, thinly sliced

3½ teaspoons extra virgin olive oil

1 teaspoon kosher salt

¼ cup roughly chopped sun-dried tomatoes (about 4 whole)

1 cup ricotta cheese

½ teaspoon freshly ground black pepper

1 teaspoon finely chopped fresh thyme leaves

½ teaspoon finely chopped fresh oregano leaves

Pinch of crushed red pepper flakes

4 boneless, skin-on chicken breasts (about 1½ pounds total)

Crusty bread, for serving (optional)

LET'S COOK:

1. Preheat the oven to 425°F with a rack in the center position. Line a sheet pan with aluminum foil or parchment paper.

2. Spread the chard on the prepared baking sheet and sprinkle the sliced garlic on top. Drizzle with 3 teaspoons of the olive oil and

½ teaspoon of the salt and toss to combine. Set aside.

3. Mix together the sun-dried tomatoes, ricotta, black pepper, the remaining ½ teaspoon salt, and the thyme, oregano, and red pepper flakes in a small bowl to combine. Set aside.

4. Using a sharp knife, carefully slice the chicken breasts horizontally in half lengthwise, leaving one edge intact, allowing you to open the chicken breasts like a book. Open up the chicken "books" and divide the filling between them, spreading it on one side of each. Close the breasts, making sure they're skin side up. Place the stuffed chicken breasts on

top of the chard and drizzle them with the remaining ½ teaspoon olive oil.

5. Roast until the chicken is cooked through (an instant-read thermometer inserted into the thickest part of the meat should register 165°F) but still juicy, 30 to 40 minutes.

6. If you're a fan of extra crisp chicken skin, set the oven to broil and place a rack 4 inches from the heat. Broil the chicken and chard, watching carefully, until the skin is good and crisped, 1 to 2 minutes.

7. Serve the chicken and chard hot, with a side of crusty bread if you like.

CHICKEN PARMESAN

SERVES 4 TO 6

Chicken Parmesan is one of those classic Italian-American dishes, a favorite of pretty much everyone with taste buds. I often feel guilty scarfing down restaurant versions, though, since they're usually deep-fried and smothered in cheese. Luckily, the homemade version doesn't have to be quite so caloric. Instead of frying, we'll bake our chicken in a crisp panko coating; that way we won't have to think twice about loading on the cheese. Heck of a compromise, if you ask me.

Pasta is the traditional accompaniment to chicken Parmesan, but a green salad and some toasted crusty bread are also great alongside.

Olive oil cooking spray
1½ cups panko breadcrumbs
2 teaspoons garlic powder
2 teaspoons dried oregano
2 tablespoons sweet or smoked paprika
1 teaspoon kosher salt
½ cup all-purpose flour
½ teaspoon freshly ground black pepper

2 large eggs
4 to 6 boneless, skinless chicken breasts or cutlets, each about ½ inch thick (about 1½ pounds total)
1 jar (24 ounces) good-quality marinara sauce (I love Rao's)
6 to 8 slices provolone cheese
¼ cup shredded Parmesan cheese

LET'S COOK:

1. Preheat oven to 400°F with a rack in the upper third. Generously mist a sheet pan with cooking spray.

2. Stir together the panko, garlic powder, oregano, paprika, and ½ teaspoon of the salt in a large bowl to combine. In another large bowl, whisk together the flour, the remaining ½ teaspoon salt, and the pepper. In a third shallow bowl, whisk together the eggs.

3. Dip each chicken cutlet first in the flour mixture, shaking off any excess, then in the eggs, and finally in the panko mixture, patting to coat thoroughly on both sides. Place the breaded chicken cutlets on the prepared pan. Mist the chicken with cooking spray to lightly coat.

4. Bake the chicken until the panko has browned and the cutlets are almost entirely cooked through (they'll no longer feel squishy when you poke them), about 15 minutes.

5. Remove the pan from the oven. Top each chicken cutlet with about ½ cup marinara sauce (use up the jar) and the provolone and Parmesan, and return to the oven. Bake until the cheese is melted and bubbly, an additional 10 minutes.

6. Serve hot.

CHICKEN LEGS WITH FENNEL & ORANGE

SERVES 4

I love the classic pairing of fennel and citrus. It does well here with the addition of a bit of saffron and some meaty chicken legs. Finishing the dish in the broiler helps the fennel and orange slices brown and caramelize at the edges, and renders the chicken skin crisp and golden. This dish is great over a bit of rice (see page 191), so serve some up, will ya?

½ cup orange juice (preferably freshly squeezed)
Generous pinch saffron threads (see Note)
½ teaspoon grated orange zest
4 tablespoons extra virgin olive oil
1 teaspoon kosher salt
3 small bulbs fennel, trimmed and cut into ½-inch wedges (see box, page 61)

4 bone-in, skin-on chicken thighs (about 1½ pounds)
4 bone-in, skin-on chicken drumsticks (about 1 pound)
Pinch of freshly ground black pepper
1 small orange (such as a mandarin or clementine), peeled and sliced into ¼-inch-thick rounds

LET'S COOK:

1. Preheat the oven to 425°F with a rack in the center position. Line a sheet pan with aluminum foil or parchment paper.

2. Whisk together the orange juice, saffron, orange zest, 2 tablespoons of the olive oil, and ½ teaspoon of the salt in a medium-size bowl. Add the fennel wedges and toss to coat. Arrange the fennel on the prepared pan and pour any remaining liquid on top.

3. Place the chicken pieces on the sheet pan around the fennel, spacing them evenly apart. Rub the chicken pieces with the remaining 2 tablespoons olive oil and sprinkle them with the remaining ½ teaspoon salt and the pepper. Arrange the orange slices atop and around the chicken.

4. Bake until the juices run clear when the thickest part of the thighs are pricked with a knife, 35 to 40 minutes. Remove the pan from the oven. Set the oven to broil and

place a rack 4 inches from the heat. Place the pan under the broiler and cook, keeping a close eye on the chicken so it doesn't burn, until the chicken skin is deeply crisp and golden, about 3 minutes.

5. Serve hot.

NOTE: Saffron's uniquely sweet, grassy flavor and signature golden color is difficult to replace, and though it is considered the most expensive spice, a little really does go a long way. Find it in spice shops and at most supermarkets (Trader Joe's usually sells theirs for a steal).

WAIT, WHAT?

FENNEL

Let's use fennel! It's easy. First, let's find it: Fennel is probably next to the onions or leeks at the grocery store. You'll know it by its white, bulbous base, which has a bunch of green, stalky fingers coming out the top. Sometimes the stalks are covered in delicate, lacy fronds.

To cut the fennel, first slice off the frond-y fingers with a chef's knife. Cut the bulb in half from top to bottom. Look inside—you'll see a tough, white core at the center. Cut out the core and you're good to go; you can slice up the fennel just like you would an onion. And save those fronds! They're wonderful chopped up and used as a garnish like any other fresh herb. Though raw fennel tastes pretty strongly of anise or licorice, cooked fennel is a totally different beast—sweeter, softer, kind of herbal—so even if you don't love the raw flavor, give the roasted version a try.

BUFFALO CHICKEN DRUMSTICKS & CHARRED ROMAINE

SERVES 4

My little sister knows her way around a chicken wing—she learned the skill in college, like many bar-hopping coeds before her. She can tear through a basket of hot wings in less time than it takes to order them. Though I love the flavor of Buffalo chicken wings, I've never really been able to enjoy them with that kind of aplomb. The process of finding the small bits of wing meat and carnivorously ripping them off with my teeth has never been a pleasant one; there's just not enough meat there to warrant that kind of sticky, messy effort—at least, not for me. But a drumstick? Now there's a worthy adversary.

Here, meaty roasted drumsticks get slathered in a supremely spicy, homemade Buffalo sauce and served with broiler-charred romaine and cooling blue cheese dressing. It's like college, only better, because we no longer sleep on a futon and our hallways don't smell as much like stale beer. (For the most part.)

Olive oil cooking spray
2½ to 3 pounds chicken drumsticks (about 10)
Kosher salt and freshly ground black pepper
4 tablespoons (½ stick) unsalted butter, melted

½ cup hot sauce (such as Cholula or Frank's Red Hot)
2 large romaine lettuce hearts, halved lengthwise
½ cup blue cheese dressing, homemade (see box, page 64) or store-bought
¼ cup crumbled blue cheese

LET'S COOK:

1. Preheat the oven to 425°F with a rack in the center position. Line a sheet pan with aluminum foil, and place a wire rack on top of the foil. Mist the wire rack with cooking spray.

2. Rinse the drumsticks and pat them dry with paper towels. Season them all over with ½ teaspoon salt and ½ teaspoon pepper, and place them, spaced evenly apart, on the prepared rack.

3. Bake the drumsticks until the skin has crisped and they are cooked through (an instant-read thermometer inserted into a drumstick, not touching bone, should register 165°F), 30 to 35 minutes.

4. Meanwhile, in a small bowl whisk together the butter, hot sauce, and salt and pepper to taste.

5. After the drumsticks have reached 165°F, brush them with the Buffalo sauce and return them to the oven to bake for an additional 5 minutes. Remove the pan from the oven, and baste the drumsticks again with sauce. Set them aside to rest.

6. While the chicken rests, set the oven to broil and place a rack 4 inches from the heat. Line another sheet pan with aluminum foil or reuse the same pan (carefully removing the chicken legs and lining the hot pan with a fresh piece of foil). Mist the foil with cooking spray. Line up the halved romaine, cut side up, on the prepared pan. Broil the romaine until the leaves are charred at the edges but still crunchy, 1 to 2 minutes.

7. Drizzle the blue cheese dressing on the romaine, and sprinkle with the crumbled blue cheese.

8. Serve the drumsticks and broiled romaine immediately, with the remaining Buffalo sauce on the side.

DIY OR BUY?

BLUE CHEESE DRESSING

I like to make my own salad dressings, whenever possible, to avoid a lot of sneaky, weird ingredients and preservatives that are often hiding in store-bought bottles. If you're low on time, though, Marie's Chunky Blue Cheese is a good option (find it in the produce section at the supermarket). To make your own, simply mash 4 ounces crumbled blue cheese (about 1 cup) with ⅔ cup mayonnaise, ¼ cup plain Greek yogurt, ¼ cup buttermilk, 1 tablespoon apple cider vinegar, and 1 teaspoon honey. Mix everything together until smooth. Add a handful of chopped chives or scallion greens and season to taste with salt and pepper. The dressing will keep for about a week in an airtight container in the refrigerator.

CHICKEN & BLACK BEAN ENCHILADAS

SERVES 4

Thank goodness for rotisserie chickens. I love knowing that if dinner inspiration is low, I can stop at most any big grocery store, pick up a rotisserie chicken, and in not that much time at all have anything from plain drumsticks dipped in a mixture of mayonnaise and sriracha sauce (see box, page 53) to warm, cheesy chicken and black bean enchiladas.

The best part about these enchiladas is that they're easily customizable. Prefer pinto beans to black? Swap out! Have some leftover corn on the cob hanging around? Cut it off the cob and add it in! You can even use a preshredded Mexican blend cheese if you like, though I happen to love the salty bite of classic Cotija—or feta, in a pinch. Since the rice (frozen, hooray!) cooks right on the pan with the enchiladas, all you need to round this out is a few tortilla chips, a bowl of hot salsa, and maybe some smooth sour cream for dipping.

You will end up with a few cups of leftover chicken filling after making the enchiladas—save it for a quick, next-day taco salad, or tuck it into some scrambled eggs for breakfast the next morning.

---

2 cups shredded cooked chicken

1 can (4 ounces) diced green chiles, drained

2 cups enchilada sauce, store-bought or homemade (see box, page 66)

¼ teaspoon cayenne pepper

1 cup canned black beans, rinsed and drained

¼ cup chopped scallions (white and light green parts only)

1 cup crumbled Cotija cheese (about 5 ounces; see Note, page 19)

¼ cup plus 2 tablespoons chopped fresh cilantro leaves

10 small (6-inch) tortillas (I like to use whole grain tortillas, which are a mixture of corn and wheat)

3 cups frozen rice (white or brown, unthawed)

1 avocado, pitted, peeled, and sliced, for serving

1 lime, cut lengthwise into wedges, for serving

LET'S COOK:

1. Preheat the oven to 375°F with a rack in the center position. Line a sheet pan with aluminum foil or parchment paper.

2. Combine the chicken with the chiles, ½ cup of the enchilada sauce, the cayenne, black beans, scallions, ½ cup of the Cotija, and ¼ cup chopped cilantro in a large bowl. Mix well.

3. Spread 1 cup of the remaining enchilada sauce on the prepared pan, using a spoon or spatula to even it out and leaving a 1-inch border between the sauce and the edges of the pan.

4. Lay a tortilla on a work surface and place ¼ cup of the chicken filling toward one end, packing it into a straight line. Roll up the tortilla tightly around the filling and, beginning at one end of the pan, place it seam side down on top of the sauce (the enchiladas will lie across the width of the pan). Repeat with the remaining tortillas and filling, forming a tight row of enchiladas down the center of the pan. Save any leftover filling for another use.

5. Arrange the rice on the exposed sauce around the enchiladas. Pour the remaining ½ cup enchilada sauce on top of the enchiladas, spreading to cover as best you can, and sprinkle them with the remaining ½ cup Cotija. Cover the entire pan with aluminum foil and bake until the rice is tender and enchiladas are hot through, 25 to 30 minutes.

6. Sprinkle the hot enchiladas with the remaining 2 tablespoons chopped cilantro, and serve with slices of avocado and lime.

DIY OR BUY?

ENCHILADA SAUCE

Store-bought enchilada sauce is fine, but it often contains some suspect ingredients like MSG and artificial coloring. It's a snap to make your own—not to mention so much tastier. Here's how.

Whisk together 3 tablespoons canola oil and 2 tablespoons flour in a saucepan over medium-high heat until lightly browned. Add 2 tablespoons chili powder, 1 teaspoon garlic powder, and 1 teaspoon ground cumin, whisking until smooth. Add 2 tablespoons tomato paste. Whisk in 2 cups chicken broth and 1 teaspoon dried oregano. Bring to a simmer and let it reduce for 15 minutes. Add salt to taste.

There you have it! Allow the sauce to cool before using. It will keep for about a week in an airtight container in the refrigerator.

CLASSIC ROAST CHICKEN WITH MUSTARDY POTATOES

SERVES 2 TO 4

L earning to make a whole roast chicken is one of those "teach a man to fish" skills. It's something that seems difficult but is actually quite simple, and it really ups your kitchen game. You'll never go hungry if you can master the art of the roast chicken. Mixed metaphors aside, I implore you: Don't be scared of a whole bird. Get a good one from your butcher (or choose a roaster at the grocery store: Look for secure, unbroken packaging and firm white or yellow—never gray—skin) and try it once. I bet you'll feel empowered (and full-bellied) afterward. Put this roast chicken in your recipe wheelhouse, and you won't just eat for a lifetime—you'll eat well.

Note that you'll need about a foot of butcher's twine to truss the chicken (fancy for "tie its feet together," see box, page 69)—you can ask your butcher to comp you some, or if he's not the generous sort, you can find it at the supermarket.

---

1 lemon

2 yellow onions, cut into 2-inch chunks

2 pounds baby potatoes (also called new potatoes or creamers), halved (or left whole if really tiny)

¼ cup whole-grain Dijon mustard

¾ cup extra virgin olive oil

1½ teaspoons finely chopped fresh rosemary leaves, plus 2 sprigs

1 tablespoon roughly chopped fresh thyme leaves, plus 4 sprigs

Kosher salt and freshly ground black pepper

1 whole roasting chicken (4 to 5 pounds)

1 bay leaf

2 or 3 cloves garlic

3 tablespoons unsalted butter, at room temperature

LET'S COOK:

1. Preheat the oven to 425°F with a rack in the center position.

2. Cut the lemon in half widthwise and squeeze the juice into a small bowl; remove any seeds. Set the squeezed halves aside.

3. Place the onions and potatoes in a large bowl and add the lemon juice, mustard, olive oil, chopped rosemary, chopped thyme, and ½ teaspoon each of salt and pepper. Spread the vegetables in an even layer on a sheet pan. Set aside.

4. If there's a little goody bag of giblets inside the chicken cavity, remove and discard it. Use a sharp knife to trim the chicken of any excess fat in and around the cavity. Pat the skin dry with paper towels. Liberally salt and pepper the chicken both inside and out. Stuff the cavity with the reserved lemon halves, the sprigs of rosemary and thyme, the bay leaf, and the garlic cloves. Rub the butter onto the chicken skin. Sprinkle the skin again with ½ teaspoon each of salt and pepper. Place the chicken, breast side up, on top of the potatoes and onions. Tie the legs together tightly with butcher's twine and tuck the wings under the body of the chicken.

5. Roast the chicken and potatoes until an instant-read thermometer inserted in the thigh registers at least 145°F and the juices run clear when you pierce the thickest part of the thigh, 1 to 1½ hours. If the potatoes look like they're overbrowning, remove them from the pan with a spatula and set them aside until you're ready to serve.

6. Allow the chicken to rest for 10 minutes before slicing it into pieces and serving with the onions and potatoes.

TEACH ME HOW
TO TRUSS A CHICKEN
Trussing your chicken (or turkey, duck, etc.), aka tying it up with twine, is an important step toward an evenly cooked bird. There are many ways to do it, and trussing the whole bird (including the neck and wings) is common, but I find it's easiest and equally effective just to tie up the legs and tuck the wings under themselves. To do this, start with about a foot of twine. Slide the twine horizontally under the tail. Pull the ends of the twine up and over the legs, drawing them in toward the body, and tie a tight double knot over the skinny part of the legs to secure the truss. Trim any excess twine, then take the wings and tuck them securely under the body. Trussed! Trust.

PHILLY CHICKEN SAUSAGE & PEPPERS WITH BASIL-GARLIC BREAD

SERVES 4

Growing up in the suburbs of Philadelphia gave me an early appreciation for Italian sausage and peppers (hello, Wawa Shorti sandwich). In the City of Brotherly Love, garlicky peppers and onions are cooked until melt-y soft and fragrant, then piled on a hoagie roll with crisp and spicy Italian sausage. It's perfection. My version lightens things up a bit with chicken sausage and then heavies things up with some buttery basil-garlic bread. Wash it all down with some cold beer or a tall glass of water (pronounced "wudder," obviously).

Not into chicken sausage? Feel free to substitute your favorite variety of fresh sausage instead—bratwurst or spicy pork sausage sound good to me.

FOR THE SAUSAGE & PEPPERS
Olive oil cooking spray (optional)
2 large yellow onions, sliced into ¾-inch-thick wedges
10 ounces cremini mushrooms, trimmed and halved (about 2 cups)
1 large red bell pepper, stemmed, seeded, and sliced into 1-inch-wide strips
6 to 8 cloves garlic, peeled
½ teaspoon dried oregano
½ teaspoon kosher salt
⅛ teaspoon crushed red pepper flakes
¼ cup plus 1 teaspoon extra virgin olive oil

8 Italian-style chicken sausages (I like to use a mix of mild and spicy), pricked a few times with a fork

FOR THE BASIL-GARLIC BREAD
1 loaf ciabatta or Italian bread, sliced almost through horizontally (so that the loaf opens like a book)
4 tablespoons (½ stick) unsalted butter, melted
5 cloves garlic, roughly chopped
1 cup packed fresh basil leaves
½ teaspoon kosher salt
½ teaspoon freshly ground black pepper
¼ cup extra virgin olive oil

LET'S COOK:

1. Preheat the oven to 425°F with racks in the upper and lower thirds. Line a sheet pan with parchment paper, or use aluminum foil and mist the foil with cooking spray.

2. Toss together the onions, mushrooms, bell pepper, and garlic with the oregano, salt, red pepper flakes, and ¼ cup olive oil on the prepared pan. Arrange the vegetables in a single layer, place the sausages on top, spacing them evenly apart, and drizzle with the remaining teaspoon olive oil.

3. Bake on the upper rack until the veggies are lightly charred and the sausages are browned and cooked through, 45 to 60 minutes.

4. While the sausages bake, assemble the basil-garlic bread: Brush the cut sides of the ciabatta with the melted butter (like you're making a melted butter sandwich); set it aside.

5. Combine the garlic, basil, salt, pepper, and olive oil in a blender or food processor and blend until smooth and pesto-like. Use a spoon to spread the puree on both insides of the ciabatta. Close up the bread and wrap it with aluminum foil.

6. Bake the bread, placing it directly on the lower rack of the oven, for the last 5 to 7 minutes of sausage baking time. It's done when it's heated through.

7. Remove both pans from the oven. When the bread has cooled enough to handle, remove it from the foil and slice it into four sections. Serve warm, alongside the hot sausages and vegetables.

PESTO CHICKEN TURNOVERS

SERVES 4 TO 8

I discovered chicken turnovers at sleep-away camp. When I was a young girl of nine, my parents shipped me off to overnight camp on Cape Cod, and I probably would have been homesick, except I loved the chicken turnovers at the dining hall (and also the fresh air and constant opportunities to show off my lip-synching skills). I'm long past my summer-camping days, but it turns out that with the help of some frozen puff pastry, rotisserie chicken, and good pesto, making turnovers at home is a breeze. They're a little different from the camp dining hall version, but eating them as an adult makes me want to break out my Umbro shorts, hair bandanas, and Ace of Base mixtape—so I think we can all agree that the recipe is a success.

All-purpose flour, for rolling out
   the dough
1 box (17.3 ounces) frozen puff pastry,
   both sheets thawed according to
   package directions (see Note,
   page 15)
2½ cups shredded cooked chicken
   (store-bought rotisserie chicken
   is fine)

1 cup Pesto Sauce (page 44)
   or good-quality store-bought
   basil pesto
1 cup frozen peas, unthawed
1 large egg, beaten
2 tablespoons grated Parmesan
   cheese
Freshly ground black pepper

LET'S COOK:

1. Preheat the oven to 400°F, with racks in the upper and lower thirds. Line two sheet pans with parchment paper.

2. On a well-floured surface, carefully unfold the puff pastry sheets. Use a sharp knife to cut each into four pieces. Use a floured rolling pin to roll each piece into a 7-by-9-inch rectangle. Set the pastry rectangles on one of the prepared pans, layering them between pieces of parchment if necessary. Place the puff pastry in the refrigerator to chill while you mix up the filling.

3. Mix together the chicken, pesto, and peas in a medium-size bowl. Place a heaping ½ cup of filling onto the

bottom half of each pastry rectangle, leaving a small border at the bottom. Carefully fold the top half of the pastry over the filling, lining up the edges. Press the edges with the tines of a well-floured fork to seal. Arrange the turnovers on the prepared pans, spacing them evenly apart.

4. Brush each turnover with beaten egg and sprinkle with Parmesan cheese and black pepper.

5. Bake the turnovers, switching the pans from upper to lower and lower to upper halfway through cooking, until the pastry is a deep golden brown and the turnovers are starting to bubble at the seams, 25 to 30 minutes.

6. Enjoy the turnovers hot from the oven.

CRISPY CHICKEN STRIPS & BISCUITS

SERVES 4

Homemade chicken nuggets are one of my mom's specialties. I distinctly remember the first time she made them for my sisters and me—we definitely thought she used magic. In actuality she used a frying pan and a healthy (as in unhealthy) amount of oil.

My baked version uses toasted panko for color and crispness, and homemade biscuits for a quick and tasty side. Just split the biscuits, slather with your favorite sauce (personally I like to go with barbecue), and stuff with juicy baked chicken strips for the best kind of dinnertime sandwich. A heap of green salad on the side balances it all out nicely.

FOR THE CHICKEN

3 boneless, skinless chicken breasts
   (about 1½ pounds total)
3 tablespoons Worcestershire sauce
1 teaspoon kosher salt
½ teaspoon garlic powder
½ cup all-purpose flour
½ teaspoon baking soda
3 cups panko breadcrumbs
Olive oil cooking spray
1 tablespoon chopped fresh thyme
   leaves
⅛ teaspoon cayenne pepper
3 large egg whites

Dipping sauce of your choice,
   for serving

FOR THE BISCUITS

2 cups all-purpose flour, plus extra
   for working the dough
1 tablespoon baking powder
¼ teaspoon baking soda
2 teaspoons sugar
1 teaspoon kosher salt
6 tablespoons (¾ stick) cold unsalted
   butter, cut into small cubes
¾ cup cold buttermilk
1 large egg white, beaten, for dabbing
   the biscuits (optional)
2 tablespoons chopped fresh chives
½ teaspoon freshly ground black
   pepper

LET'S COOK:

1. Preheat the oven to 450°F with a rack in the center position.

2. Trim the chicken breasts of fat, then slice them on a diagonal into 1-inch-thick strips. Place the chicken strips in a large zip-top bag, and add the Worcestershire, ½ teaspoon of the salt, and the garlic powder. Seal the bag, shake to coat, and allow the chicken to marinate in the refrigerator for 30 minutes.

3. Meanwhile, whisk together the remaining ½ teaspoon salt with the flour and baking soda in a small bowl. Set aside.

4. Toast the breadcrumbs: Spread the crumbs in an even layer on a sheet pan and mist them evenly with cooking spray. Bake, stirring occasionally, until golden brown, 5 to 8 minutes. Remove from the oven and set them aside to cool. Leave the oven on.

5. Line a second sheet pan with parchment paper and prepare the biscuits: Whisk together the flour, baking powder, baking soda, sugar, and salt in a medium-size bowl. Add the butter and use your hands or a pastry cutter to work it in until the flour mixture looks like pebbly sand. Work quickly to avoid letting the butter become too warm.

6. Pour the buttermilk over the flour mixture and use a fork to bring everything together into a shaggy dough. Knead the dough in the bowl once or twice (try to avoid overmixing) to pick up any sandy pieces at the bottom of the bowl.

7. Turn out the dough onto a lightly floured work surface and use your hand to pat it out into a ¾-inch-thick slab. Using a floured 2½-inch biscuit cutter, cut out as many biscuits as you can, gently repatting the dough together when necessary; you should get 6 to 8 biscuits.

8. Place the biscuits on the prepared pan, dab the tops with some water (or egg white, if you like), and sprinkle with chives and black pepper. Bake the biscuits until risen and golden brown, about 18 minutes. Remove the biscuits from the oven and set them aside to cool. Leave the oven on.

9. While the biscuits bake and cool, prepare your chicken-coating assembly line: Transfer the toasted panko to a medium-size bowl, add the thyme and cayenne, and stir to combine. Set a wire rack on the now-empty sheet pan and place it to one side; place the bowl of panko next to it. Whisk the egg whites until frothy in a second medium-size bowl; place this next to the panko. Place the reserved flour mixture next to the egg whites.

10. Remove the chicken strips from the marinade (discard the marinade) and pat them dry with paper towels. One by one, coat each chicken strip first in the flour mixture, then in the egg whites, shaking off any excess, and finally in the panko mixture, until totally coated. Place the breaded chicken strips on the wire rack, spacing them closely together to fit. Mist the strips lightly with cooking spray.

11. Bake the chicken strips until deeply browned and cooked through, 10 to 14 minutes.

12. Serve the chicken strips warm, alongside the fresh biscuits and plenty of dipping sauce.

Chapter 4

FISH BUSINESS

It took me years to get up the nerve to eat fish that didn't come frozen, in stick form. Don't get me wrong, fish sticks definitely have their merits, but I've happily come to appreciate the real deal—I'm talking fresh, healthful dishes like Asparagus & Black Cod in Parchment (page 96) and Swordfish Cacciatore (page 102). Besides the flavor factor, one of the best things about fish is how quickly it cooks. It's magical! We can rely on the dishes in this chapter—like Soy-Mustard Salmon & Broccoli (page 84), or Fancy Tuna Melts (page 104)—to come together in a snap, either for seamless entertaining or for getting dinner on the family table pronto. Glad we took all the fishiness out of this fish business.

WARM TUNA NIÇOISE SALAD

SERVES 4

The thought of a true *salade niçoise* takes me back to my time in culinary school—to our big midterm exam, in fact. My classmates and I all pulled numbers out of a hat (out of a chef's toque, naturally) to see which classic French dishes we'd have to make to pass the test. No one wanted to pull the niçoise, because of all of the *stuff* that went into it—so many different elements! Potatoes, beans, olives, tomatoes, eggs, herbs, anchovies! All needed to be boiled or blanched or chopped separately, and all needed to make it onto the plate before the time ran out. I'm getting sweaty palms just thinking about it.

Happily, my own version doesn't involve much more than some light chopping and the unceremonious throwing together of things on a sheet pan. My classic niçoise ingredients (French-style *haricots verts*, baby potatoes, tomatoes, olives, anchovy vinaigrette) all roast together in a hot oven—no blanching necessary. And then I top it all off with some lightly dressed tuna fillets—the lovely jarred kind—and sliced hard-boiled eggs (see box, page 80). To hell with midterms, anyway.

About that jarred tuna: I like the way those fancier fillets look on this salad, but if you can't find any at your market (they're typically sold next to the regular cans at Whole Foods or other upscale grocery stores), any kind of solid canned tuna, such as albacore in water or oil, works just fine.

---

1 small shallot, finely diced

1 tablespoon Dijon mustard

½ teaspoon anchovy paste (see Note)

½ cup apple cider vinegar

½ cup extra virgin olive oil

½ teaspoon freshly ground black pepper

2 tablespoons chopped fresh tarragon leaves

1 pound haricots verts or green beans, ends trimmed

1 pound baby potatoes (I like the multicolored ones in red, white, and purple), cut in ½-inch wedges

2 cups cherry or grape tomatoes

½ cup niçoise or kalamata olives, pitted

2 jars (7 ounces each) tuna fillets in water or olive oil

4 hard-boiled large eggs, quartered or sliced

Kosher salt

LET'S COOK:

1. Preheat the oven to 425°F with a rack in the center position. Line a sheet pan with aluminum foil or parchment paper.

2. In a small container with a tight-fitting lid, combine the shallot, mustard, anchovy paste, vinegar, olive oil, pepper, and tarragon. Seal the container and shake it vigorously to combine and emulsify the dressing. Set aside.

3. Evenly spread the haricots verts, potatoes, tomatoes, and olives in a single layer on the prepared pan. Drizzle the veggies with ⅓ cup of the dressing and toss to combine. Bake the vegetables, rotating the pan halfway through, until everything is browned and puckery and the potatoes are knife-tender, 20 to 30 minutes.

4. Meanwhile, drain the tuna fillets and place them in a bowl. Drizzle them with 2 to 3 tablespoons of the dressing and toss to coat.

5. When the vegetables are done, remove them from the oven and, while they're still warm, arrange the dressed tuna and the hard-boiled eggs on top. Sprinkle the eggs with a pinch of salt and serve the salad immediately, with extra dressing alongside.

NOTE: Anchovy paste is sold in a squeezable tube, usually by the tomato paste or canned fish, in many grocery stores.

TEACH ME HOW

TO HARD-BOIL EGGS

There are a few different ways to achieve the perfect hard-boiled egg. I'm talking smooth-and-creamy-centered, without that chalky, rubbery texture or dreaded gray ring of gross around the yolk. I find the simplest way is to place eggs in a saucepan, cover them with cold water, bring the pot to a boil, then immediately cover the pot and turn off the heat. Let the eggs sit in the hot water for 13 minutes, then drain the pot under cold, running water to quickly cool the eggs and stop them from overcooking. All that's left to do is peel, sprinkle with salt, and enjoy!

LEMON-HERB SOLE ON CRISPY POTATO RAFTS

SERVES 4

When I saw the idea for this recipe in an old, dog-eared copy of *Cook's Illustrated* (a personal bible of sorts), I knew I had to make my own version. Discovering garlicky potato "rafts" was, to me, the best thing since the acceptance of wearing yoga pants in public. They're hot and crisp and supremely garlicky, a noble base for the delicately light, flaky, herb-, lemon-, and butter-flavored fish fillets. A smattering of oven-frizzled capers tops it all off perfectly.

I use fillets of sole, when I can find them, though haddock, halibut, or cod are also good choices. Serve these with a simple green salad or a few slices of baguette and some salted butter, if you like.

1½ pounds russet potatoes (about 2 medium), unpeeled and scrubbed, sliced into ¼-inch-thick rounds
2 tablespoons extra virgin olive oil
4 cloves garlic, minced (roughly 1 tablespoon)
½ teaspoon kosher salt
½ teaspoon freshly ground black pepper

4 skinless fillets sole or other firm white fish (each 5 ounces and 1 to 1½ inches thick)
4 tablespoons (½ stick) unsalted butter
1 lemon, thinly sliced
8 sprigs fresh thyme
2 tablespoons capers, drained

LET'S COOK:

1. Preheat the oven to 425°F with a rack in the center position. Line a sheet pan with parchment paper.

2. In a large bowl, toss the potatoes with the olive oil, garlic, salt, and pepper until thoroughly coated.

3. Assemble four potato rafts by overlapping potato slices on the prepared pan in rectangular mounds. Each raft should consist of 3 or 4 shingled rows and be roughly 4 by 6 inches; use 3 or 4 slices of potato per row.

4. Roast the potatoes, rotating the pan halfway through, until golden brown and beginning to crisp, about 30 minutes. Remove the pan from the oven.

5. Blot the fish fillets dry with a paper towel. Place one, skinned side down, centered on top of each potato raft. Top each piece of fish with 1 tablespoon butter, 2 lemon slices, and 2 sprigs thyme. Scatter the capers atop the fish and around the pan.

6. Return the pan to the oven and roast until the fish is flaky and opaque, about 15 minutes.

7. Transfer the potato rafts and accompanying fillets to individual plates, ideally with a big spatula. Serve hot.

ORANGE-GINGER SALMON WITH LENTILS & GREEN BEANS

SERVES 4

Though perhaps not the prettiest belle at the dinner ball, this dish is a perfectly perfect weeknight meal, when flavor, ease, and good-health all meet to high-five. Bright orange flavor shines through the soft, rich base of crème fraîche, and the ginger sings a subtle yet satisfying tune. If you really love ginger and are hoping for more spice, feel free to increase the amount called for here.

A quick pot of brown rice (or precooked rice in a microwaveable bag, let's be real) would round out this wholesome meal nicely. If you can find it and can also afford to spend a little more, it's best to use wild Alaskan salmon, which is higher in omega-3 fatty acids and lower in toxins than farmed.

The salmon is best served warm, though it also makes an excellent next-day leftovers lunch straight from the refrigerator.

---

2 pounds green beans, ends trimmed

1 can (15 ounces) lentils, rinsed and drained

4 tablespoons extra virgin olive oil

1½ teaspoons kosher salt

½ cup crème fraîche (or sour cream in a pinch)

1 tablespoon freshly grated orange zest

Juice of ½ orange

1 teaspoon grated fresh ginger

½ teaspoon freshly ground black pepper

4 skinless fillets salmon (5 ounces each, about 1½ inches thick)

2 scallions (white and light green parts only), thinly sliced

---

LET'S COOK:

1. Preheat the oven to 450°F with a rack in the center position. Line a sheet pan with aluminum foil or parchment paper.

2. Place the green beans and lentils on the prepared pan, drizzle with 3 tablespoons of the olive oil and sprinkle with 1 teaspoon of the salt, and toss to coat evenly. Spread the beans and lentils into an even layer on the pan.

3. Whisk together the crème fraîche, orange zest, orange juice, ginger, the remaining ½ teaspoon salt, the pepper, and the remaining tablespoon of olive oil in a small bowl until smooth.

4. Arrange the salmon fillets skinned side down on top of the green beans and lentils, spacing them evenly apart. Spoon the crème fraîche mixture generously on top of each salmon fillet, spreading it to coat the fish. Drizzle any leftover sauce over the green beans and sprinkle the scallions over all.

5. Bake the salmon to desired doneness: 8 minutes for rare, 13 minutes for medium-rare, and 17 minutes for well-done.

6. Serve the salmon hot with the green beans and lentils.

SOY-MUSTARD SALMON & BROCCOLI

SERVES 4 TO 6

Living with someone from the Pacific Northwest (in my case that'd be my Seattle native husband, Ben) means eating a lot of salmon. Which is entirely fine by me. It's been fun thinking up delicious new ways to serve the meaty fillets; since they're so sturdy and strongly flavored themselves, salmon fillets can stand up to other bold ingredients like grainy mustard, brown sugar, and soy sauce. Roasted broccoli is a favorite of mine (its concentrated flavor and crisp-edged florets can't be beat) so it was a natural pairing here. Serve with a side of brown rice to fill out this healthy and hearty meal.

---

4 heaping cups fresh broccoli florets (about 2 pounds)

¼ cup extra virgin olive oil

¼ cup plus 1 tablespoon soy sauce

Kosher salt and freshly ground black pepper

1 tablespoon dark brown sugar

1 tablespoon Dijon mustard

2 teaspoons whole-grain mustard (such as country Dijon or spicy brown)

2 teaspoons freshly squeezed lemon juice

4 to 6 skinless fillets salmon (about 5 ounces each)

LET'S COOK:

1. Preheat the oven to 425°F with a rack in the center position. Line a sheet pan with aluminum foil or parchment paper.

2. Spread the broccoli florets on the prepared pan, drizzle with the olive oil and ¼ cup of the soy sauce, and sprinkle with a pinch each of salt and pepper. Roast the broccoli until it just starts to brown at the edges, about 20 minutes.

3. Meanwhile, make the glaze for the salmon: Whisk together the brown sugar, Dijon mustard, whole-grain mustard, the remaining 1 tablespoon soy sauce, and lemon juice in a small bowl until smooth.

4. Remove the broccoli from the oven. Arrange the salmon fillets, skinned side down, atop the broccoli. Spoon the glaze over the fish and return the pan to the oven. Roast for 10 minutes, until the salmon is nearly cooked through.

5. Remove the pan from the oven, set the oven to broil, and place a rack 4 inches from the heat. Place the pan under the broiler for about 3 minutes to fully thicken the glaze and brown the tops of the fillets.

6. Serve the salmon and broccoli hot, warm, or at room temperature.

SALMON WITH ROASTED CUCUMBERS & DILLED YOGURT SAUCE

SERVES 4

Here, roasted cucumbers make for a more interesting take on the classic match of salmon, cucumbers, and dill. This was my first go at roasting cucumbers, and now I'm obsessed. I still enjoy raw cucumbers for snacking, but I love what the oven does to this humble vegetable at dinnertime. The dry heat gives a cuke a chance to brown and softly yield but still maintain its refreshing crunch.

---

1 large red onion, cut into 1-inch chunks (about 3 cups)

4 or 5 Persian cucumbers (see box, opposite), sliced into ¾-inch-thick rounds (about 3 cups)

¼ cup extra virgin olive oil

Kosher salt and freshly ground black pepper

4 skinless fillets salmon (each about 1 inch thick; 1½ pounds total)

1½ cups plain Greek yogurt

¼ cup chopped fresh dill

Juice of 1 lemon

LET'S COOK:

1. Preheat the oven to 425°F with a rack in the center position. Line a sheet pan with aluminum foil or parchment paper.

2. Toss together the onion, cucumber, olive oil, ½ teaspoon salt, and ¼ teaspoon pepper on the prepared pan, and spread them out evenly in a single layer. Roast, rotating the pan halfway through, until the vegetables start to pucker and brown, about 20 minutes.

3. Push the vegetables to the perimeter of the pan to make room for the salmon. Place the salmon fillets in the middle of the pan in a single layer, leaving about an inch between them, and sprinkle with ¼ teaspoon salt and ¼ teaspoon pepper. Return the pan to the oven and roast the salmon until its internal temperature registers 130°F on a thermometer for medium-well, about 10 minutes. (Feel free to adjust the cooking time if you like your salmon on the rarer or more well-done side.)

4. Meanwhile, whisk together the yogurt, dill, lemon juice, and salt and pepper to taste in a small bowl.

5. Serve the salmon and vegetables warm, topped with the cool dilled yogurt sauce.

WAIT, WHAT?

PERSIAN CUKES

I like Persian cucumbers for this recipe because they're thin-skinned so I don't have to peel them; they have few seeds; and their small size is perfect for cutting into pretty, fat rounds for roasting. If you can't find Persian cucumbers, though, substitute English or hothouse cukes, which are larger in size but similar in taste and texture.

ROASTED ARCTIC CHAR & ASPARAGUS WITH PISTACHIO GREMOLATA

SERVES 4

This dish is as tasty as it is beautiful. Pink-fleshed Arctic char is closely related to both salmon and lake trout, with a flavor somewhere between the two. If you can't find any Arctic char, feel free to substitute either trout or salmon in its stead. Gremolata sounds impressive, but it is just a simple Italian condiment of chopped parsley, garlic, and lemon zest. Our version has some chopped pistachios, too, for an extra salty, crunchy bite. It brings a little zing to a straightforward meal of roasted fish and bright asparagus with sweet red onion and concentrated pops of cherry tomato.

Olive oil cooking spray (optional)
1 bunch asparagus (roughly 1 pound total)
¼ cup extra virgin olive oil
Kosher salt and freshly ground black pepper
4 skinless fillets Arctic char (5 to 6 ounces each)
½ medium red onion, sliced into ¼-inch-thick half-moons

½ lemon, sliced into ¼-inch-thick rounds
½ cup cherry or grape tomatoes
Grated zest of 1 lemon
1 clove garlic, minced
½ cup packed fresh flat-leaf parsley leaves, roughly chopped
½ cup roasted, salted, and shelled pistachios, roughly chopped

---

LET'S COOK:

1. Preheat the oven to 350°F, with a rack in the center position. Mist a sheet pan with cooking spray or line it with parchment paper.

2. Gently bend one asparagus spear between your fingers and snap off the bottom where it breaks easily. Line up the rest of the bunch and slice off the bottoms at the same distance from the tips. Place the trimmed asparagus on the prepared pan, drizzle with the olive oil, and sprinkle with ½ teaspoon each of the salt and pepper. Toss to coat, and spread the asparagus in an even layer.

3. Place the Arctic char fillets on top of the asparagus, evenly spaced apart, and sprinkle with an extra pinch of salt and pepper. Scatter the onion, lemon slices, and cherry tomatoes around and on top of the char.

4. Bake until the asparagus is crisp-tender and the char is almost opaque, 20 to 30 minutes.

5. While the fish cooks, mix together the lemon zest, garlic, parsley, and pistachios in a small bowl—this is your gremolata.

6. Sprinkle the gremolata over the char and asparagus before serving warm.

TILAPIA TACOS WITH ZUCCHINI & FRESH MANGO SALSA

SERVES 4 TO 6

Broiling is a quick and easy way to prepare fish, especially tilapia fillets, which are so thin that they need only a few minutes under the flame. Tilapia also has the benefit of being relatively inexpensive and widely available. Its mild flavor proves a great canvas for a bold slather of spicy chipotles in adobo, accented with fresh cilantro and lime. You could easily just serve this dish over rice (see page 191), although nestling some flaky fish, tender zucchini, and bright salsa in a soft tortilla is a pretty great move.

---

1 medium-size zucchini, sliced into ⅛- to ¼-inch-thick rounds
4 tablespoons extra virgin olive oil
Kosher salt
¾ teaspoon ground cumin
1 cup loosely packed fresh cilantro leaves, plus extra for serving
1 canned chipotle chile in adobo sauce, chopped, with 1 teaspoon adobo sauce
½ teaspoon grated lime zest
5 tablespoons freshly squeezed lime juice (from 2 to 4 limes)

6 fillets tilapia (about 5 ounces each)
½ cup chopped scallions (white and light green parts only)
8 to 12 small (6-inch) corn or flour tortillas
1 large ripe mango, peeled, pitted, and cut into ½-inch cubes
1 large ripe avocado, pitted, peeled, and cut into ½-inch cubes
½ jalapeño pepper, stemmed, seeded, and diced
Freshly ground black pepper

LET'S COOK:

1. Preheat the oven to broil with one rack about 4 inches from the heat, and another rack in the center position.

2. In a large bowl, toss the zucchini with 1 tablespoon of the olive oil, ¼ teaspoon salt, and ¼ teaspoon of the cumin. Arrange the zucchini in a single layer around the perimeter of a sheet pan. Set aside.

3. In a blender or food processor, combine the cilantro, chipotle, adobo sauce, lime zest, 3 tablespoons of the lime juice, the remaining

½ teaspoon cumin, 2 tablespoons of the olive oil, and 1 tablespoon water and puree until smooth. Transfer the cilantro sauce to a shallow bowl.

4. Dredge the tilapia in the cilantro sauce to coat both sides. Arrange the fillets in a single layer in the center of the prepared pan (discard any leftover sauce). Scatter half of the scallions over the tilapia.

5. Broil the zucchini and fish on the upper rack until the zucchini is soft and puckery and the tilapia is just cooked through, 5 to 10 minutes.

6. Meanwhile, stack the tortillas, wrap them tightly in aluminum foil, and place them directly on the center rack to warm through while the fish cooks.

7. Toss together the mango, avocado, jalapeño, and the remaining 2 tablespoons lime juice, 1 tablespoon olive oil, and chopped scallions in a medium-size bowl. Season the salsa to taste with salt and pepper.

8. Serve the tilapia and zucchini hot from the oven over warm tortillas, topped with the salsa and extra cilantro.

PECAN "FRIED" FISH WITH TARTAR SAUCE

SERVES 4

When I was a kid I spent my summers in Montauk, New York, splashing in the waves near my grandparents' house and licking tartar sauce off my fingers after eating fried clams at Gosman's Dock. Though Montauk fried clams are harder for me to come by these days (it's a bit of a trek from the West Coast), I can still get my fill of tartar sauce (homemade, this time!) and crisp seafood with this oven-baked, nut-crusted fish feast. I like using cod, since it's tasty and affordable, but any thick white fish such as haddock or sea bass will do. Some sliced raw cucumbers sprinkled with salt would be a refreshing side.

1½ cups raw pecan halves
1½ cups panko breadcrumbs
3 tablespoons minced fresh parsley
   leaves
Olive oil cooking spray
½ cup all-purpose flour
Kosher salt
2 large eggs
1¼ cups mayonnaise
Freshly ground black pepper

½ teaspoon smoked paprika
1¼ pounds skinless cod or other
   thick white fish, cut into 4 pieces
   (each 1½ inches thick)
2 tablespoons capers, drained
2 tablespoons sweet relish
1 tablespoon freshly squeezed
   lemon juice
½ teaspoon Worcestershire sauce

LET'S COOK:

1. Preheat the oven to 350°F with a rack in the center position.

2. In a blender or a food processor, pulse the pecans until they look like coarse meal. Transfer them to a sheet pan, stir in the panko to combine, and toast until the crumbs are golden brown, about 10 minutes.

3. Allow the pecan mixture to cool before transferring it to a shallow bowl. Mix in 2 tablespoons of the parsley.

4. Place a wire rack over the now-empty sheet pan and mist it with cooking spray.

5. Whisk together the flour and 1 teaspoon salt in another shallow bowl. In a third bowl, whisk together the eggs, ¼ cup of the mayonnaise, ½ teaspoon pepper, and the smoked paprika until smooth.

6. Pat the fish dry on both sides with paper towels. One at a time, dredge a fish piece in flour, then dunk it in the mayonnaise mixture to coat. Shake off any excess mayonnaise, then dip the fish in the pecan mixture, pressing to coat all sides fully. Place the breaded fish on the prepared rack and mist each fillet lightly with cooking spray. Repeat with the remaining fish.

7. Bake until the fish flakes apart when gently prodded with a paring knife, 18 to 23 minutes.

8. Meanwhile, whip up the tartar sauce: Whisk together the remaining 1 cup mayonnaise, 1 tablespoon parsley, the capers, sweet relish, lemon juice, Worcestershire, and ½ teaspoon pepper in a small bowl. Taste and adjust the seasoning to your liking.

9. Serve the fish hot, with the tartar sauce on the side for dipping.

ASPARAGUS & BLACK COD IN PARCHMENT

SERVES 4

Cooked ever-so-briefly (12 minutes!) in parchment, asparagus and black cod steam gently in the oven, giving us crisp-tender vegetables and moist, flaky fish fillets. Butter, salty olives, fresh herbs, and bright citrus give the flavor some good, clean punch. Simple preparation, stunning presentation. You are a domestic god/goddess.

Don't be intimidated by parchment packets; they'll change the way you cook forever! A bit of simple cutting—you've made homemade Valentines before, right?—is all you need to do to wow the pants off your dinner guests. Or socks? I guess wowing their socks off would be more appropriate? Just . . . let's wow 'em. (And for more guidance on cutting and folding the parchment, see the pics that follow.)

---

2 bunches asparagus, bottom 2 inches of each spear removed
4 skinless fillets black cod (5 ounces each; see Note)
Juice of ½ orange
4 teaspoons extra virgin olive oil

1 teaspoon kosher salt
2 teaspoons roughly chopped fresh tarragon leaves
4 heaping tablespoons chopped, pitted marinated green olives

LET'S COOK:

1. Preheat the oven to 400°F with racks in the upper and lower thirds.

2. Cut four sheets of parchment paper, each 18 inches long and 15 inches wide. Fold each piece of parchment in half (short side to short side). Use scissors to cut each folded piece so that when you open the parchment it looks like a big, fat heart (sort of like you're making a parchment Valentine).

3. Divide the asparagus into four equal bunches. Place one bunch of asparagus on each piece of parchment, on one side of the heart, just next to the center crease. Place one fish fillet on top of each bunch of asparagus.

4. Drizzle the orange juice over the fish fillets, then drizzle each with 1 teaspoon of the olive oil. Sprinkle each with ¼ teaspoon of the salt,

½ teaspoon of the tarragon, and 1 heaping tablespoon of the olives.

5. Seal the parchment packages: Fold the empty half of each heart over the filling and crimp the edges in overlapping folds as you go, until each package is completely closed up and airtight.

6. Carefully place the closed packets on two sheet pans (two packets per pan), and bake, rotating the pans halfway through and switching them from upper to lower and vice versa, until the asparagus is crisp-tender and the cod is opaque (it's okay to unfold an edge to peek inside one of the packets), 12 to 15 minutes.

7. Slide each packet onto a plate and carefully cut open the packets (watch out for the steam), or let each guest open his or her packet at the table for a particularly dramatic presentation.

NOTE: Black cod (sometimes also called sablefish or butterfish) is a superior fish for cooking in parchment—its white flesh is delicate yet firm in texture and boasts a rich, buttery flavor. If you can't find it, substitute another firm white-fleshed fish, such as tilapia or sea bass.

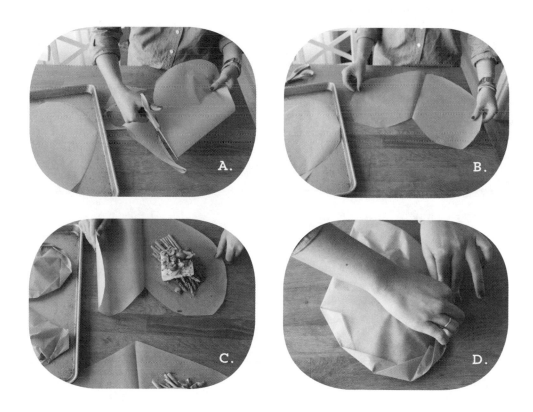

CILANTRO-LIME STEAMED HALIBUT & SPICY COCONUT RICE

SERVES 4

We're cooking in parchment again! The trick to the success of this meal, I've found, is frozen precooked rice. Sold in boxes or bags in many grocery stores, this stuff is one clever shortcut, and it's *good*. So throw away any reservations you have about the freezer section and give yourself a little present of moist, citrusy, coconut-scented halibut and rice. A stunner, this one, all wrapped up in a neat little package.

Note that if your fish fillets are thinner or thicker than 1 inch, you may need to adjust the cooking time by about 5 minutes (less time for thinner fillets, more time for thicker).

---

2 cups frozen precooked white rice (unthawed)

1 cup canned coconut milk (regular or light)

Juice of 1 lime

½ teaspoon crushed red pepper flakes

1 cup frozen shelled edamame (unthawed)

Kosher salt and freshly ground black pepper

4 skinless fillets halibut (each 1 inch thick; about 2 pounds total)

4 teaspoons chopped fresh cilantro leaves

2 limes, sliced into thin rounds

LET'S COOK:

1. Preheat the oven to 400°F with a rack in the center position.

2. Stir together the rice, coconut milk, lime juice, red pepper flakes, edamame, and a pinch of salt in a medium-size bowl. Set aside.

3. Cut four sheets of parchment paper, each 18 inches long and 15 inches wide. Fold each piece of parchment in half (short side to short side). Use scissors to cut each folded piece so that when you open the parchment it looks like a big, fat heart (sort of like you're making a parchment Valentine).

4. Spoon the rice mixture onto one side of each heart, just next to the crease. Lay a halibut fillet on top of each rice pile and sprinkle each fillet with salt, pepper, and 1 teaspoon of chopped cilantro. Arrange 3 or 4 overlapping lime slices atop each fillet.

5. Seal the parchment packages: Fold the empty half of each heart over the filling and crimp the edges in overlapping folds as you go, until each package is completely closed up and airtight.

6. Carefully place the closed packets on two sheet pans (two packets per pan), and bake until the fish is opaque, about 20 minutes (feel free to unfold the edge to peek inside one of the packets toward the end to check the fish).

7. Carefully open the packets (watch out for the steam) and slide the rice and fish into bowls, or transfer the packets to plates so each guest can open his or her own at the table. Serve immediately, while the rice and fish are still warm.

CITRUS-MISO ROASTED WHOLE FISH

SERVES 2

Don't freak out. You *can* roast a whole fish! Yes, with the head and eyes and everything. Once you find the freshest fish available, you can have your fishmonger do the dirty work, gutting and scaling the fish (and if you're really weirded out, she can cut off the head for you, too), so all you have to do is stuff the thing with aromatics, drizzle it with miso dressing, and let it cook in a hot oven. I promise you'll find the process empowering, and the flavor? Incredible. When fish is roasted whole, the words "dry" and "overcooked" leave our fish-for-dinner vocabulary. Instead, we'll use words like "rich," "succulent," "tender," and "flavorful." And that's no fish story. This dish does well with a simple side of buttery rice or, even better, the Spring Rice Pilaf on page 191.

3 blood oranges, skin-on, sliced
    ¼-inch thick
1 jalapeño pepper, stemmed and
    sliced into ¼-inch-thick rounds
2 whole snappers or branzino
    (1 to 1½ pounds each), scaled,
    gutted, and rinsed
½ teaspoon kosher salt

1 lemon, sliced ¼-inch thick
¼ cup white miso paste (see Note)
¼ cup extra virgin olive oil
¼ cup freshly squeezed lemon juice
2 tablespoons honey
3 scallions (whites and light green
    parts only), roughly chopped

LET'S COOK:

1. Preheat the oven to 400°F with a rack in the center position. Line a sheet pan with aluminum foil or parchment paper.

2. Arrange some of the orange slices on the sheet pan, reserving at least 4 for stuffing the fish. Scatter all but 6 slices of the jalapeño over the oranges.

3. Use a sharp knife to score the fish skin on both sides, making a few shallow slashes in the sides of each fish. Sprinkle the cavities of the fish with the salt and place them, side by side, on the orange-lined pan. Stuff the fish with the remaining orange and jalapeño slices and the lemon slices.

4. Whisk together the miso, olive oil, lemon juice, and honey in a small bowl. Spread the miso dressing over the fish, flip the fish and spread the second side with the miso dressing, and drizzle any extra dressing over the oranges on the pan. Scatter the scallions over all.

5. Roast the fish until a knife inserted near the fish's backbone reveals flaky, opaque flesh, 20 to 30 minutes.

6. Fillet the fish at the table for added drama: Use a sharp knife to remove the fillets from the whole fish, working horizontally from tail to gills (the flesh will pretty much fall off the bones). Serve hot.

NOTE: White miso paste is a seasoning made from fermented soybeans, traditionally used in Japanese food. It brings a light, mellow umami flavor wherever it's used, from soups to sauces and salad dressing. Find it in the refrigerated section at your local Asian market; many regular grocery stores sell it these days, too.

TEACH ME HOW
TO BUY A WHOLE FISH
There are a few things to look for when buying whole fish at the market: bright, clear eyes (not cloudy or sunken); firm flesh (it should bounce back when you touch it, not leave an indentation); bright red gills; and a clean, ocean-y smell (fresh fish won't smell "fishy"). Always buy your fish, whole or otherwise, from a reputable vendor who knows their stuff.

SWORDFISH CACCIATORE

SERVES 4

Although *cacciatore* (which means "hunter" in Italian) is normally a word associated with chicken, it turns out that the basic elements of a cacciatore-style sauce—tomatoes, onions, peppers, herbs, and wine—pair fantastically with a meaty fillet of fish. Swordfish is one of the meatiest varieties out there (almost steak-like!) so it can stand up to the bold flavors of a classic cacciatore. I added mushrooms to the mix because I happen to love them, but if you're not a fan, feel free to leave them out. I've heard that southern Italian cooks use red wine in their cacciatore and northern Italians swear by white, but I'm not Italian, so I just use what I have on hand (feel free to do the same).

If you can't find swordfish, tuna steaks or thick fillets of halibut or mahi mahi would substitute nicely.

---

1 medium-size yellow onion, thinly sliced

8 ounces cremini mushrooms, sliced ¼ to ½ inch thick

1 red bell pepper, stemmed, seeded, and sliced into ¼-inch-wide strips

3 cloves garlic, thinly sliced

Kosher salt and freshly ground black pepper

½ teaspoon dried oregano

¼ cup plus 1 tablespoon extra virgin olive oil

1 can (28 ounces) crushed tomatoes, with their juice

½ cup red or white wine

4 swordfish steaks (each ¾ to 1 inch thick; about 2¼ pounds total)

¼ cup capers, drained

2 tablespoons roughly chopped fresh parsley leaves, for garnish

---

LET'S COOK:

1. Preheat the oven to 425°F with a rack in the center position.

2. Combine the onion, mushrooms, bell pepper, garlic, ¼ teaspoon salt, ¼ teaspoon pepper, the oregano, and ¼ cup olive oil on a sheet pan and toss well to coat the vegetables. Arrange the veggies in a single layer and roast until softened and lightly browned, about 20 minutes. Remove the pan from the oven.

3. Stir together the crushed tomatoes and wine in a large bowl and season with a pinch each of salt and pepper. Pour this over the roasted vegetables in the pan, and carefully stir to combine. Pat the swordfish steaks dry on both sides with a paper towel. Sprinkle the steaks all over with a pinch of salt and pepper and arrange them atop the vegetables in the pan. Drizzle the fish with the remaining tablespoon of olive oil and scatter the capers on top of the fish.

4. Return the pan to the oven and bake until the sauce has thickened slightly and the fish is just cooked through, about 15 minutes.

5. Sprinkle the parsley on top of the fish steaks and serve hot, with plenty of the tomato-vegetable sauce spooned over it all.

FANCY TUNA MELTS

SERVES 4

Tuna melts made "fancy" have become my go-to meal when I've pretty much got no time to make dinner but still have an appetite for something warm and luxurious. Small touches like basing the melt on chewy store-bought naan bread, mixing the tuna with crisp apple and briny capers, and topping it all with flavorful braided string cheese, sun-dried tomatoes, and a handful of tender baby greens (I like mâche rosettes) or salt-and-vinegar potato chips turn ho-hum tuna melts into midweek showstoppers.

Naan is a kind of Indian flatbread, similar to pita bread (though a bit softer in texture). I buy it packaged in the bread aisle at Whole Foods, but if you have trouble finding it, go ahead and substitute your favorite pocketless pita or flatbread. As for braided string cheese, which is traditionally Armenian and so very delicious—it can be found in the fancier cheese section at most grocery stores. If you can't get your hands on any, substitute marinated mozzarella cheese (bocconcini).

---

4 naan breads (from two 8.8-ounce packages), cut in half widthwise

1 large can (12.8 ounces) chunk light tuna in water, drained

1 large shallot, finely diced

½ cup diced unpeeled apple (I like Pink Lady apples for their crunch)

¼ cup capers, drained, plus 1 tablespoon reserved caper brine

1 heaping tablespoon chopped fresh dill

1½ tablespoons Dijon mustard

¼ cup mayonnaise

5 ounces braided string cheese marinated in oil and herbs, drained if liquid-y

Sun-dried tomatoes packed in oil, drained, for topping (optional)

Mâche rosettes or other baby greens, for topping (optional)

Salt-and-vinegar or other potato chips, for topping (optional)

LET'S COOK:

1. Preheat the oven to 375°F with a rack in the center position. Line a sheet pan with aluminum foil or parchment paper.

2. Arrange 4 naan bread halves on the prepared pan. Mix together the tuna, shallot, apple, capers and caper brine, fresh dill, mustard, and mayonnaise in a medium-size bowl until combined. Evenly distribute the

tuna salad, in big, heaping scoops, among the naan breads. Break and pull the string cheese apart and lay the strands evenly over the sandwiches. Arrange the remaining naan halves around the sandwiches.

3. Bake until the tuna salad is warmed through and the cheese is melted, about 10 minutes.

4. Top each open-faced sandwich with sun-dried tomatoes and mâche or with handfuls of potato chips if you like. Press the sandwiches closed with the remaining naan bread halves. Enjoy the tuna melts warm from the oven.

HONEY-ORANGE SHRIMP WITH BABY BOK CHOY

SERVES 4

This is sort of like the sheet pan version of a sweet and spicy stir-fry. We just marinate the shrimp while some glazed baby bok choy gets a head start in the hot oven, then all we have to do is toss the shrimp on top and wait for the oven to turn them pink and lovely. A big bowl of jasmine rice is a natural pairing here.

1½ pounds 26/30 count raw shrimp, peeled and deveined, tails removed
1 teaspoon grated orange zest
¼ cup plus 3 tablespoons freshly squeezed orange juice
¼ cup extra virgin olive oil
2 tablespoons hot sauce (such as Cholula's or Frank's Red Hot)
1 tablespoon Dijon mustard

2 cloves garlic, minced
Olive oil cooking spray
2 tablespoons unsalted butter, melted
2 tablespoons honey
1 tablespoon soy sauce
Pinch of crushed red pepper flakes
1 pound baby bok choy, sliced lengthwise into quarters

LET'S COOK:

1. Place the shrimp, orange zest, ¼ cup of the orange juice, the olive oil, hot sauce, mustard, and garlic in a medium-size bowl or gallon-size zip-top bag, and toss to combine (or seal the bag and shake gently). Cover the bowl and marinate the shrimp in the refrigerator for 20 to 30 minutes.

2. Meanwhile, preheat the oven to 400°F with a rack in the center position. Mist a sheet pan with cooking spray.

3. Whisk together the butter, honey, soy sauce, red pepper flakes, and the remaining 3 tablespoons orange juice in a small bowl. Place the bok choy on the sheet pan, drizzle with the dressing, and toss to coat. Spread out the bok choy in a single layer.

4. Roast the bok choy, rotating the pan halfway through, until it starts to brown and the sauce has thickened, about 25 minutes.

5. Add the shrimp and its marinade to the pan in a single layer over the bok choy, and roast until the shrimp are bright pink and just cooked through, an additional 8 to 10 minutes.

6. Serve hot.

BALSAMIC SHRIMP & SUMMER VEGETABLES

SERVES 4

Sweet and tangy balsamic vinegar really shines paired with a heap of warm-weather vegetables and juicy shrimp. When I can, I like to buy shrimp that have already been peeled and deveined; it saves me both time and a goopy mess in the kitchen. After the shrimp are cleaned and you've gotten some basic chopping out of the way, this bright, summery dish comes together in a snap. Letting the peeled shrimp marinate while the vegetables cook is a simple way to amp up the flavor, so don't skip that step.

Olive oil cooking spray

2 medium-size zucchini, sliced into ½-inch-thick half-moons

1 yellow summer squash, sliced into ½-inch-thick half-moons

1 medium-size red or orange bell pepper, stemmed, seeded, and cut into 1-inch chunks

1 cup cherry tomatoes, halved

1 medium-size red onion, cut into 1-inch chunks

Kosher salt and freshly ground black pepper

¼ cup plus 1 tablespoon extra virgin olive oil

3 tablespoons balsamic vinegar

Juice of 1 lemon

1¼ pounds 26/30 count raw shrimp, peeled and deveined, tails on

½ teaspoon Worcestershire sauce

¼ cup roughly chopped fresh basil leaves

Crusty bread or couscous (cooked according to package directions), for serving

---

LET'S COOK:

1. Preheat oven to 375°F with one rack in the center position and another 4 inches from the heat. Mist a sheet pan with cooking spray.

2. Toss the zucchini, yellow squash, bell pepper, tomatoes, and onion on the prepared pan with ½ teaspoon salt, ½ teaspoon pepper, ¼ cup of the olive oil, 2 tablespoons of the vinegar, and the lemon juice. Roast the vegetables on the center rack until softened and beginning to brown at the edges, about 20 minutes. Remove the vegetables from the oven.

3. Meanwhile, place the shrimp in a large bowl. Add ¼ teaspoon salt, the remaining 1 tablespoon olive oil, 1 tablespoon vinegar, and the Worcestershire sauce and toss gently. Let the shrimp marinate at room temperature while the vegetables cook.

4. Set the oven to broil. Scatter the shrimp, with their marinade, over the vegetables in a single layer. Broil on the upper rack until the shrimp tails are charred and the shrimp are just cooked through, about 5 minutes.

5. Scatter the basil over the dish, and enjoy warm, with bread or a side of couscous.

SHRIMP & POLENTA WITH CRISPY PANCETTA TUILES

SERVES 4

H ere, thin slices of precooked polenta are transformed into sweet rounds of crisp-edged, creamy-centered satisfaction (it helps that they're cooked in pancetta drippings), and oven roasting yields particularly sweet and juicy shrimp. It's all topped with a pancetta tuile, which is like a thin and crisp baked pork chip—these should be served with pretty much everything, as far as I'm concerned. The dish is a bit of an Italian slant on shrimp and grits, and it's pretty perfect weeknight fare, though it would also be a welcome addition to the brunch table.

8 to 10 very thin slices round unsmoked pancetta
1 tube (18 ounces) precooked polenta, sliced into ½-inch-thick rounds (about 16 slices)
½ pint cherry tomatoes, halved
1½ tablespoons plus 1 teaspoon extra virgin olive oil
Kosher salt and freshly ground black pepper

1 tablespoon freshly squeezed lemon juice
1 or 2 cloves garlic, minced
½ teaspoon dried oregano
½ teaspoon Worcestershire sauce
1 teaspoon chopped fresh chives
1 generous pound 26/30 count raw shrimp, peeled and deveined, tails removed, blotted gently with paper towels to dry

LET'S COOK:

1. Preheat the oven to 400°F with a rack in the center position. Line a sheet pan with parchment paper. Line a plate with paper towels.

2. Place the pancetta rounds side by side on the prepared pan and bake until crisp, 5 to 7 minutes. Remove to the lined plate to cool and drain; set aside (keep the parchment on the sheet pan).

3. Place the polenta rounds on the used sheet pan, right on top of the pancetta drippings, positioning them closely together so they form a kind of raft.

4. In a large bowl, toss together the cherry tomatoes with 1 teaspoon of the olive oil, ¼ teaspoon salt, and ¼ teaspoon pepper. Scatter the tomatoes around and on top of the polenta. Bake the polenta and tomatoes for about 10 minutes.

5. Meanwhile, whisk together the remaining 1½ tablespoons olive oil with the lemon juice, garlic, oregano, Worcestershire sauce, ¼ teaspoon salt, ¼ teaspoon pepper, and the chives in a large bowl. Add the shrimp and toss to coat. Set them aside at room temperature to marinate while the polenta and tomatoes cook.

6. After the polenta and tomatoes have baked for 10 minutes, arrange the shrimp on top in a single layer (make sure the shrimp do not overlap) and return the pan to the oven. Bake until the shrimp are pink and just cooked through, an additional 8 to 10 minutes.

7. Serve the shrimp, tomatoes, and polenta warm, with the pancetta tuiles on top.

Chapter 5

MEATS, MAINLY

....

We didn't eat a ton of red meat in my family when I was growing up, though we did enjoy our fair share of hamburgers and meatloaf. As I've gotten older, I've learned to appreciate more robust dishes using steak, lamb, and pork, such as buttery Beef Tenderloin with Frizzled Leeks & Fennel (page 115), or Thick-Cut Pork Chops with Warm Apple-Cabbage Slaw (page 125). I often turn to these heartier, showstopping recipes for special occasions.

I've found lean, quick-cooking meats (like a roasted Pork Tenderloin with Squash, Apples & Onion, page 129, or a Fajita Flank Steak with Peppers & Onion, page 113) to do exceptionally well using the sheet pan method, and I even managed to perfect baby back ribs (page 127)! From my dad's famous Barbecue Meatloaf (see page 119) to Roasted Sausage & Red Grapes with Polenta & Gorgonzola (page 133), this chapter is where you'll find the real meat of the matter.

FAJITA FLANK STEAK WITH PEPPERS & ONION

SERVES 4 TO 6

It's a fiesta! All on one pan. Skirt steak is traditionally used for fajitas, but I like the leaner, equally thin cut of flank steak. If you can't find it, skirt, flatiron, or hanger steaks make good substitutes.

Be sure to give the meat plenty of time to soak up the bright, garlicky marinade—anywhere from 2 to 12 hours should do it. The thin flank is easy to overcook, so a quick blast of heat in the broiler is all it needs; keep an eye on it and use a thermometer to ensure the perfect degree of doneness.

And don't forget the fajita fixings! We'll need some tortillas, salsa, sour cream, cheese, maybe even some sliced avocado, for good measure.

2½ pounds flank steak

4 cloves garlic, minced

¼ cup plus 2 tablespoons extra virgin olive oil

3 tablespoons Worcestershire sauce

¼ cup freshly squeezed lime juice (from 2 to 4 limes)

1 tablespoon ground cumin

1 tablespoon chili powder

1 tablespoon sugar

¼ teaspoon crushed red pepper flakes

1 teaspoon kosher salt

Olive oil cooking spray

4 bell peppers (any color), stemmed, seeded, and thinly sliced

1 yellow onion, thinly sliced

8 to 12 small (6-inch) flour or corn tortillas, for serving

¼ cup chopped fresh cilantro leaves

Salsa, sour cream, sliced avocado, and Cotija cheese (see Note, page 19), for serving

---

LET'S COOK:

1. Place the flank steak in a large zip-top bag or a shallow glass baking dish. Whisk together the garlic, olive oil, Worcestershire sauce, lime juice, cumin, chili powder, sugar, red pepper flakes, and salt in a small bowl. Reserve ¼ cup of the marinade for the vegetables and pour the rest over the flank steak, turning it to coat. Close up the bag or cover the baking dish and marinate the steak in the refrigerator for at least 2 hours, and up to 12.

2. When you're ready to cook, preheat the oven to 450°F with one rack about 4 inches from the broiler, another rack in the center position, and another in the bottom position. Line a sheet pan with aluminum foil, and mist it with the cooking spray.

3. Toss the peppers and onion with the reserved ¼ cup marinade in a large bowl and spread them evenly on the prepared pan. Roast on the center rack until softened and starting to brown, 10 to 15 minutes.

4. Remove the pan from the oven and turn the oven to broil. Wrap a stack of tortillas in aluminum foil and set it aside.

5. Push the peppers and onion to the perimeter of the pan. Remove the flank steak from the marinade, allowing any excess liquid to drip off the meat, and place it in the center of the pan, surrounded by the vegetables.

6. Place the pan on the top rack and broil the steak, flipping it once, until it begins to char on the outside and an instant-read thermometer inserted into the thickest part of the meat registers 125°F for rare or 135°F for medium-rare, 3 to 5 minutes per side.

7. While the steak cooks, place the foil-wrapped tortillas on the bottom rack to warm through. Once the steak is finished cooking, remove the pan from the oven and turn the oven off. Leave the tortillas in the oven to continue warming while the steak rests.

8. Allow the steak to rest, loosely covered with foil, for 10 minutes before slicing it thinly against the grain. Sprinkle with the cilantro.

9. Serve the steak warm with the peppers and onion and tortillas. Pass the salsa, sour cream, avocado, and cheese at the table.

BEEF TENDERLOIN WITH FRIZZLED LEEKS & FENNEL

SERVES 4

Crispy leeks over rich, buttery, tender beef—this is a special occasion meal. Whether you're celebrating a big birthday, a sweet anniversary, a well-deserved promotion, a date night, or just because, make sure you're ready to shell out some beans for a fresh beef tenderloin at the butcher shop or grocery store. I don't mean to deter you—this sumptuous dish is totally worth it—just to prepare your conscience (and wallet).

The tenderloin is one of the leanest, most tender cuts of beef (it's the same cut that gives us filet mignon), so it's important to treat it with care. Have the butcher trim the fat and silverskin for you, if you're uncomfortable handling it yourself. Tie it compactly with butcher's twine (for tips on trussing, see the box on page 69).

And don't let leftovers go to waste—a few slices of beef piled on a soft roll with some deli-counter horseradish sauce makes a truly decadent next-day lunch.

---

3 large leeks, white and light green parts only, thinly sliced into half-moons and well rinsed (see box, page 116)

3 or 4 cloves garlic, thinly sliced

1 small bulb fennel, stalky fingers removed, cored, and thinly sliced (see box, page 61)

¼ cup plus 1 tablespoon extra virgin olive oil

1½ teaspoons kosher salt

1 teaspoon freshly ground black pepper

1 beef tenderloin roast (2½ to 3 pounds), trimmed of excess fat and silverskin

1 tablespoon finely chopped fresh rosemary

1½ teaspoons ground fennel seed

LET'S COOK:

1. Preheat the oven to 400°F with a rack in the center position.

2. Place the leeks, garlic, and fennel on a sheet pan, drizzle with ¼ cup of the olive oil, sprinkle with ½ teaspoon each salt and pepper, and toss to combine. Spread the vegetables in an even layer and set a wire rack on top.

3. Pat the beef tenderloin dry with paper towels. If the tenderloin is an uneven thickness, tuck the skinny tapered end underneath and tie it tightly with butcher's twine. Continue to tie up the roast at ½-inch intervals, to help it keep its shape during cooking.

4. Stir together the remaining tablespoon olive oil, 1 teaspoon salt, ½ teaspoon pepper, the rosemary, and fennel seed in a small bowl to form a loose paste. Rub the paste on all sides of the beef, coating it entirely. Place the beef on the wire rack over the vegetables.

5. Roast the tenderloin until an instant-read thermometer inserted into the thickest part of the meat registers 130°F for medium-rare, 35 to 45 minutes. The vegetables should be quite crisp and frizzled.

6. Allow the meat to rest, uncovered, for 10 to 15 minutes before transferring it to a cutting board. Remove the butcher's twine and slice the meat into ½-inch-thick slices. Serve topped with the frizzled vegetables.

TEACH ME HOW
TO CLEAN A LEEK

Leeks, those taller, milder cousins of onions and garlic, grow in sandy soil and tend to accumulate a healthy amount of grit and dirt. To clean them, first rinse them under cold water to remove any visible grime. Slice off the stringy roots and the tough dark green parts of the stalk, then cut the leek lengthwise, from white end to green, into two long halves. Slice the leek into thin half-moons. Place the slices into a large bowl and add cold water to cover. Use your hands to gently agitate the leeks, dislodging any grit, which will sink to the bottom. Scoop the leeks from the water. Repeat the process with fresh water, if necessary.

BROILED STEAK & ASPARAGUS WITH FETA CREAM SAUCE

SERVES 4

This dish is deliciously simple. Beautiful sirloin tip steaks (which are nice and lean, and cheap to boot) and fresh asparagus are broiled to perfection—in 10 minutes! And while the broiler works its magic, all we need to do is whip up a salty, creamy, tangy feta sauce in the blender.

If asparagus isn't your thing, feel free to swap out another quick-cooking vegetable, such as sliced summer squash or some bright cherry tomatoes.

Olive oil cooking spray
2 bunches asparagus
5 tablespoons extra virgin olive oil
¾ teaspoon kosher salt
½ teaspoon freshly ground black pepper

2 sirloin tip steaks (each 1 to 1½ inches thick; about 2¼ pounds total)
1 cup (about 6 ounces) crumbled feta cheese
½ cup sour cream
2 tablespoons apple cider vinegar
¼ cup finely chopped fresh chives

LET'S COOK:

1. Preheat the broiler with a rack about 4 inches from the heat. Line a sheet pan with aluminum foil and mist a wire rack about the size of the sheet pan with cooking spray.

2. Snap off the bottom of one asparagus spear, to see where it breaks easily. Line up the rest of the bunch and slice off the bottoms at the same spot. Place the trimmed asparagus on the prepared pan, drizzle with 3 tablespoons of the olive oil, sprinkle with ¼ teaspoon salt and ¼ teaspoon black pepper, and toss to coat. Arrange the asparagus in a single layer around the perimeter of the pan and set the wire rack on top, nudging the asparagus aside as needed so the rack lies flat and even.

3. Blot the steaks dry with a paper towel. Season both sides with the remaining ½ teaspoon salt and ¼ teaspoon pepper. Place the steaks on the wire rack.

4. Place the pan under the broiler (the steaks should be about an inch from the heat). Broil, flipping the steaks

once, until well browned and charred at the edges, 4 to 5 minutes per side for medium-rare. (If you prefer your steak more or less done, adjust the cooking time accordingly.)

5. While the steaks and asparagus cook, make the feta cream sauce: Combine the feta cheese, sour cream, remaining 2 tablespoons olive oil, and cider vinegar in a food processor or blender. Puree the ingredients

until smooth. Add salt and pepper to taste and give the sauce one last pulse. Pour the sauce into a bowl and fold in the chives.

6. Remove the pan from the broiler and allow the steak and asparagus to rest for 10 minutes on the rack. Transfer the steak to a cutting board before slicing it thinly against the grain. Serve the steak and asparagus with the feta cream sauce.

BRUCE'S BARBECUE MEATLOAF & POTATOES

SERVES 4 TO 6

This meatloaf is my dad Bruce's culinary pride and joy. His repertoire in the kitchen is small but solid; he's great with cereal, SpaghettiOs, and meatloaf. The recipe is his go-to "special occasion, Dad's cooking" dinner, and it's full of all of his favorite things (such as diced onions and barbecue sauce). It's a smoky, sweet, tangy version of regular (boring?) meatloaf, and it's fantastic. Dad usually serves his famous loaf with tiny whole roasted potatoes, but using Yukon golds, sliced thin, really brings things to a new level, flavor-wise.

Dad bakes his meatloaf right on the pan, but I've found that elevating the loaf on a wire rack over the potatoes prevents everything from getting soggy and really perfects the dish. Trust me on this one, Pops.

2½ pounds (about 4 medium-size) Yukon gold potatoes, unpeeled, scrubbed, sliced into ¼-inch-thick rounds
¼ cup extra virgin olive oil
½ teaspoon kosher salt
1 tablespoon plus ½ teaspoon garlic powder

2 pounds lean ground beef
1 large yellow onion, diced (about 2 cups)
2 cups barbecue sauce (I love Sweet Baby Ray's or Stubb's)
½ cup plain dried breadcrumbs

LET'S COOK:

1. Preheat the oven to 375°F with a rack in the center position. Line a sheet pan with aluminum foil or parchment paper.

2. Place the potatoes on the prepared pan, drizzle with the olive oil, sprinkle with the salt and the ½ teaspoon of garlic powder, and toss to coat. Spread the potatoes in an even layer and set a wire rack on top.

3. Fold a piece of aluminum foil into a 10-by-6-inch rectangle and place it in the center of the wire rack. Use a skewer or a fork to poke little holes evenly throughout the rectangle of foil—this will help with heat circulation and keep the meatloaf from steaming in its own fat.

4. Gently combine the beef, onion, the remaining tablespoon garlic powder, 1½ cups of the barbecue sauce, and the breadcrumbs in a large bowl. Without squishing and squeezing too much, form the meat mixture into a loaf on top of the foil rectangle.

5. Place the pan in the oven. Bake the meatloaf and potatoes for 30 minutes, then brush the top of the loaf with the remaining ½ cup barbecue sauce.

6. Return the pan to the oven and bake the meatloaf and potatoes until the potatoes are tender and an instant-read thermometer inserted into the center of the meatloaf registers 150°F, about 45 minutes more.

7. Allow the meatloaf to cool slightly before slicing. Serve with the potatoes.

CHEESEBURGERS WITH BACON & CHARRED ONION

SERVES 4

I created this recipe for my dad, who would probably eat a cheeseburger every day for the rest of his life if my sisters and I would let him (we are his nagging daughters, though, so we won't). The broiler is a quick and mess-free way to get juicy, flavorful hamburgers, in this case topped with sharp Cheddar cheese, crisp bacon, and charred onions.

---

8 slices bacon (about 8 ounces)
1 pound ground beef (I like to use 85% lean)
2 tablespoons Worcestershire sauce
1 tablespoon garlic powder
½ teaspoon kosher salt
½ teaspoon freshly ground black pepper

1 yellow onion, sliced into ¾-inch-thick rounds
4 thick slices sharp Cheddar cheese (about 6 ounces)
4 soft hamburger buns
Ketchup, mustard, pickles, or your own favorite burger condiments (optional)

LET'S COOK:

1. Preheat the oven to 375°F with one rack about 4 inches from the broiler and another rack in the center position. Line a sheet pan with aluminum foil. Line a plate with paper towels.

2. Lay the bacon slices flat on the prepared pan. Bake on the center rack, flipping halfway through, until crisp, about 20 minutes.

3. While the bacon is cooking, gently mix together the beef, Worcestershire, garlic powder, salt and pepper in a large bowl. Divide and shape the meat into four equal patties, each about ¾ inch thick.

4. Transfer the bacon to the plate and set aside to drain. Carefully pour the bacon grease from the pan and replace the aluminum foil.

5. Set a wire rack on the sheet pan and turn on the broiler. Place the burger patties on the rack with some space between them. Arrange the onion slices around the burgers (if the rack's not big enough and some onions spill onto the pan itself, that's fine).

6. Broil the burgers and onions on the upper rack for 3 minutes per side for medium-rare. Top the burgers with the Cheddar and broil until the cheese is melted and bubbly, an additional 30 to 60 seconds.

7. Serve the burgers on the buns, topped with the charred onions, crisp bacon, and all your favorite condiments.

MAKE IT MINE

THE PERFECT CHEESEBURGER

Everyone's got their own version of the perfect cheeseburger, so if Cheddar, bacon, and charred onions aren't your thing, feel free to play around with burger toppings to nail your own! A few suggestions, if I may:

- California Dreamburger: Prepare with pepperjack cheese, top with avocado slices and sprouts.

- BlueBQ Burger: Prepare with blue cheese, top with sliced red onion and barbecue sauce.

- Reuben Burger: Prepare with Swiss cheese, top with sauerkraut and Thousand Island dressing.

- Salty Spainburger: Prepare with manchego cheese, top with sliced ham or prosciutto and olive tapenade.

CHINESE FIVE SPICE PORK CHOPS WITH NECTARINES

SERVES 4

When I was a kid, my baseball team was called the Pork Chops. We excelled at batting, fielding, and postgame trips to Dairy Queen. To this day, I have trouble not associating pork chops with the smell of fresh-cut grass and the promise of ice cream. It follows, then, that I really enjoy a good pork chop.

This recipe uses thin-cut chops so they cook quickly, surrounded by sweet stone fruit and sharp scallions. A marinade of soy sauce, brown sugar, rice vinegar, fresh ginger, sesame oil, and Chinese five spice powder completes the rich and complex flavor profile of the dish. Round out the meal by serving the chops with a pot of jasmine rice or some quick-cooking couscous.

If nectarines aren't in season, apples or pears would be a nice substitute.

¼ cup canola oil
¼ cup packed brown sugar
¼ cup low-sodium soy sauce
2 tablespoons rice vinegar
1 piece (2 inches) fresh ginger, peeled and finely grated
1 teaspoon Chinese five spice powder

1 teaspoon toasted (dark) sesame oil
6 boneless pork chops (each ½ inch thick), trimmed of visible fat
5 nectarines, unpeeled, pitted, and cut into ¾-inch slices
¼ cup chopped scallions (white and light green parts only)

LET'S COOK:

1. Whisk together the oil, sugar, soy sauce, vinegar, ginger, five spice powder, and sesame oil in a medium-size bowl until combined. Place the pork chops in a gallon-size zip-top bag, add the marinade, and seal the bag. Turn the pork chops over in the marinade to coat fully.

Place the bag in the refrigerator and let the chops marinate for at least 4 hours, and up to overnight.

2. When you're ready to cook, preheat the oven to 425°F with a rack in the center position. Line a sheet pan with aluminum foil or parchment paper.

3. Using kitchen tongs, transfer the marinated pork chops to the prepared sheet pan, spacing them evenly apart. Reserve the marinade. Place the nectarine slices in a medium-size bowl, add ¼ cup of the marinade, and toss to coat. Arrange the nectarines around the pork chops.

4. Bake until the pork chops are just cooked through (an instant-read thermometer inserted into the thickest part of the meat should register 140°F to 145°F) and the nectarines have softened and browned, 15 to 20 minutes. Serve immediately.

WAIT, WHAT?

CHINESE FIVE SPICE POWDER

A blend of (surprise!) five spices often used in Chinese cuisine, this powder brings elements of sweet, spice, and warmth to many dishes, both sweet and savory. It's typically made up of some combination of star anise, Chinese cinnamon, cloves, Sichuan pepper, and fennel seed, though it can also contain additions like ground ginger, nutmeg, turmeric, black pepper, or cardamom. You can find it in the spice aisle at most supermarkets.

THICK-CUT PORK CHOPS WITH WARM APPLE-CABBAGE SLAW

SERVES 4

Thick, meaty, bone-in pork chops get a hit of freshness from a tart, mustardy marinade, and a warm apple-cabbage slaw brings the dish a much-needed bit of sweetness and crunch. Napa cabbage is sometimes referred to as Chinese cabbage, and I like its mild flavor and light, yellow green color here. If you can't find it, feel free to substitute another type of cabbage, such as red, green, or savoy.

Olive oil cooking spray
½ head napa cabbage, shredded (about 6 cups)
2 Granny Smith apples, unpeeled, cored and sliced into thin matchsticks
3 tablespoons extra vigin olive oil
2 tablespoons apple cider vinegar
1 teaspoon kosher salt
¼ teaspoon freshly ground black pepper

4 bone-in pork loin chops (each 1½ inches thick; 4 to 5 pounds total)
2 teaspoons Dijon mustard
2 teaspoons pure maple syrup or honey
1 teaspoon chopped fresh thyme leaves
3 scallions (white and light green parts only), thinly sliced

---

LET'S COOK:

1. Preheat the oven to 375°F with one rack about 4 inches from the broiler and another rack in the center position. Mist a sheet pan with cooking spray.

2. Toss together the cabbage and apples with the olive oil, 1 tablespoon of the vinegar, ½ teaspoon of the salt, and the pepper on the prepared sheet pan. Place a sheet pan–size

wire rack over the slaw, and mist it with cooking spray.

3. Pat the pork chops dry with a paper towel, and season them on both sides with the remaining ½ teaspoon salt.

4. Whisk together the mustard, maple syrup, the remaining tablespoon cider vinegar, and the fresh thyme in a small bowl. Spread this over both sides of the pork chops. Place the chops evenly apart on the rack over the slaw.

5. Bake until an instant-read thermometer inserted into the thickest part of the meat (but not touching the bone) registers 130°F, about 35 minutes.

6. Remove the pan from the oven and turn the oven to broil.

7. Broil the pork chops and slaw until the chops are golden-crusted and the thermometer registers 145°F.

8. Remove the pork chops from the wire rack to rest on a cutting board, loosely covered with aluminum foil, for 10 minutes while you mix the scallions into the slaw.

9. Serve the chops warm, topped with heaps of slaw.

BAKED BABY BACK RIBS & POTATOES

SERVES 4

I live in a small apartment in a bustling city, so for me, backyards and barbecue grills are the stuff of pipe dreams. Still, perfectly tender baby back ribs are well within reach. A slow and steady stint in the oven followed by a quick broil does the trick! A mixture of dry rub, barbecue sauce, some Dijon mustard, and liquid smoke ensures knock-out flavor, and a side of creamy-centered potatoes seals the deal. Who needs a grill, anyway?

1 tablespoon Dijon mustard
1 teaspoon liquid smoke (optional)
3 tablespoons dark brown sugar
1½ tablespoons garlic powder
2 teaspoons kosher salt
2 teaspoons sweet or smoked paprika
2 teaspoons ground mustard (such as Colman's)
1 teaspoon ground cumin
¼ teaspoon cayenne pepper

4 pounds baby back ribs, trimmed of silverskin
1 pound medium-size Yukon gold potatoes, unpeeled, scrubbed and quartered
1 tablespoon extra vigin olive oil
1 teaspoon Old Bay seasoning
¾ cup barbecue sauce (I like Sweet Baby Ray's or Stubb's), plus extra for serving

LET'S COOK:

1. Preheat the oven to 325°F with one rack about 4 inches from the broiler and another rack in the center position.

2. Place the Dijon mustard in a small bowl, add the liquid smoke, if using, and stir together to combine. Whisk together the brown sugar, garlic powder, salt, paprika, ground mustard, cumin, and cayenne in a medium-size bowl.

3. Brush both sides of the ribs with the Dijon mustard and sprinkle with the spice mix to coat. Pat the spice mix into the meat so it sticks. Wrap the ribs tightly in aluminum foil and place them in the center of a sheet pan.

4. Combine the potatoes, olive oil, and Old Bay in a large bowl and toss to coat. Place the potatoes on the pan around the package of ribs.

5. Bake for 1½ hours, gently flipping the package and stirring up the potatoes halfway through cooking.

6. Carefully transfer the package of ribs to a platter or another sheet pan and remove the foil. Return the ribs (without the foil) to the center of the pan in a single layer, meaty side up. Brush them all over with the barbecue sauce.

7. Bake until a knife slides easily into the thickest part of the meat, an additional 30 minutes. Keep an eye on the potatoes during this part of the baking—if they're getting too dark, remove them to a serving bowl, cover with aluminum foil to keep warm, and set them aside.

8. When the ribs are knife-tender, remove the pan from the oven. Scoop the potatoes into a serving bowl and cover with aluminum foil to keep warm.

9. Turn the oven to broil and broil the ribs on the top rack until they are slightly charred in spots, about 3 minutes.

10. Allow the ribs to rest for about 10 minutes before slicing them between the bones. Serve the ribs with the potatoes and extra barbecue sauce.

DIY OR BUY?
BARBECUE SAUCE

It's pretty simple to whip up your own homemade barbecue sauce, and there are roughly a million different ways to do it. Most standard-issue red barbecue sauces involve some mixture of ketchup or tomato sauce, mustard, vinegar, sugar, onion or garlic, molasses, and spices—every region of the country seems to have its preferred way of doing it. I'm all for homemade, but I won't lie: More often than not, I'll grab a bottle of the stuff at the market. There are quite a few good-quality store-bought options out there, depending on your personal tastes. I grew up on Sweet Baby Ray's (which I love), and recently discovered Stubbs (I particularly like the smoky mesquite flavor), which is richly flavored and doesn't rely on high fructose corn syrup, unlike most other store-bought options.

PORK TENDERLOIN WITH SQUASH, APPLES & ONION

SERVES 4 TO 6

We didn't eat a ton of pork in my house when I was growing up, but since my time in culinary school, I've learned to appreciate the merits—and there are many—of "the other white meat." (Did anyone else think that ad campaign was kind of weird?) Anyway, roasting a pair of lean pork tenderloins is one of the simplest ways to ease into a world beyond beef and chicken—and let me tell you, this new world is a juicy and flavorful one. Butternut squash, apples, red onion, and garlic are a sweet, savory, autumn-inspired backdrop for the rich, tender meat, but feel free to swap out the winter squash and apples for whatever's in season (zucchini and tomatoes in summer, baby artichokes and ramps in spring, perhaps).

---

4 cups chopped, peeled butternut squash (about ¾-inch chunks; about 1 large squash)

2 Granny Smith apples, peeled, cored, and cut into ¾-inch chunks

1 large red onion, cut into ½-inch-thick chunks

3 cloves garlic, thinly sliced

¼ cup extra virgin olive oil

1½ teaspoons kosher salt

1 teaspoon chopped fresh thyme leaves

2 pork tenderloins (1 pound each), trimmed of all visible fat

2 teaspoons dried herbes de Provence (see box, page 50)

1 teaspoon ground mustard (such as Colman's)

½ teaspoon freshly ground black pepper

LET'S COOK:

1. Preheat the oven to 450°F with a rack in the center position. Line a sheet pan with aluminum foil or parchment paper.

2. Toss together the squash, apples, onion, garlic, olive oil, ½ teaspoon salt, and the thyme on the prepared pan until well combined. Spread out the vegetables evenly.

3. Place the pork tenderloins on a plate. Pat them dry with a paper towel, then rub them with the remaining 1 teaspoon salt, the herbes de Provence, ground mustard, and

pepper until coated on all sides. Place the tenderloins on top of the vegetables in the sheet pan, leaving some space between the two pieces of meat.

4. Roast the pork and vegetables for 15 minutes, then use kitchen tongs to flip the tenderloins over. Continue to roast until the vegetables are browned and an instant-read thermometer inserted into the thickest part of the pork registers 145°F, an additional 10 to 15 minutes.

5. Allow the pork to rest, loosely covered with aluminum foil, for 10 minutes before transferring them to a cutting board to slice. Serve the ribs with the potatoes and extra barbecue sauce.

ROASTED BRUSSELS SPROUTS & PANCETTA PASTA

SERVES 4 AS A MAIN DISH, 4 TO 6 AS A SIDE (WITHOUT PASTA)

It seems like vegetables go in and out of fashion, and I feel like lately Brussels sprouts are having their day. It's like they get to sit at the vegetable cool table, which is otherwise occupied by kale, avocado, and cauliflower. Brussels sprouts for prom queen!

Charred Brussels sprouts and crisp pancetta are hearty and warming piled atop a simple bowl of pasta (which I realize isn't exactly sheet pan friendly, but we can bend the rules just this once). If you decide to skip the pasta, though, the roasted Brussels also make a nice side dish for a meatier main of chicken, pork, beef, or lamb.

To really up the festive vibe, scatter some shaved Parmesan cheese, bright pomegranate arils (aka the seeds), or toasted nuts on top of the dish before serving.

1 pound dried pasta, such as spaghetti
  or fettuccine
3 tablespoons extra virgin olive oil,
  plus extra for coating the pasta
2 pounds Brussels sprouts, trimmed
  and halved vertically
4 ounces pancetta, diced
1 shallot, thinly sliced
3 or 4 cloves garlic, minced

½ teaspoon fresh thyme leaves
½ teaspoon kosher salt
½ teaspoon freshly ground black
  pepper
¼ cup dry white wine or water
Shaved Parmesan cheese,
  pomegranate seeds, or toasted
  walnuts or pine nuts, for garnish
  (optional)

LET'S COOK:

1. Set a large pot of water to boil over high heat. When at a rolling boil, drop the pasta into the pot and cook according to package directions until al dente. Set aside a cup of the pasta water before draining the noodles. Transfer the drained pasta back into the pot, toss with a drizzle of olive oil to coat, and cover to keep warm.

2. While the water is coming to a boil, preheat the oven to 425°F with a rack in the center position.

3. Toss together the Brussels sprouts, 3 tablespoons olive oil, pancetta, shallot, garlic, thyme, salt, and pepper on a sheet pan until everything is combined and well coated in oil. Spread the Brussels

sprouts in a single layer and roast until the pancetta is crisp and the Brussels sprouts are browned and charred in spots, 20 to 30 minutes.

4. Remove the pan from the oven and stir the wine into the still-hot sprouts, scraping the bottom of the pan to release any flavorful brown bits into the dish.

5. Carefully transfer the contents of the sheet pan to the waiting pasta and use kitchen tongs to toss everything together. If the pasta looks dry or clumpy, add the reserved pasta water by the quarter cup to loosen.

6. Serve warm, with a scattering of Parmesan, pomegranate seeds, or toasted nuts, if you like.

ROASTED SAUSAGE & RED GRAPES WITH POLENTA & GORGONZOLA

SERVES 4

The basics of this dish are a well-balanced equation—sweet fruit, salty meat, mild polenta, and sharp cheese. (Just regular math, you know.) The end result is a winner, and you can make it your own by customizing the basic parts to suit your fancy. Prefer spicy sausage? Yes. Tomatoes instead of grapes? If that's what you've got. Goat cheese for Gorgonzola? Fine. Just keep the basic balance, and dinner will hit all the right notes.

Olive oil cooking spray
1 tube (18 ounces) precooked polenta
1 small red onion, sliced into ¼-inch-thick half-moons
2 cups red seedless grapes
2 tablespoons extra virgin olive oil
¼ teaspoon kosher salt

6 links hot or mild Italian sausage (about 1½ pounds total)
1 teaspoon fresh thyme leaves
2 tablespoons crumbled Gorgonzola cheese (plus an optional extra 2 tablespoons for serving)

LET'S COOK:

1. Preheat the oven to 425°F with one rack about 4 inches from the broiler and another in the center position. Mist a sheet pan with cooking spray.

2. Remove the polenta from its packaging and slice it into ¼- to ½-inch-thick rounds. Place them in a single layer on the prepared pan.

3. Toss the red onion and grapes with the olive oil and salt in a medium-size bowl. Scatter them over the polenta. Arrange the sausages evenly around the grapes and onions, and prick each sausage once or twice

with a fork. Sprinkle all with the fresh thyme leaves.

4. Bake until the sausages are cooked through and the grapes are starting to wrinkle, about 30 minutes.

5. Remove the pan from the oven and turn the oven to broil. Scatter 2 tablespoons of the Gorgonzola over the sausages. Broil to melt the cheese and brown the sausages, 3 minutes.

6. Serve the sausages over the polenta, onions, and grapes, with another 2 tablespoons Gorgonzola for topping, if you like.

HERBED LEG OF LAMB WITH CRISPY SWEET POTATOES

SERVES 8

L eg of lamb is rich, hearty fare, so I like to balance it by roasting the meat over a bed of thinly sliced sweet potatoes. Plenty of fresh herbs and a bit of brown sugar help round out the deep flavors of the dish; you'll probably want to file this one under the "special occasion" category.

If you'd rather use a boneless leg of lamb, that's totally fine, just make sure it's tied up well before roasting (see box, page 69, for instructions on trussing) and adjust the cooking time accordingly; you'll want to check it for doneness 10 or 15 minutes earlier than a bone-in roast.

3½ pounds sweet potatoes, unpeeled, scrubbed, cut in half lengthwise then sliced into ¼-inch-thick half-moons
¼ cup extra virgin olive oil
3½ teaspoons kosher salt
1 teaspoon freshly ground black pepper

1 bone-in leg of lamb (5 to 7 pounds), trimmed of fat and silverskin
3 cloves garlic, thinly sliced
1 tablespoon finely chopped fresh rosemary leaves
1 tablespoon roughly chopped fresh thyme leaves
2 tablespoons packed dark brown sugar

LET'S COOK:

1. Preheat the oven to 425°F with a rack in the center position.

2. Place the sweet potatoes on a sheet pan, drizzle with the olive oil, sprinkle with 1½ teaspoons salt and ½ teaspoon pepper, and toss to coat. Spread the potatoes in an even layer on the sheet pan. They'll overlap— that's fine.

3. Using a paring knife, pierce the meat at roughly 2-inch intervals all over. Stuff each cut with a slice of garlic.

4. Combine the rosemary, thyme, and brown sugar with the remaining 2 teaspoons salt and ½ teaspoon pepper in a small bowl. Rub the herb mixture all over the meat. Set the meat on top of the potatoes.

TEACH ME HOW

TO CARVE A LEG OF LAMB

Carving a piece of meat on the bone can be tricky. To start, cut a few thin slices from the bottom end of the roast (opposite the exposed bone) to create a flat surface on which to rest the leg while you carve; you'll carve the meat holding the leg bone up at a 45-degree angle to the cutting board. Next, make a series of slices perpendicular to the bone, making sure to cut all the way down to the bone, slicing against the grain of the meat. Now turn your knife so it's parallel to the bone and make one long slice down the bone, in order to free all of the slices you just cut. Finally, turn the leg over and repeat the process on the other side.

Done! Don't forget to save the bone with all those meaty, leftover bits attached—you can use it to enrich your homemade (or store-bought) beef stock, or to add flavor to a pot of hearty lentil or split pea soup.

5. Roast the lamb for 30 minutes, then lower the oven temperature to 350°F.

6. Continue roasting, rotating the pan halfway through, until an instant-read thermometer inserted into the thickest part of the meat (but not touching the bone) registers 135°F for medium-rare, another 45 to 60 minutes.

7. Transfer the lamb to a cutting board and allow it to rest, uncovered, for 15 minutes before slicing the meat off the bone, against the grain. Serve with the sweet potatoes.

RACK OF LAMB WITH HERBY BREADCRUMBS & BUTTERED CARROTS

SERVES 4

This feels like a celebration dinner. Rack of lamb just sounds highbrow (and has a high price tag to prove it), but its rich flavor and stunning presentation are worth the price, and both are secretly pretty simple to achieve. Toss some carrots with melted butter and herbs, slap a garlicky, herby breadcrumb mixture on the meaty rack, and throw it all, unceremoniously, into the oven. Forty minutes later the whole house (or tiny studio apartment, as the case may be) smells rich and savory, and you're looking at a pan of gorgeously browned, breadcrumb-crusted lamb racks and buttery glazed carrots.

Celebration? Maybe. Or maybe it's just Thursday night. Either way, we're crushing it.

Olive oil cooking spray
2 racks of lamb (8 chops each), frenched (see box, page 139)
1 teaspoon kosher salt
1 teaspoon freshly ground black pepper
2 pounds carrots, peeled and cut into 3-inch-long, ¾-inch-thick sticks
6 tablespoons (¾ stick) unsalted butter, melted

¼ cup plus 1 tablespoon extra virgin olive oil
1 teaspoon finely chopped fresh rosemary leaves
1 cup plain dried breadcrumbs
2 teaspoons dried oregano
1 teaspoon freshly grated lemon zest
¼ cup finely chopped fresh mint leaves
¼ cup Dijon mustard
4 cloves garlic, minced

LET'S COOK:

1. Preheat the oven to 425°F with a rack in the center position. Mist a sheet pan with cooking spray.

2. Season the lamb racks on both sides with a generous ½ teaspoon each of salt and pepper. Set them aside on the work surface.

3. Place the carrots on the prepared pan, drizzle with the butter and 1 tablespoon of the olive oil, and sprinkle with the rosemary and the

remaining salt and pepper. Toss to combine. Spread the carrots in an even layer. Mist a sheet pan–size wire rack with cooking spray and place it on top of the carrots.

4. Mix together the breadcrumbs, oregano, lemon zest, and mint in a small bowl. Add the mustard, ¼ cup olive oil, and garlic and stir well to incorporate and moisten the breadcrumbs.

5. Place the lamb racks, with the ribs curving down, on the prepared wire rack. Spread and press the breadcrumb coating onto the lamb in a thick layer, making sure to cover the ends, too. Some of the breadcrumbs will fall onto the carrots during this process—that's fine.

6. Roast until the carrots are fork-tender and brown in spots, and an instant-read thermometer inserted into the thickest part of the meat (but not touching any bone) registers 130°F for medium-rare, about 40 minutes.

7. Transfer the lamb to a cutting board and allow the meat to rest, covered loosely with aluminum foil, for at least 10 minutes before slicing the rack into individual chops. When you slice the meat, a good amount of the breadcrumb coating will fall onto the cutting board, so use one large enough to capture all of the crumbs.

8. Serve the lamb chops and carrots with the rescued breadcrumbs sprinkled on top.

WAIT, WHAT?

FRENCHING A LAMB CHOP

A rack of lamb that's been "frenched" simply means the tips of the rib bones have been trimmed of all meat, fat, and membrane, in order to cleanly expose the bone. This is entirely for aesthetic reasons; a lamb rack looks neat and elegant after it's been frenched. In all likelihood, your butcher will sell you a rack of lamb that's already been frenched, but if you're not sure, just ask.

APPLE, PROSCIUTTO & RADICCHIO PIZZA

SERVES 4 TO 6

This pizza! It looks like a Pollock and tastes like a dream. A sweet and salty dream, on a thin and crunchy crust.

Using rapid-rise yeast makes this whole wheat, no-knead pizza dough a snap. Sold in small packets in the baking aisle, rapid-rise (aka quick-rise) yeast helps the dough rise in just an hour. And unlike other kinds of yeast (like "active dry" or "instant active dry"), rapid-rise yeast allows our dough to be mixed quickly and makes it ready to bake after only one rise.

So yes, the pizza is homemade, and yes, it's totally worth it. Don't be scared—you'll see that yeast and bread flour are no big deal (bread flour's higher gluten content is better suited for stretching pizza dough—though if all you have is all-purpose, go ahead and use it here). Any and all thoughts of intimidation can take a hike—we *are* going to get flour everywhere. It's fine. It's pizza! With crisp, sweet apples, salty ham, and wilted radicchio, an unexpected—but fun and well-balanced—trio of toppings.

2¾ cups bread flour, plus extra for working the dough

1 cup whole wheat pastry flour

2½ teaspoons rapid-rise yeast (from about two ¼-ounce packets)

¾ teaspoon kosher salt

¾ teaspoon sugar

1½ cups plus 2 tablespoons warm water

3 tablespoons extra virgin olive oil

1½ cups shredded sharp Cheddar cheese (about 6 ounces)

2 ounces (about 3 slices) prosciutto, cut into small strips

1 small green apple, unpeeled, cored, and sliced into ⅛-inch-thick wedges

½ head radicchio, shredded (roughly 2 cups)

Freshly ground black pepper

LET'S COOK:

1. Whisk together the flours, yeast, salt, and sugar in a large bowl. Add the warm water and mix with a wooden spoon or rubber spatula to form a shaggy but cohesive dough. If mixing it gets too difficult, just use your hands to work the dough instead.

2. Cover the bowl of dough with plastic wrap and then a clean kitchen towel. Set it aside at room temperature to rise until the dough has doubled in size, about 1 hour.

3. Meanwhile, preheat the oven to 500°F with a rack in the upper third. Drizzle 2 tablespoons of the olive oil onto a sheet pan, then tilt the pan around to evenly distribute the oil—you want the pan liberally oiled.

4. When the dough has risen, turn it out onto a lightly floured work surface. Use a sharp, floured knife to cut the dough into two equal pieces. Leave one piece out on the work surface. (Wrap the other tightly in plastic wrap, place it in a zip-top bag, and store it in the freezer for later use. Thaw it overnight in the fridge, then let it come to room temperature before using.)

5. Place the piece of pizza dough you're using on the sheet pan. Flour your hands and press and stretch the dough into the pan, until it nearly reaches the edges. (If it rips, just press it back together.) If the dough starts to spring back and shrink while you're pressing it out, allow it to rest for 5 minutes, then resume pressing. You should end up with a flat, roughly ½-inch-thick rectangle of dough.

6. Brush the dough all the way to the edges with the remaining tablespoon of olive oil. Sprinkle ¾ cup of the cheese over the dough, leaving about a ½-inch border around the edges for the crust. Layer the prosciutto, apple, and radicchio over the first layer of cheese, then top with the remaining cheese. Grind some black pepper on top of it all.

7. Bake the pizza until the crust is deeply brown and the cheese is browned and bubbly, 18 to 20 minutes.

8. Let the pizza cool slightly before slicing it into squares or rectangles. Serve hot.

DIY OR BUY?
PIZZA DOUGH
I think everyone should try making their own pizza dough at least once, but if you don't have the time or it's just not your thing, hit up your local pizza parlor instead of grabbing some packaged dough from the grocery store. In most cases, pizza places are happy to sell you a ball of fresh dough, and it's guaranteed to taste better than anything you can find on a supermarket shelf.

ITALIAN MEAT & CHEESE STROMBOLI

SERVES 6 TO 8

I want to say that stromboli was invented when a boy in a Philadelphia pizza shop wanted to take his slice to go but instead of waiting for a proper box, he just rolled the thing right up and walked out with a stromboli. But that would be a total fabrication and this is not a book of fiction. Still, it's safe to say that stromboli is pretty much nothing more than a very meaty, very cheesy pizza rolled up into a log, baked, sliced, and dipped into warm marinara sauce.

Making the dough from scratch is fun and rewarding, but if you don't have the time or energy and want to go the store-bought route, think about asking your local pizzeria if they'll sell you a ball of the fresh stuff.

All-purpose or bread flour, for working the dough

½ recipe pizza dough (page 140) or 1 pound store-bought pizza dough

¼ cup good marinara sauce (store-bought, such as Rao's, or homemade), plus extra for dipping

8 ounces thinly sliced Italian deli meats, such as prosciutto, salami, pepperoni, and capicola

4 ounces sliced provolone cheese

4 ounces sliced mozzarella cheese (use low-moisture, such as Sargento, not fresh mozzarella)

1 tablespoon extra virgin olive oil

½ teaspoon freshly ground black pepper

½ teaspoon garlic powder

LET'S COOK:

1. Preheat the oven to 375°F with a rack in the center position. Line a sheet pan with parchment paper.

2. On a lightly floured surface, roll out the pizza dough to a rough rectangle about 10 by 14 inches.

3. Spread the marinara sauce over the rectangle, leaving an inch-wide border around the edges. Layer the meat and cheese over the sauce.

4. Starting from one of the long edges, roll the stromboli up into a log. Place the log seam side down on the prepared sheet pan, and fold down the open ends, tucking them under the log to seal it shut.

Brush the log with the olive oil and sprinkle the top with the pepper and garlic powder.

5. Bake the stromboli until quite brown all over, about 30 minutes. Some of the cheese may leak out a bit; that's fine.

6. Let the stromboli cool for a few minutes, so the insides are no longer molten.

7. While the stromboli cools, warm some extra sauce in a small saucepan over low heat, or place it in a small bowl and microwave it on high for 30 to 60 seconds.

8. Slice the stromboli into inch-wide pieces and serve it with the warm marinara sauce alongside for dipping.

LASAGNA'D HASSELBACK POTATOES

SERVES 6

Are you the kind of person who doesn't like the foods on your plate to touch? If so, I'm sorry for this. I'm a mixer-and-mingler, and I find it's usually for the best. Most often, I want my food to touch. I'll sometimes push my salad up next to my chicken, just to help everyone get along on the plate. Mixing is how perfect combinations are born! For example: This recipe is a mash-up of creamy lasagna and Hasselback potatoes, which are like baked potatoes 2.0—thin, vertical slices down but not all the way through the potato help expose surface area and result in supremely crispy potato fans. Two classic dishes, mixed-and-matched on the way to delicious.

If you want to make this a vegetarian dish, simply omit the pancetta and you're good to go.

---

6 thin slices pancetta (about 3 ounces)

6 medium-size russet potatoes, unpeeled, well scrubbed

8 cloves garlic, thinly sliced

6 tablespoons vegetable oil

6 tablespoons (¾ stick) unsalted butter, cut into ½-inch chunks

1¼ teaspoons kosher salt

¾ teaspoon freshly ground black pepper

1 container (15 ounces) ricotta cheese

1 cup shredded mozzarella cheese (low-moisture, such as Sargento, not fresh)

1¼ cups shredded Parmesan cheese

½ teaspoon garlic powder

1 teaspoon dried oregano

1 cup good marinara sauce (store-bought, such as Rao's, or homemade)

1 cup sun-dried tomatoes in oil, drained and chopped

¼ cup chopped fresh basil leaves

LET'S COOK:

1. Preheat the oven to 425°F with a rack in the center position.

2. Lay the pancetta slices in a single layer on a sheet pan, and bake them until crisp, 3 to 5 minutes. Remove from the oven and set aside on a piece of paper towel to drain. Do not wash the pan.

3. Cut a small slice off a long side of each potato to form a flat surface on which the potato can lie without wobbling. Working with one potato at a time, lay a chopstick or butter

knife on each long side of the potato and use a sharp knife to make thin, vertical slices down the potato but not all the way through, about ⅛ inch apart. The chopsticks will prevent you from cutting all the way through the potatoes; you should end up with a potato that fans out. Place the potatoes on the sheet pan.

4. Shove the garlic slices between some of the potato slices, distributing them evenly. Drizzle each potato with 1 tablespoon of the oil and top with the butter chunks, evenly distributing the butter between the potatoes. Sprinkle the potatoes with 1 teaspoon of the salt and ½ teaspoon of the pepper.

5. Bake the potatoes until they are tender when pierced between slices with a paring knife, about 1 hour.

6. While the potatoes are baking, stir together the ricotta and mozzarella with ¼ cup of the Parmesan in a medium-size bowl. Mix in the garlic powder, oregano, and remaining ¼ teaspoon salt and ¼ teaspoon pepper.

7. When the potatoes are tender, remove the pan from the oven and sprinkle the potatoes generously with the remaining 1 cup Parmesan. Spoon the marinara sauce on top. Evenly spread the ricotta mixture on top of the marinara. Scatter the sun-dried tomatoes over all. Return to the oven and bake until the toppings are warm and melt-y, an additional 10 minutes.

8. Crumble the reserved pancetta into small pieces. Sprinkle the lasagna"d potatoes with the crumbled pancetta and chopped basil. Serve warm.

PEPPERONI FRENCH BREAD PIZZA

SERVES 4 TO 6

When I was about nine years old, I made my dad buy a French bread pizza from the freezer section at the grocery store. I was psyched when he agreed; I mean, to a nine-year-old, frozen French bread pizza is like the Holy Grail of dinners! We baked it (in the toaster oven, obviously) and sat down to eat it together. I thought it was great, but Dad declared it "just okay." He even made that twisting hand motion—the one that I'm pretty sure is the universal sign for "eh."

I was upset at having led my father astray, so from that day on we started equating mediocrity with the phrase "French bread." Oh, that new television show? French bread. Dad's new haircut? Freeeench bread (twisting hand motion). Better luck next time.

I'm happy to say that I've since switched the association of French bread from mediocrity to the sublime. When you skip the freezer section and buy a fresh baguette, this dinner transforms from a nine-year-old's dream into a taste of perfection for palates of all ages, complete with warm and melt-y toasted (real!) cheese. No one could call this version "French bread."

I like to serve the pizzas with a big green salad on the side.

---

1 large baguette, cut in half and then sliced through horizontally to make 4 long pieces
1½ to 2 cups good marinara sauce (I like Rao's)
2 ounces sliced pepperoni

8 ounces fresh mozzarella cheese, thinly sliced
About ½ cup shredded Parmesan cheese
½ teaspoon dried oregano
Coarsely ground black pepper

LET'S COOK:

1. Preheat the oven to 350°F with one rack about 4 inches from the broiler and another rack in the center position. Line a sheet pan with aluminum foil or parchment paper.

2. Place the baguette slices cut side up on the prepared sheet pan. If your baguettes are on the softer side, toast them on the center rack of the oven for 5 to 7 minutes to crisp them up. (If they're already pretty crisp, skip this step.)

3. Spoon the marinara sauce evenly over each baguette piece. Top with most of the pepperoni (reserve a few slices) and the mozzarella. Arrange the remaining pepperoni slices atop the mozzarella and sprinkle the Parmesan, oregano, and some pepper, over it all.

4. Bake the pizzas on the center rack until the baguettes are hot and the cheese is good and melt-y, about 20 minutes.

5. Move the pan to the upper rack and turn the oven to broil. Broil the pizzas until the cheese is brown and bubbling, 1 to 2 minutes.

6. Cut the pizzas into smaller pieces, if you like, and serve hot.

Chapter 6

HOLD THE MEAT, PLEASE

I adore vegetables. And grains and legumes and tofu, too. They make my body feel good, and win an extra gold star of approval for being both relatively cheap and often quite quick to prep and cook. I enjoy meat too much to ever become a vegetarian, but hearty, big-flavor recipes like Baked Sweet Potatoes with Cannellinis & Baby Spinach (page 175), and Sesame Snap Peas & Baked Tofu with Spicy Peanut Sauce (page 170) could make me think twice. You'll find those recipes, along with so many more substantial meatless wonders, in the chapter ahead.

ROASTED CRISP-TOPPED EGGPLANT WITH CHICKPEAS

SERVES 6

I find eggplant to be kind of a polarizing vegetable—people seem to either love it or hate it. I'm in the love camp (peace, love, and eggplant). Here, the delicate flavor (and sometimes tricky texture) of baked eggplant is elevated by a supremely crisp herb-cheese-and-garlic-laden topping. Creamy chickpeas in rich tomato sauce provide a solid base on which the crisp-topped eggplant can really shine.

This is a light, healthy meal that feeds a moderate crowd, especially when served alongside a simple pot of rice or pasta. If you can splurge for a jar of upscale marinara sauce (such as Rao's or Il Mulino), I think it's worth it here, since the dish has so few components and thus presents a quality-over-quantity situation.

---

2 cans (15 ounces each) chickpeas, rinsed and drained

1 jar (28 ounces) good marinara sauce

1 large or 2 small eggplants, stemmed and sliced into ½-inch-thick rounds (about 1¼ pounds)

¼ cup plus 3 tablespoons extra virgin olive oil

1 teaspoon salt

1 cup panko breadcrumbs

Heaping ½ cup grated Parmesan cheese

½ teaspoon fresh rosemary leaves, chopped

1 teaspoon fresh thyme leaves, chopped

½ teaspoon freshly ground black pepper

1 teaspoon herbes de Provence (see box, page 50)

2 tablespoons roughly chopped garlic (about 4 cloves)

LET'S COOK:

1. Preheat the oven to 425°F with a rack in the center position. Line a sheet pan with aluminum foil or parchment paper.

2. Stir together the chickpeas and marinara sauce in a medium-size bowl until combined. Spread the mixture evenly on the prepared sheet pan. Arrange the eggplant slices on top of the chickpeas, overlapping them very slightly. Drizzle the eggplant with ¼ cup of the olive oil and sprinkle ½ teaspoon of the salt. Cover the pan loosely with aluminum foil and roast until the eggplant has softened, about 30 minutes.

3. Meanwhile, make the breadcrumb topping: Stir together the panko, Parmesan, rosemary, thyme, remaining ½ teaspoon salt, the pepper, herbes de Provence, garlic, and the remaining 3 tablespoons olive oil in a medium-size bowl to combine.

4. When the eggplant has roasted for 30 minutes, remove the pan from the oven and uncover it. Sprinkle the breadcrumb mixture in a thick layer on top of the eggplant slices. Roast uncovered, rotating the pan halfway, until the eggplant is tender and the breadcrumbs are deeply toasted brown, an additional 20 to 25 minutes.

5. Serve hot.

WAIT, WHAT?

PANKO

Unsure about panko? It may sound fancy, but panko is just the name for Japanese breadcrumbs. Unlike regular breadcrumbs, which can be pretty dense when packed together, panko flakes are delightfully large, light, and crunchy. Their bigger size and flat shape are ideal for achieving a crisp and airy texture when baked in the oven.

HEARTY RATATOUILLE WITH GOAT CHEESE

SERVES 8

Depending on whom you ask, ratatouille is either a popular animated film starring a culinarily-inclined rat named Remy, or a traditional French dish of stewed summer vegetables. Either way, it's a highly enjoyable experience. Remy (the rat) makes a beautiful version of ratatouille (the dish) in *Ratatouille* (the movie) with meticulously layered zucchini, eggplant, bell peppers, and tomatoes; I've tried to make mine equally beautiful.

My version of ratatouille uses all of the usual vegetable suspects— peppers, eggplant, zucchini, and squash—but I've added sliced potatoes to the mix, which I think helps to heft it up. A smattering of soft goat cheese adds even more flavor and texture.

Served with a good crusty bread or over penne pasta or rice, this humble and hearty ratatouille makes for a deeply satisfying vegetarian meal.

Olive oil cooking spray

1 can (12 ounces) tomato puree

3 cloves garlic, thinly sliced

½ medium yellow onion, finely chopped

Kosher salt and freshly ground black pepper

2 tablespoons unsalted butter, cut into small cubes

1 large red bell pepper

1 large Chinese eggplant or other long, skinny eggplant (see box, page 154)

1 large zucchini

1 large yellow squash

3 or 4 smallish Yukon gold potatoes, unpeeled (about ¾ pound)

2 tablespoons extra virgin olive oil

1 teaspoon chopped fresh thyme leaves

4 ounces soft goat cheese

1 tablespoon roughly chopped fresh basil leaves

Crusty bread, for serving

LET'S COOK:

1. Preheat the oven to 375°F with one rack about 4 inches from the broiler and another rack in the center position. Mist a sheet pan with cooking spray.

2. Dump the tomato puree onto the prepared sheet pan. Add the garlic, onion, ½ teaspoon salt, and ¼ teaspoon pepper, and toss together to combine. Use a rubber spatula to spread the puree evenly over the pan, distributing the garlic and onion throughout and pushing the sauce into the corners of the pan. Drop the butter cubes over all, spacing them evenly apart.

3. Cut off the top of the pepper, and carefully pull out the seeds and membrane. Use a sharp knife to slice the pepper into ⅛- to ¼-inch-thick rounds, then slice the rounds into thirds—you'll end up with a bunch of small curved pepper pieces.

4. Trim the ends off the eggplant, zucchini, and squash. Slice each into thin rounds, ⅛- to ¼-inch thick. Slice the potatoes into rounds of the same thickness.

5. Carefully arrange the vegetables over the tomato sauce and butter, overlapping them in a deliberate pattern going from short end to short end of the pan. You'll be able to see a bit of tomato sauce at the sides of the pan, but the vegetable layer should be tight enough that you don't see much.

6. Drizzle the vegetables with the olive oil, sprinkle with the thyme and an extra pinch each of salt and pepper. Bake the ratatouille on the center rack until the vegetables are tender and the tomato sauce is bubbling up at the edges, 30 to 40 minutes.

7. Remove the pan from the oven and turn the oven to broil. Break the goat cheese into large crumbles and scatter them evenly over the ratatouille. Broil to gently melt the cheese, about 1 minute.

8. Sprinkle the chopped basil on top of the ratatouille and serve warm with plenty of crusty bread for scooping up the vegetables and sauce.

WAIT, WHAT?

CHINESE EGGPLANT

Did you know that eggplants, like tomatoes, are actually fruits, not vegetables? It's true! And there are thousands of varieties out there, running the gamut in size, shape, and color. Chinese eggplants are long and skinny, with thin skin and a pretty, deep purple hue. I like them for ratatouille because of their small circumference (they match up nicely with the zucchini and yellow squash), but you can easily swap out another type, such as Japanese, Italian, or white eggplants, all of which are widely available in most grocery stores.

ROASTED BEET & ORANGE SALAD WITH PISTACHIOS & FETA

SERVES 2 AS A MAIN, 4 AS A SIDE DISH

Some days I find myself accidentally eating cookies for lunch. When this happens, it feels good to have a bright, fresh salad for dinner. I love the combination of sweet roasted beets, juicy oranges, sharp onions, and tangy cheese. Pistachios add great color and crunch. It's fun to switch things up and use golden beets and deeply red blood oranges, though easier-to-find red beets and navel oranges work just as well.

For a heartier vegetarian meal, serve this with a scoop of quinoa, cooked according to package directions, and a thickly sliced avocado half. If it's a meaty meal you want, this salad would do nicely next to a few pieces of rotisserie chicken from the market.

---

3 pounds beets, trimmed, peeled, and cut into 1-inch chunks (see box, page 157)

¼ cup extra virgin olive oil, plus extra for drizzling

¼ cup freshly squeezed orange juice (about 1 small orange)

½ teaspoon kosher salt

1 medium shallot, cut in half lengthwise and thinly sliced

4 oranges, peel and white pith removed, sliced into suprêmes (see box, page 157) or ½-inch-thick half-moons

¼ cup shelled, salted pistachios

4 ounces (about 1 cup) crumbled feta cheese

¼ cup chopped fresh chives

Freshly ground black pepper

LET'S COOK:

1. Preheat the oven to 425°F with a rack in the center position.

2. Toss the beets with the olive oil, orange juice, and salt on a sheet pan and spread them in an even layer.

3. Roast, shaking and rotating the pan halfway through cooking, until the beets have softened and are starting to brown at the edges, about 30 minutes.

4. Sprinkle the shallots over the beets and roast until the shallots are

golden brown and the beets are fork-tender, an additional 15 minutes.

5. While the beets are still warm, transfer them to a bowl, add the oranges, pistachios, feta, and chives, and toss to combine. Drizzle the salad with a bit of extra olive oil, and top with a pinch of pepper.

6. Serve the salad warm or at room temperature, or chill in the refrigerator. It will keep, in an airtight container, for about 4 days.

TEACH ME HOW

TO SUPRÊME AN ORANGE

Getting delicate segments of citrus, without a hint of skin or membrane, is surprisingly easy, even if the name for doing it—suprêming—sounds fussy and highbrow. Start by slicing ½ inch off the top and bottom of an orange, exposing the glittering flesh within. Rest the fruit on one of the cut ends, and use a sharp paring knife to slice off the remaining peel and pith, making downward curving slices from top to bottom, following the shape of the fruit. Finally, slice in between the dividing membranes to remove the individual segments, which should be bright and beautiful.

TO PREP A BEET

Buying and prepping fresh beets can be intimidating, but there's not much to it, I promise. When you buy beets, look for the ones with their green tops still attached. If the greens look nice and crisp, you can bet that beet is fresh!

Peeling fresh beets can be a pain, but a Y-shaped peeler makes it easy. Just hold the beet at the green-top end and use the peeler to carefully shave off the skin from top to root. From there, it's easy to chop the beets up into smaller pieces for salad. And save the greens! They're great sautéed or roasted with some olive oil and garlic.

ROASTED FENNEL PANZANELLA

SERVES 4

❝ P anzanella" is just a fancy way to say "bread salad," which is to say "carb salad," which is to say delicious. The foundation of a good bread salad is, naturally, some good day-old bread, but since I can never count on having a stale baguette on hand, I like to use a fresh one and toast it until it's dry. The roasted fennel, fresh tomatoes, hunks of provolone cheese, and bright, lemony dressing make this particular panzanella stand out from other, more classic versions.

---

1 baguette, cut into bite-size pieces
(about 5 cups)
2 bulbs fennel, stalky fingers removed
(reserve a few fronds), cored and
cut into 1-inch chunks (see box,
page 61)
¾ cup extra virgin olive oil
Kosher salt and freshly ground black
pepper

2 cups cherry tomatoes, halved
½ pound block provolone cheese,
cut into ½-inch chunks
1 teaspoon Dijon mustard
1 teaspoon freshly grated lemon zest
¼ cup freshly squeezed lemon juice
(about 1 large lemon)
½ cup roughly chopped fresh basil
leaves

LET'S COOK:

1. Preheat the oven to 400°F with a rack in the center position.

2. Spread the bread cubes on a sheet pan and toast until lightly browned and crunchy, about 10 minutes. Transfer the croutons to a large bowl.

3. Spread the fennel chunks in a single layer on the empty sheet pan. Drizzle with ¼ cup of the olive oil and sprinkle with a pinch each of salt and pepper. Roast the fennel until the edges are nice and brown, about 30 minutes. Let cool slightly.

4. Add the fennel to the croutons, then add the tomatoes and cheese.

5. Make the dressing: Put the mustard in a small container with a lid, and add the lemon zest, lemon juice, and a pinch each of salt and pepper. Pour the remaining ½ cup olive oil into the container, cover it, and shake like the dickens to make a smooth vinaigrette. Taste it and adjust the seasoning.

6. Drizzle the vinaigrette over the bread salad and toss to coat. Sprinkle the basil and reserved fennel fronds on top, and serve immediately.

CAESAR SALAD GARLIC BREAD

SERVES 4

Here's a way not to feel guilty about eating garlic bread for dinner: Top it with greens! And add protein, too, in the form of anchovies (all those healthful essential fatty acids!) and cheese (all that calcium!). Somebody tell me this counts as health food.

We'll transform a traditional Caesar salad by substituting cheesy garlic bread for croutons and piling some fresh, lightly dressed romaine on top. In traditional Caesar salad fashion, there's plenty of anchovy flavor and Parmesan cheese to go around.

---

1 loaf ciabatta bread, cut in half horizontally

8 tablespoons (1 stick) unsalted butter, at room temperature

5 cloves garlic, minced

Pinch of kosher salt

Pinch of freshly ground black pepper

1 cup shredded Parmesan cheese, plus extra for sprinkling

2 teaspoons anchovy paste (see box, page 161)

2 tablespoons freshly squeezed lemon juice (about ½ large lemon)

1 teaspoon Worcestershire sauce

1 teaspoon Dijon mustard

1 heaping tablespoon mayonnaise or plain Greek yogurt

½ cup extra virgin olive oil

2 hearts of romaine lettuce, very roughly chopped

LET'S COOK:

1. Preheat the oven to 400°F with a rack in the center position. Line a sheet pan with aluminum foil or parchment paper.

2. Place the ciabatta halves cut side up on the prepared sheet pan. Reserve 1 teaspoon of the garlic and mix the rest with the butter, salt, and pepper in a small bowl until combined. Generously spread the garlic butter over the ciabatta, being sure to reach every nook and cranny. Sprinkle 1 cup of the Parmesan over the garlic butter. Bake the bread until it is well toasted and the cheese has melted, 12 to 15 minutes.

3. Meanwhile, make the dressing: Whisk together the reserved garlic, anchovy paste, and lemon juice in a medium-size bowl until smooth. Add the Worcestershire sauce, mustard, and mayonnaise and whisk to combine. Whisk in the olive oil in a slow stream until the dressing is smooth and emulsified.

4. Place the chopped romaine in a large bowl and toss with enough dressing to lightly coat it. You'll have plenty of dressing left over.

5. Remove the bread from the oven and pile the salad on top of it. Sprinkle some extra Parmesan cheese on top and drizzle with a bit of the dressing. Return the salad-topped bread to the oven and bake until the romaine has just begun to wilt but is still nice and crunchy inside, about 5 minutes.

6. Carefully slice the leafy garlic bread into pieces and enjoy warm from the oven.

DIY OR BUY
CAESAR SALAD DRESSING

Make your own Caesar dressing! The store-bought versions are usually full of all kinds of preservatives and fake stuff—no thanks. From-scratch is pretty simple; a bit of whisking and we're pretty much done.

Anchovy paste is widely available in most markets and specialty stores, usually in the same section as the canned tomatoes and tomato paste (otherwise, find it near the canned fish). If you can't find any, you can make your own by mincing about 6 anchovy fillets until smooth.

SPAGHETTI SQUASH "NOODLE" BOWLS

SERVES 4

I've discovered the key to happiness, and this is it. Happiness, of course, is an enormous bowl of hot pasta smothered with tomato sauce and cheese, eaten entirely and blissfully guilt-free. The secret, of course, is that our "noodles" are not actually noodles at all, but rather the more healthful (yet equally satisfying) spaghetti squash, in all of its toothsome and noodle-like glory.

Spaghetti squash are those yellow football-ish-shaped winter squash. When cooked, the squash's flesh is easily raked with a fork into long, skinny, noodle-like strands—a supremely satisfying activity, as you'll soon find out. The squash noodles are faintly sweet and slightly crunchy, like pasta cooked al dente.

---

2 small spaghetti squash
   (2 to 3 pounds each)
4 tablespoons extra virgin olive oil
¾ teaspoon kosher salt
¾ teaspoon freshly ground black
   pepper
1 cup chopped cremini or baby bella
   mushrooms (3 to 4 ounces)

1 small shallot, diced
2 cups good-quality marinara
   (I like Rao's)
15 to 20 small balls fresh mozzarella
   cheese (bocconcini, about
   1¾ ounces), sliced in half
4 to 6 leaves fresh basil leaves, roughly
   chopped, for garnish

LET'S COOK:

1. Preheat the oven to 425°F with racks in the upper and lower thirds. Line a sheet pan with parchment paper.

2. Using a very sharp chef's knife, carefully cut the two spaghetti squash in half lengthwise. (If the squash give you a really tough time, heat them, one at a time, in the microwave on high power for 3 to 4 minutes to soften.) Use a spoon to scoop out and discard the seeds.

3. Place the squash halves cut side up on the prepared sheet pan, and drizzle 2 tablespoons of the olive oil over them. Season with ½ teaspoon salt and ½ teaspoon pepper. Turn the squash over (skin side up) and bake on the lower rack until the squash has softened

significantly and browned at the edges, 35 to 40 minutes. Let the squash cool to the touch on the sheet pan.

4. When you put the squash in to bake, toss together the mushrooms, shallots, the remaining 2 tablespoons olive oil, ¼ teaspoon salt, and ¼ teaspoon pepper on a separate sheet pan, spreading them out in an even layer. Bake on the upper rack until softened and starting to brown, about 30 minutes. Let the mushrooms and shallots cool to the touch on the sheet pan.

5. Pour the marinara sauce into a large bowl. When the squash are cool enough to handle, flip them over and use a fork to scrape the flesh from

the shells, taking care to leave the shells intact (these will become the "bowls"). You will end up with long strands of squash "noodles." Add the squash strands and the mushrooms to the sauce and stir together to thoroughly combine.

6. Divide the squash noodle mixture among the empty squash bowls. Place the mozzarella on top.

7. Bake the squash on the lower rack until the filling is hot and the mozzarella has melted and browned in spots, about 10 minutes. (If the sauce looks a bit watery after baking, carefully spoon the extra liquid out of the bowl.)

8. Serve the squash pasta bowls hot, garnished with the fresh basil.

ROASTED SQUASH SALAD BOWLS

SERVES 4

These pretty squash "bowls" are a light, simple weeknight meal and an easy way to make it look like you're an effortless whiz in the kitchen, dinner party–wise. The toughest part here is actually chopping the squash in half while keeping all ten fingers intact, but I've got you covered. Simply microwave the whole squash (one at a time, please) for 1 to 2 minutes before cutting. This little trick will soften the squash and make them worlds easier to halve before roasting.

I enjoy these salad bowls as light and healthy fare on weekdays, but if you're serving them to company, consider hefting up the meal by pairing these with a rotisserie chicken from the market (can you tell I'm big into these?).

2 medium-size acorn squash (about 4 pounds total)
3 tablespoons extra virgin olive oil
4 tablespoons (½ stick) unsalted butter
1 teaspoon kosher salt
1 teaspoon freshly ground black pepper

1 teaspoon chopped fresh thyme leaves
4 teaspoons dark brown sugar
4 to 5 cups wild or baby arugula
Juice of 1 lemon
Shaved Parmesan cheese, for garnish

LET'S COOK:

1. Preheat the oven to 350°F with a rack in the center position. Line a sheet pan with aluminum foil or parchment paper.

2. Using a sharp chef's knife, carefully cut the acorn squash in half lengthwise (your knife should be parallel to the squash's grooves). Use a spoon to scoop out and discard the seeds and fibers—you will be left with four pieces of squash that look a bit like bowls.

3. Place the squash, cut side up, on the prepared sheet pan, and drizzle the insides with 2 tablespoons olive oil, rubbing to coat. Place 1 tablespoon of the butter in each squash bowl and sprinkle ½ teaspoon of the salt, ½ teaspoon of the pepper, and the

brown sugar and chopped thyme over all the squash.

4. Roast the squash until browned in spots and fork-tender, 45 to 60 minutes. Let the squash halves cool slightly.

5. While the squash are cooling, place the arugula in a medium-size bowl.

Drizzle with the lemon juice and remaining tablespoon olive oil, then sprinkle with the remaining salt and pepper. Toss lightly to coat.

6. Place the squash on plates. Pile the arugula salad high inside the bowls, and top with the Parmesan cheese. Serve immediately.

GREEK STUFFED ROLY-POLY SQUASH

SERVES 4 TO 6

When I lived in San Francisco, I acquired quite a few vegetarian friends. I enjoy cheeseburgers too much to join their ranks, but I admire and certainly respect their (sadly bacon-noninclusive) choice. So I took to peppering my Monday night dinner-and-HBO-series-watching parties with these roly-poly squash, scooped clean and stuffed with couscous and bright, salty Greek flavors. If the "roly-poly" alone doesn't make you want to hug yourself, the sight of these colorful, hearty little squash bowls brimming with olives, feta, and almonds surely will.

Roly-polies are in season in late summer and can be found at farmers' markets or in the produce aisle of your supermarket. They're also called Eight-Ball squash.

6 roly-poly squash
¼ cup extra virgin olive oil
Kosher salt and freshly ground black pepper
¼ cup uncooked couscous
¼ cup chicken broth or water
3 cloves garlic, minced
¼ cup ricotta cheese
1 teaspoon freshly grated lemon zest

1 cup (about 4 ounces) crumbled feta cheese
½ cup kalamata olives, pitted and chopped
1 tablespoon capers, drained
3 tablespoons chopped roasted, salted almonds
1 tablespoon chopped fresh chives
1 tablespoon chopped fresh mint leaves

LET'S COOK:

1. Preheat the oven to 400°F with a rack in the center position. Line a sheet pan with aluminum foil.

2. Using a sharp chef's knife, cut the tops off the squash about ¾ inch down from the stem. Use a spoon to scoop out and discard the seeds and meaty flesh of each, leaving little squash cups roughly ¼ inch thick. Place the squash cups, cut side up, on the prepared sheet pan. Drizzle each squash inside and out with 1 teaspoon olive oil and sprinkle each with a pinch of salt and pepper.

3. Roast the squash until their skins begin to pucker, about 15 minutes. Remove from the oven and let them cool to the touch on the pan. Leave the oven on.

4. While the squash are cooling, in a large bowl combine the couscous, chicken broth, garlic, ricotta, lemon zest, feta, olives, capers, 1 tablespoon of the almonds, the chives, mint, 1 teaspoon salt, and ½ teaspoon pepper. Stir together until thoroughly incorporated.

5. When the squash cups are cool enough to handle, divide the stuffing among them, filling each to the top. Sprinkle the remaining chopped almonds on top, and drizzle each squash with another teaspoon olive oil.

6. Return the filled squash to the oven and bake until the skin of the squash is quite puckered and the almond topping is good and brown, about 30 minutes.

7. Allow to cool slightly before serving warm.

ISRAELI COUSCOUS–STUFFED PEPPERS

SERVES 4 TO 6

We're cooking couscous inside peppers. Because it's fun to cook foods inside other foods (with the exception of turducken, which just seems like overkill). A quick jaunt in the oven renders the couscous creamy and fragrant with cheese and rosemary, while the peppers gently soften but still maintain a satisfyingly crunchy bite. One of my testers had a major problem with tippy peppers (read: upended peppers, and couscous all up in the crevices of the oven floor), so be sure to slice a thin layer from the bottom of your peppers to give them a level surface on which to stand.

Meaty note: To bulk up this recipe (and take it out of the vegetarian sphere), a handful of cooked spicy sausage meat thrown into the filling is really pretty great. With or without meat, a simple green salad or hunk of crusty bread makes a nice complement.

---

6 red, orange, or yellow bell peppers
1⅓ cups uncooked Israeli couscous
1 tablespoon extra virgin olive oil
2 cups vegetable broth or chicken broth
½ teaspoon kosher salt
¼ teaspoon freshly ground black pepper

1 cup packed baby spinach leaves
¾ teaspoon chopped fresh rosemary leaves
½ cup crumbled soft goat cheese, plus an extra few tablespoons for topping
Crusty bread, for serving (optional)

LET'S COOK:

1. Preheat the oven to 375°F with a rack in the upper third. Line a sheet pan with parchment paper.

2. Slice a sliver off the bottom of each pepper to make a flat surface, being careful not to cut through to the inner cavity. Cut the top off of each pepper (about an inch below the stem) to make a stem-topped lid; set the tops aside. Scoop out and discard the seeds and membranes, making 6 pepper "cups." Stand the pepper cups upright on the prepared sheet pan, leaving a few inches between each pepper.

3. Stir together the couscous, olive oil, broth, salt, pepper, spinach, rosemary, and goat cheese in

a medium-size bowl until well combined. Spoon the stuffing into the peppers, distributing the liquid evenly and filling each pepper three-quarters full. Place the tops back on each pepper.

4. Bake the peppers until they look a little puckery and the couscous has absorbed much of the liquid, about 30 minutes.

5. Remove the tops and sprinkle the filling with extra goat cheese. Continue baking, uncovered, until the cheese is melt-y and browned, an additional 5 to 10 minutes.

6. Let the stuffed peppers cool slightly before serving warm (place the tops back on for a fun presentation) with hunks of crusty bread.

WAIT, WHAT?
ISRAELI COUSCOUS
Did you know that Israeli couscous is pretty much just pasta? It's made from semolina or wheat flour, is much bigger than regular couscous, and is sometimes called "pearl couscous" because of its spherical shape. Its nutty flavor and chewy texture make it perfect for this stuffed pepper recipe, but feel free to substitute another small pasta such as orzo, ditalini, or pastina (tiny stars), if you like.

SESAME SNAP PEAS & BAKED TOFU WITH SPICY PEANUT SAUCE

SERVES 4

I'll be honest—when tofu and I first met, we didn't make a love connection. I thought tofu was bland and soggy and totally hippy-dippy weird. (I'm not sure what it thought about me.) To be fair, I think the first time I tried tofu was in seventh grade at the food court in the King of Prussia Mall. It was probably before a trip to Hot Topic and after a stroll through Wet Seal.

Truth is, when improperly handled, tofu *can* be bland and soggy, but it turns out that a small amount of love (and peanut butter) can turn hippy-dippy weird into Asian-inspired awesome. Try this and you'll see.

---

1 package (12 to 14 ounces) firm tofu
4 cups sugar snap peas (about 1 pound), ends trimmed and strings removed
1 tablespoon sesame seeds
3 tablespoons extra virgin olive oil
2 tablespoons soy sauce
1 tablespoon plus 1 teaspoon toasted sesame oil
Pinch of kosher salt

1 heaping tablespoon creamy peanut butter
2 teaspoons sriracha sauce (see box, page 53)
1 tablespoon light brown sugar
1 tablespoon freshly squeezed lime juice (about 1 lime)
¼ cup roasted, salted cashews, roughly chopped

LET'S COOK:

1. Drain and press the tofu: Line a plate or cutting board with two sheets of paper towels and place the tofu on top. Lay two more sheets of paper towel on top of the tofu and press down gently—we're trying to dry it thoroughly. Replace the damp paper towels with fresh ones and press again. Leave the second set of paper towels on the tofu and lay a heavy plate or cutting board on top. Leave it to press for 15 minutes. (You could also do this in the morning and let the tofu press in the refrigerator all day until you're ready to make dinner.)

2. While the tofu is being pressed, preheat the oven to 375°F with a rack in the center position. Line a sheet pan with parchment paper.

3. Combine the snap peas with the sesame seeds, 1 tablespoon of the olive oil, 1 tablespoon of the soy sauce, 1 teaspoon of the sesame oil, and a pinch of salt in a large bowl and toss to coat. Spread the snap peas in a single layer on the prepared sheet pan.

4. Make the peanut sauce in the same bowl you used for the snap peas: Whisk together the peanut butter, sriracha, the remaining 2 tablespoons olive oil, 1 tablespoon soy sauce, and 1 tablespoon sesame oil, and the brown sugar and lime juice.

5. Remove the weight and paper towels from the tofu. Use a sharp knife to cut the block into 8 equal slices, ½ to ¾ inch thick.

6. Dredge the pieces of tofu in the peanut sauce and place them on top of the snap peas, spacing the tofu pieces evenly apart. Drizzle any extra peanut sauce over all.

7. Bake until the snap peas are puckered and browned and the sauce on top of the tofu has thickened, 25 minutes.

8. Remove the pan from the oven and sprinkle the chopped cashews over all. Serve immediately.

THAI GREEN CURRY EGGPLANT BOATS WITH TOFU

SERVES 4 TO 6

As a kid, I wasn't the most adventurous eater, and I didn't try Thai food until college. Now I eat curry whenever possible—you know, to make up for lost Thai.

I love ordering take-out from the many Thai restaurants in my neighborhood, but it's surprisingly easy to cook a Thai curry at home, and these eggplant "boats" are particularly fun. You can usually find green curry paste (or red, which is a fine substitute) in the Asian food aisle at the grocery store.

---

1 package (12 to 14 ounces) extra
　firm tofu

3 large eggplants, stemmed

2 tablespoons green curry paste

1 can (14 ounces) light coconut milk

2 tablespoons packed light brown
　sugar

1 tablespoon rice vinegar

1 tablespoon soy sauce

2 teaspoons kosher salt

½ teaspoon crushed red pepper flakes

1 orange, red, or yellow bell pepper,
　stemmed, seeded, and chopped

½ cup canned sliced bamboo shoots,
　drained

3 scallions (white and light green parts
　only), chopped

1 tablespoon chopped fresh basil
　leaves, plus extra for garnish

2 cups frozen rice (white or brown,
　unthawed)

LET'S COOK:

1. Drain and press the tofu: Line a plate or cutting board with two sheets of paper towels, and place the tofu on top. Lay two more sheets of paper towel on top of the tofu and press down gently—we're trying to dry it thoroughly. Replace the damp paper towels with fresh ones and press again. Leave the second set of paper towels on the tofu and lay a heavy plate or cutting board on top. Leave it to press for 15 minutes. (You could also do this in the morning and let the tofu press in the refrigerator all day, until you're ready to make dinner.)

2. While the tofu is being pressed, preheat the oven to 375°F with a rack in the center position. Line a sheet pan with aluminum foil or parchment paper.

3. Using a sharp chef's knife, cut the eggplants in half lengthwise. Use a spoon to scoop out and discard the centers, leaving ½ inch of meat inside the skin. This will ensure that the eggplants will keep their shape in the oven. Place the hollowed eggplants, cut side up, on the prepared sheet pan.

4. Put the green curry paste in a medium-size bowl and slowly whisk in the coconut milk until smooth. Whisk in the brown sugar, rice vinegar, soy sauce, salt, and red pepper flakes. Fold in the bell pepper, bamboo shoots, scallions, and 1 tablespoon of chopped basil.

5. Remove the paper towels from the tofu and cut it into bite-size chunks. Add the tofu pieces to the curry mixture, folding gently to combine.

6. Evenly distribute the frozen rice among the eggplant boats, then pile the green curry atop the rice.

7. Bake until the eggplants are quite soft but not yet falling apart and the filling is bubbly, 50 to 60 minutes.

8. Let the eggplant boats cool briefly, garnish with the extra basil, and serve warm.

BAKED SWEET POTATOES WITH CANNELLINIS & BABY SPINACH

SERVES 4

This is a simple yet flavorful and satisfying meal in a bright and healthful package. Tender roasted sweet potatoes are filled with creamy white cannellini beans, a sweet and briny mix of raisins, capers, and herbs, then topped with a gently wilted baby spinach salad. If you have the foresight to roast the potatoes ahead of time, all it takes is a quick reheat in the oven or microwave and a piling on of toppings, and dinner can be ready in less time than it takes to decide what to eat for dessert. (May I suggest chocolate?)

4 medium-size sweet potatoes, unpeeled, scrubbed and pricked all over with a fork
1 can (15 ounces) cannellini beans, rinsed and drained
¼ cup capers, drained
¼ cup golden raisins
1 tablespoon freshly squeezed lemon juice (about ½ lemon)

½ teaspoon herbes de Provence
1 teaspoon kosher salt
½ teaspoon freshly ground black pepper
Pinch of crushed red pepper flakes, or to taste
1 tablespoon plus 1 teaspoon extra virgin olive oil
4 cups packed fresh baby spinach

LET'S COOK:

1. Preheat the oven to 400°F with a rack in the center position. Line a sheet pan with aluminum foil or parchment paper.

2. Place the sweet potatoes on the prepared sheet pan and bake until soft enough to pierce easily with a paring knife, about 1 hour. Set aside on the sheet pan to cool to the touch.

3. Meanwhile, stir together the beans, capers, raisins, lemon juice, herbes de Provence, salt, pepper, red pepper flakes, and 1 teaspoon of the olive oil in a medium-size bowl.

4. When the sweet potatoes are cool enough to handle, use a paring knife to split each one open lengthwise, taking care not to cut all the way

through. (We're going to fill them like loaded baked potatoes.) Gently press the short ends of each potato together to expose the soft flesh and create a nice crater for the filling.

5. Use a spoon to distribute the bean mixture among the potatoes. Toss the spinach with the remaining tablespoon olive oil in the same bowl you used for the beans. (The bowl will have some delicious "dressing" still clinging to it.)

6. Stuff a big handful of spinach (about 1 cup) inside and on top of each bean-filled potato (they'll be overfilled and the spinach will overflow onto the baking sheet—that's okay).

7. Return the sheet pan to the oven and bake the potatoes until the spinach has wilted and everything is warmed through, 5 to 10 minutes. Serve the loaded potatoes hot from the oven.

TEACH ME HOW

TO "QUICK-BAKE" A BAKED SWEET POTATO
Don't have an hour to wait for those potatoes to roast? Just nuke 'em! Scrub the potatoes, prick them all over with a fork, place them on a microwave-safe dish, and cover them with a damp paper towel. Microwave the potatoes on high in 5-minute increments, until cooked through (they will take 15 to 20 minutes total). Cool, slice open, and continue with the rest of the recipe.

SMOKED CHEDDAR & APPLE GRILLED CHEESE

SERVES 4 TO 6

Standing over a skillet and making sandwiches to order is a drag. Another one for the sheet pan win column: multiple grilled cheeses at once!

Everyone has their thing when it comes to the "perfect" grilled cheese; personally, I love the combination of smoked Cheddar (or smoked Gouda, if there's no Cheddar to be had), crisp apple, and peppery arugula. In summertime, I like to substitute fresh peaches for apples. Also, I swear by a light coating of mayonnaise on both sides of the bread for an extra crisp and luxurious sandwich.

---

4 tablespoons (½ stick) butter
¼ cup mayonnaise
12 slices sourdough bread (each about ½ inch thick, preferably from a high-quality bakery loaf)
12 slices smoked Cheddar cheese

1 apple, unpeeled, cored and thinly sliced (Honeycrisp and Pink Lady are nice varieties here)
1 heaping cup fresh baby arugula, plus extra for serving
Chips, for serving (optional)

LET'S COOK:

1. Preheat the oven to 400°F with a rack in the center position.

2. Place the butter on a sheet pan, and put it in the hot oven to melt, 2 to 5 minutes.

3. Meanwhile, evenly spread the mayonnaise over both sides of the bread slices. Lay half of the bread slices on a work surface and top each with 1 slice of cheese, a layer or two of sliced apple, and a small mound of arugula. Top each arugula mound with 1 of the remaining cheese slices, then the remaining bread, to form 6 sandwiches.

4. Remove the hot pan from the oven and carefully tilt it to coat the surface with the melted butter. Place the sandwiches on the sheet pan. Set a second (clean) sheet pan on top of the sandwiches, pressing down a bit to compress them. With the second pan still in place, bake the sandwiches until the bottoms are golden brown, about 10 minutes.

5. Remove the top pan, carefully flip the sandwiches with a spatula, re-cover them, and return them to the oven. Continue baking until the bread is toasted and the cheese is melted and bubbling, an additional 10 minutes.

6. Serve the sandwiches hot from the oven, with chips or extra greens on the side.

MAKE IT MINE

GRILLED CHEESE PAIRINGS
There are so many options when it comes to grilled cheese pairings! Here are just a few of my favorites.

- Brie + fig jam

- Fresh mozzarella + sliced tomato + fresh basil

- Swiss cheese + sautéed mushrooms + caramelized onions

- Smoked Gouda + sliced turkey + bread-and-butter pickles

PORTABELLA CAP PIZZAS WITH GARLIC KNOTS

SERVES 2 TO 4

I feel like I should have called this book *Let's Think of Ways to Eat Pizza*— that's sort of what we're doing here, after all (check out pages 140, 147, and 148 to see what I mean). To be fair, it's really not a bad life motto, as far as life mottos go.

This one is a fresh and healthy (traditional crustless) version, which happens to be vegetarian to boot. Bright Mediterranean flavors in the form of artichokes, tomatoes, garlic, and goat cheese come together atop tender, meaty portabella mushroom caps, the result of which should please meatless friends and carnivores alike. Plus we're throwing in some garlic knots! Here's to pizza night, refined and redefined.

---

4 large portabella mushrooms, wiped of dirt, stemmed
Kosher salt
¾ cup chopped, drained jarred or canned artichoke hearts
1 cup chopped tomato (about 1 medium-size tomato)
4 ounces goat cheese, crumbled
¼ cup grated Parmesan cheese
¼ teaspoon garlic powder

1 teaspoon dried oregano
Freshly ground black pepper
Crushed red pepper flakes
6 cloves garlic, minced
3 tablespoons extra virgin olive oil
1 tablespoon minced fresh flat-leaf parsley leaves
1 tube (8 ounces) refrigerated crescent rolls

LET'S COOK:

1. Preheat the oven to 400°F with a rack in the center position. Line a sheet pan with parchment paper.

2. Place the portabellas top down and evenly spaced on the prepared sheet pan, making sure to leave room on the perimeter and in between for the garlic knots. Sprinkle the mushrooms with a pinch of salt. Pile the artichokes, tomatoes, goat cheese, and Parmesan on top of the portabellas, dividing the toppings evenly. Season them with the garlic powder, oregano, and a pinch each of black pepper and red pepper flakes.

3. Combine the garlic, olive oil, and parsley in a small bowl. Open the crescent rolls and cut them apart into triangles where they're scored.

Working with one dough triangle at a time, tie the piece of dough in a loose knot, tucking the ends under the knot. Arrange the knots on the sheet pan around the portabellas, leaving a bit of space between knots. Brush each knot generously with the garlic mixture.

4. Bake the portabellas and knots until the portabellas are tender, the cheese has browned and melted, and the garlic knots are golden, 20 minutes. If your portabellas are particularly fat, remove the garlic knots from the pan and let the mushrooms cook until tender, an additional 5 to 10 minutes.

5. Serve the pizzas and garlic knots hot from the oven.

SERVE-WITHS

....

Sometimes chicken needs rice to go with it. And what goes better with meat than potatoes? The dishes in this chapter are these starchy "serve-withs" that help heft up a meal whenever needed. But we're not limited to just regular rice and potatoes, no sir. Here we have recipes for gussying up garlic bread, making the most of precooked polenta, improvising a quick rice "pilaf," and even whipping up a batch of simple drop biscuits to go with everything from shrimp to pork,

from beef to veggies and back again.

You'll see a fair bit of "cheating" in these recipes—that is, we'll use a bunch of already cooked, store-bought fare (frozen rice, baguettes, polenta, and so on) and dress it up for the dinner table—but who cares?

Aside from the drop biscuits, which have to be cooked at a very specific 400 degrees, the following recipes can be fudged and fiddled with, time- and temperature-wise, to cook easily alongside whatever main dish you please.

SIMPLE HASSELBACK POTATOES

SERVES 6

There's a more interesting way to do a wholesome baked potato, one that results in crisp-skinned, creamy-centered, almost French fryesque spuds: the Hasselback potato (page 145 has a recipe for a lasagna'd version). Also called Accordion Potatoes because of their shape, this thinly sliced, fanned-out-then-baked version was created in Sweden at Restaurant Hasselbacken. How do you say "thanks" in Swedish?

I find these go especially well with the Broiled Steak & Asparagus with Feta Cream Sauce (page 117), or the Pork Tenderloin with Squash, Apples & Onions (page 129). It's fine to make these potatoes alongside another recipe that cooks at a higher or lower temperature—just make sure that you adjust the potatoes' cook time accordingly.

Olive oil cooking spray
6 medium russet or Yukon gold potatoes, well scrubbed (2 to 2½ pounds total)
6 tablespoons extra virgin olive oil
1 teaspoon kosher salt

½ teaspoon freshly ground black pepper
Chopped fresh herbs, shredded Parmesan cheese, crumbled bacon, sour cream, or other favorite potato toppings, for serving (optional)

LET'S COOK:

1. Preheat the oven to 425°F with a rack in the center position. Mist a sheet pan with cooking spray.

2. Cut a small slice off a long side of each potato to form a flat surface on which the potato can lie without wobbling. Working with one potato at a time, lay a chopstick or butter knife on each long side of the potato and use a sharp knife to make thin, vertical slices down the potato but not all the way through, about ⅛ inch apart. The chopsticks will prevent you from cutting all the way through the potatoes; you should end up with a potato that fans out. Place the potatoes on the sheet pan.

3. Brush the potatoes all over (including the bottoms) with the olive oil, about 1 tablespoon each. Sprinkle them evenly with the salt and pepper. Bake them until the slits have begun to open and spread apart like fans, about 30 minutes.

4. Remove the pan from the oven and brush the tops of the potatoes with the oily pan drippings. Return the pan to the oven and bake the potatoes until crisp on the outside and knife tender within, another 30 to 40 minutes.

5. Finish the potatoes with a sprinkle of chopped herbs, shredded cheese, crumbled bacon, a dollop of sour cream, or other toppings, if you like, and serve warm.

CRISPY ROASTED POTATOES

SERVES 4 TO 6

Everyone needs a good, simple recipe for roasted potatoes—and here it is! Oven-roasting leaves potatoes crisp on the outside, soft and creamy within. Sprinkling fresh herbs on the warm potatoes is optional, but I love the brightness they bring to the final dish. I like to serve these crispy spuds alongside Chicken Legs with Fennel & Orange (page 60) or Beef Tenderloin with Frizzled Leeks & Fennel (page 115).

If you're making these potatoes to go with another recipe from this book, you can put the potatoes on a rack in the lower third of the oven, and the other pan in the upper third. If you make them with a recipe that cooks at a higher or lower temperature, simply adjust the potatoes' cook time accordingly.

2½ pounds Yukon gold potatoes, unpeeled, chopped into 1- to 1½-inch chunks
2 to 3 tablespoons extra virgin olive oil
1 teaspoon kosher salt
½ teaspoon freshly ground black pepper
2 tablespoons finely chopped fresh herbs such as flat-leaf parsley, chives, or tarragon (optional)

LET'S COOK:

1. Preheat the oven to 425°F with a rack in the center position.

2. Place the potatoes on a sheet pan and toss with the olive oil, salt, and pepper until well coated. Spread out the potatoes on the pan in an even layer.

3. Roast, rotating the pan and using a spatula to mix and turn the potato chunks halfway through cooking, until they're crisp and brown on the outside and tender on the inside, about 45 minutes.

4. Sprinkle the fresh herbs over the potatoes, if using, and serve warm.

WARM BREAD WITH HERBY GARLIC BUTTER

SERVES 6 TO 8

I t's never a bad time for garlic bread (even on a date! I promise). It's an easy side to throw together, warm and comforting, and it happily feeds a crowd. I love this garlicky herbed version alongside Chicken Parmesan (page 58), Baked Turkey Meatballs & Slow-Roasted Tomatoes (page 48), and Greek Stuffed Roly-Poly Squash (page 166). The best part is that it's easy to switch up the flavor profile of the butter to suit your favorite meal (see box, page 186).

Flavored butter (technically called "compound butter") sounds impressive but, once the butter is soft enough, is so easy to make. It can even be made ahead of time—after the butter is mixed with your add-ins of choice, just press it into a small ramekin and cover it with parchment paper—it will keep for about two days in the refrigerator.

Don't worry about warming the bread alongside another recipe that cooks at a different temperature—just keep an eye on the bread and adjust its time in the oven accordingly.

---

1 standard-size baguette or similar loaf (something crusty on the outside and tender within, like a French bâtard, Italian loaf, or ciabatta)
8 tablespoons (1 stick) unsalted butter, at room temperature
1 clove garlic, minced

1 tablespoon chopped fresh flat-leaf parsley leaves
1 tablespoon chopped fresh chives
1 tablespoon chopped fresh thyme leaves
Pinch of kosher salt

LET'S COOK:

1. Preheat the oven to 350°F with a rack in the lower third.

2. Slice the baguette in half horizontally almost all the way through (so that the loaf opens like a book).

3. Mix together the butter, garlic, herbs, and salt in a small bowl with a rubber spatula until well combined. Spread the compound butter evenly on the insides of the baguette, then close the butter sandwich and cut 1-inch-wide slices down but not all the way through the baguette. Wrap the bread in aluminum foil and place it directly on the rack. Toast the bread until it's heated throughout and the butter has melted into the baguette, about 15 minutes.

4. Serve warm.

MAKE IT MINE

COMPOUND BUTTERS

It's easy to mix and match your favorite herbs and spices into wonderfully flavored compound butters. Just start with 8 tablespoons (1 stick) unsalted butter at room temperature, then add your favorite combos. Here are some that I'm into.

• Chipotle-Lime Butter: Chop up 1 canned chipotle chile in adobo sauce, and mix it into the soft butter with the grated zest of 1 lime and a pinch of kosher salt.

• Salt & Pepper Butter: Mix 1 teaspoon of kosher salt and some freshly ground black pepper and crushed pink peppercorns (to taste) into the softened butter.

• Mediterranean Butter: Mix 1 teaspoon dried oregano, 1 teaspoon grated lemon zest, a pinch of kosher salt, and 1 teaspoon chopped fresh flat-leaf parsley leaves into the softened butter.

DROP BISCUITS

MAKES 12 BISCUITS

These are the simplest kind of biscuit, requiring exactly no rolling or cutting or rerolling—just some easy mixing, dropping, and baking are all it takes. They're tender and rich, perfect next to a pan of baby back ribs (page 127) or ratatouille with goat cheese (page 153). If you do make these to serve with another recipe from this book, make sure the biscuits go into a 400°F oven to bake (either cook everything at once at 400°F, or bake the biscuits ahead of time).

The biscuits are best the day they're made, preferably warm from the oven, although you can bake them a few hours ahead of time. Let them cool uncovered, then simply rewarm them in a 300°F oven for about 5 minutes before serving.

---

2 cups all-purpose flour
3 tablespoons sugar
1 teaspoon kosher salt
2 teaspoons baking powder

¼ teaspoon baking soda
1½ cups heavy cream
Salted butter, for serving (optional)

LET'S COOK:

1. Preheat the oven to 400°F with a rack in the center position. Line a sheet pan with parchment paper.

2. Whisk together the flour, sugar, salt, baking powder, and baking soda in a large bowl to remove any lumps. Pour in the cream and stir with a rubber spatula just until a sticky-ish, shaggy dough comes together.

3. Use a large spoon or 2-inch ice cream scoop to drop the dough onto the prepared pan in 12 even lumps, about 2 tablespoons per scoop.

4. Bake the biscuits, rotating the pan halfway through baking, until the biscuits are nicely golden brown, 18 to 20 minutes.

5. Let the biscuits cool slightly before serving warm, with pats of butter alongside if you like.

CHEESY HERB FOCACCIA

SERVES 14 TO 18

I love homemade bread, but the long process of mixing, rising, shaping, proofing, and *finally* baking often seems too much to handle. This focaccia recipe, adapted from the masterminds over at King Arthur Flour, comes together in just over an hour but tastes like you spent a full day kneading and shaping and coaxing it into existence. Full of fresh rosemary and sharp Parmesan cheese, a pan of this bread, sliced in long pieces, would be a welcome addition to any breadbasket or impressive lineup of hors d'oeuvres.

About ½ cup extra virgin olive oil
1½ cups warm water
1¼ teaspoons kosher salt
3½ cups all-purpose flour

1 tablespoon rapid-rise (sometimes labeled "instant") yeast (see Note)
4 teaspoons chopped fresh rosemary leaves
½ cup finely grated Parmesan cheese

LET'S COOK:

1. Generously grease the bottom and sides of a sheet pan with 2 tablespoons of the olive oil. Coat one side of a piece of plastic wrap with oil (it should be about the size of the sheet pan), and set it aside.

2. Pour the warm water into a large bowl and add 3 tablespoons of the olive oil, the salt, flour, yeast, 2 teaspoons of the rosemary, and ¼ cup of the Parmesan cheese. Using an electric mixer, beat on high speed until it comes together in a sticky dough, 1 minute. (Alternatively, beat vigorously by hand with a wooden spoon for 5 minutes.)

3. Turn out the dough onto the prepared pan and let it sit at room temperature to rise, covered with the greased plastic wrap and a clean kitchen towel, until the dough looks puffy and almost doubled in size, about 1 hour. About 40 minutes into this time, preheat the oven to 375°F with a rack in the center position.

4. Press the dough evenly into the sheet pan, reaching into the corners, and use your fingers to poke the dough all over, leaving the top quite dimpled. Drizzle the dough with 2 tablespoons olive oil and sprinkle it evenly with the remaining rosemary and Parmesan cheese.

5. Bake the focaccia until golden brown all over, 35 to 40 minutes.

6. Allow the bread to cool for 5 minutes before carefully turning it out onto a cutting board and slicing. Focaccia is best served on the day it's made, either warm or at room temperature.

NOTE: One tablespoon of instant yeast can be measured from two 0.25-ounce packets.

MAKE IT MINE

FOCACCIA FLAVORS

Rosemary and Parmesan are always good topping choices, but focaccia takes well to different flavor pairings, so feel free to spice it up! Try one of these combos next time.

• Sea salt + pink peppercorns

• Chopped olives + za'atar

• Cheddar cheese + fresh chives

• Grated orange zest + raisins + cinnamon sugar (for a sweeter bread)

SPRING RICE PILAF

SERVES 4

This isn't really a recipe—it doesn't involve actually cooking anything! We're just doctoring up some frozen precooked rice with a few springtime essentials to make a pilaf-inspired side. The result tastes vibrant and fresh, despite its frozen origins. The rice is warmed on a sheet pan covered with aluminum foil to keep in the moisture, a technique that's super easy and convenient if you've already got the oven going for your main dish.

If you're making this rice in conjunction with another sheet pan recipe—it'd be wonderful with the Asparagus & Black Cod in Parchment (page 96) or Curried Chicken with Cauliflower, Apricots & Olives (page 54)—place the rice in the upper third of the oven, and the main dish in the center or lower third.

---

1 bag (20 ounces) frozen rice (white or brown, unthawed, about 4 cups)
3 tablespoons extra virgin olive oil
Kosher salt and freshly ground black pepper

1 cup frozen peas (unthawed)
2 tablespoons chopped fresh mint leaves
2 tablespoons chopped fresh chives
¼ cup slivered blanched almonds

LET'S COOK:

1. Preheat the oven to 350°F with a rack in the center position.

2. Place the rice in a mound on a sheet pan, drizzle it evenly with the olive oil, and sprinkle it with a pinch each of salt and pepper. Place the frozen peas on top of the rice, then mix them together thoroughly on the pan. Spread out the rice mixture in an even layer about ½ inch thick, leaving a bare border around the pan's edges (don't spread it too thin or it may dry out). Cover the pan tightly with aluminum foil.

3. Bake the rice until warmed through, about 15 minutes.

4. Remove the foil and sprinkle the herbs and almonds over the rice. Toss to combine. Serve warm.

CHEESY BAKED POLENTA WITH MIXED HERBS

SERVES 4

A store-bought tube of polenta makes this side dish a breeze. We'll transform that polenta into creamy, cheesy, herby, corn-flavored goodness on a sheet pan, all in just 20 short minutes.

If you're making this dish to go alongside another sheet pan recipe, you can put the polenta on a rack in the lower third of the oven, and the other sheet pan in the upper third. As always, if the other recipe cooks at a higher or lower temperature, simply adjust the polenta's cook time as needed.

Olive oil cooking spray
1 tube (18 ounces) precooked polenta, sliced into ½-inch-thick rounds (about 16 slices)
2 tablespoons extra virgin olive oil
½ teaspoon kosher salt

½ teaspoon freshly ground black pepper
¼ cup shredded Parmesan cheese
¼ cup chopped fresh herb leaves such as flat-leaf parsley, tarragon, thyme, or rosemary

---

LET'S COOK:

1. Preheat the oven to 400°F with a rack in the center position. Mist a sheet pan with cooking spray.

2. Place the polenta rounds on the sheet pan, spacing them evenly apart. Drizzle evenly with olive oil and sprinkle with the salt and pepper.

3. Bake the polenta, flipping the slices halfway through cooking, until their edges are lightly browned and their centers are soft and creamy, about 20 minutes.

4. Remove the pan from the oven and sprinkle the cheese and fresh herbs on top of the polenta. Return the pan to the oven until the cheese is good and melted, about 5 minutes.

5. Serve warm.

Chapter 8

I LOVE BRUNCH

W ho doesn't, really? Weekend brunch feels so wonderfully luxurious, and brunch on a weekday? Practically sinful. Because brunch means time for leisure, time to linger. It can be quiet and romantic, or social and noisy. It can be sweet or savory, though oftentimes it's both (biscuits and bacon, anyone?).

Making brunch on a sheet pan usually means cooking for a crowd (one dozen Fresh Brioche Cinnamon Rolls, please, or maybe a Big Dutch Baby with Meyer Lemon Sugar. Recipes for both are here on pages 225 and 210). It also means skipping the stressful and annoying parts of brunchtime entertaining like standing over a skillet and cooking dozens of eggs to order. It's so easy to bake eggs (maybe over some roasted peppers and tomato sauce for Shakshuka, page 198) and other eggy dishes (like Baked Apricot French Toast, page 206) using our trusty sheet pan. Less fussing, more brunching.

So get ready for many happy, chatty, friend-filled brunch dates in your future.

GREENS & EGGS & HAM

SERVES 4 TO 6

I will eat these, Sam I Am. They're clever and healthy and perfect for hosting some friends for (a clever and healthy) brunch! We just nestle some eggs into a bed of baked kale, and top it all off with some salty feta cheese and meaty chunks of ham. It covers all our bases, especially when served with some simple toast and a big pitcher of fresh orange juice.

With friends, on the weekend, in a house, with a mouse (but no mice, because gross), let's enjoy these greens and eggs and ham.

Olive oil cooking spray
1 boneless ham steak (7 ounces), cut into ½-inch cubes
4 to 5 cups packed chopped kale
1 tablespoon extra virgin olive oil
Kosher salt

8 to 12 large eggs
½ cup crumbled feta cheese (about 2 ounces)
Freshly ground black pepper
Crusty bread, for serving

LET'S COOK:

1. Preheat the oven to 375°F with a rack in the center position. Line a sheet pan with aluminum foil and mist the foil with cooking spray.

2. Spread out the ham on the prepared pan and bake, using a spatula to mix and turn the ham occasionally, until lightly browned, 10 to 12 minutes.

3. Transfer the ham to a plate with a spatula or slotted spoon. Do not wipe up any grease from the bottom of the pan.

4. Place the kale on the sheet pan, drizzle with the olive oil, sprinkle with ½ teaspoon salt, and toss to coat. Spread out the kale in an even layer. Bake for 5 minutes.

5. Remove the pan from the oven but leave the oven on. Use a wooden spoon to make eight to twelve evenly spaced divots in the kale to accommodate the eggs. Crack an egg into each divot. Sprinkle the feta, the reserved ham cubes, and some salt and pepper on top.

6. Return the pan to the oven. Bake the eggs until the whites are set but the yolks are still runny, 10 to 15 minutes.

7. Enjoy greens and eggs and ham immediately, with some crusty bread to soak up the warm, runny yolks.

SMOKED SALMON EGG BOATS

SERVES 8

I'm intrigued by edible cooking vessels (have you noticed?). I bake things in peppers, in squashes, in eggplants—why not in loaves of bread, too? This bread boat inspiration came from a lovely food blog called Spoon Fork Bacon, and, boy, if it's not clever. Cheesy baked eggs in a carved-out loaf of bread! Creamy softness and chewy sturdiness at once. The addition of crème fraîche, smoked salmon, capers, and chives takes it all up a notch, though feel free to customize the filling to suit your taste (see the box opposite for suggestions).

A *bâtard* is an oval-shaped loaf of bread that's about 10 inches long. It usually has a few slits down the middle like a baguette, but it's shorter and fatter than that old French staple.

---

2 sourdough bâtards or 4 sourdough demi baguettes
½ cup shredded Gruyère or Swiss cheese (about 2 ounces)
4 ounces sliced smoked salmon
12 large eggs
½ cup crème fraîche (or sour cream in a pinch)

½ teaspoon kosher salt
¼ teaspoon freshly ground black pepper
3 scallions (white and light green parts only), thinly sliced
2 tablespoons capers, drained
2 tablespoons chopped fresh chives

LET'S COOK:

1. Preheat the oven to 350°F with a rack in the center position. Line a sheet pan with parchment paper.

2. Using a serrated knife, cut a V-shaped section from the top of each bread loaf, stopping the knife about ½ inch from the bottom of the loaf. Remove the loose bread tops, and scoop out a bit of the inside, too, to form the "boats." Discard the scooped bread (or save it to make homemade breadcrumbs). Place the boats on the prepared pan.

3. Evenly distribute the shredded cheese and smoked salmon between the cavities of the boats.

4. Whisk together the eggs, crème fraîche, salt, pepper, and scallions in a medium-size bowl. Pour the egg

mixture into the boats, distributing it evenly between them. Scatter the capers atop the egg filling.

5. Bake until the eggs are puffed and no longer jiggle when you shake the pan gently, 30 to 40 minutes. (If using demi baguettes, check for doneness around 20 minutes.)

6. Let the boats cool for about 5 minutes. Sprinkle them with the fresh chives, slice into 8 pieces total, and serve warm.

MAKE IT MINE
EGG BOAT FILLINGS
Not into smoked salmon and capers? Try one of these other combinations to dress up your own perfect egg boat. Just place the ingredients in the bottom of the boat before adding the eggs.

• Gruyère cheese + crumbled bacon+ sautéed mushrooms

• Feta cheese + halved cherry tomatoes + chives

• Cheddar cheese + crumbled cooked sausage + chopped scallions

SHAKSHUKA

SERVES 6 TO 8

S hak-whatta? Say it with me: shack-SHOO-kah. Shakshuka! It's just the best name ever for eggs poached in spicy tomato sauce, then topped with crumbled feta cheese and fresh parsley. A traditional Israeli dish, the simplicity and bold flavor of shakshuka make it popular not just for breakfast, but for lunch and dinner, too. And using our trusty sheet pan lets us make as many as a dozen eggs at once! So brunch (and dinner, while we're at it) is covered.

A quick word to the wise: Be sure to handle the hot peppers carefully. If you can, wear disposable gloves while you prep them and definitely wash up thoroughly with soap afterward lest you fall victim to "burny finger syndrome," an ailment whose name I just made up but whose painful sting is very real indeed.

---

2 poblano peppers, stemmed, seeded, and finely chopped
2 jalapeño peppers, stemmed, seeded, and finely chopped
1 large shallot, finely chopped
6 cloves garlic, thinly sliced
1½ teaspoons ground cumin
2 tablespoons smoked paprika
Kosher salt

3 tablespoons extra virgin olive oil
1 can (28 ounces) crushed tomatoes
12 large eggs
½ to 1 cup crumbled feta cheese (2 to 4 ounces)
½ cup roughly chopped fresh flat-leaf parsley leaves
Toast or warm pita bread, for serving

LET'S COOK:

1. Preheat the oven to 350°F with a rack in the center position.

2. Toss together the poblanos, jalapeños, shallot, garlic, cumin, paprika, ½ teaspoon salt, and the olive oil on a sheet pan until the vegetables are evenly coated.

3. Bake until the spices are fragrant and the vegetables have softened and started to brown, 10 to 15 minutes.

4. Remove the pan from the oven. Pour the tomatoes, with their juice, over the vegetables and stir to combine. Use a wooden spoon to make twelve evenly spaced divots in the sauce; the sauce will be a bit runny, but do your best. Crack the eggs into the divots, and sprinkle them with some extra salt.

5. Return the pan to the oven and bake until the eggs are cooked to your liking. (It will take 10 to 15 minutes for the whites to be set and the yolks to still be runny.)

6. Remove the eggs from the oven and sprinkle a generous amount of feta cheese and fresh parsley on top of each. Serve the shakshuka hot, with plenty of toast or warm pita bread on the side.

BISCUITS & BACON

SERVES 4 OR 5

This right here is the way brunch should be. Cooking bacon in the oven is a total revelation; our little sheet pan trick gives us perfectly flat, extra crisp bacon strips with nary a grease burn in sight. And our rich, flaky buttermilk biscuits bake right in the bacon fat, the benefits of which I shouldn't even have to explain. I mean, the whole thing is basically an insight into the (smoky, buttery, bacon-y) glories of heaven. If you have thoughts of making a bacon biscuit sandwich once you pull this pan out of the oven, go with those thoughts. Drizzle it with honey, even. You are in excellent company.

If you must, you can make this dish a few hours in advance—just be sure to rewarm everything in a low oven (about 300°F) before serving for an optimal biscuit-bacon experience.

---

8 to 10 slices thick-cut bacon
2 cups all-purpose flour, plus extra
   for shaping the biscuits
1 tablespoon baking powder
¼ teaspoon baking soda
2 teaspoons sugar

1 teaspoon kosher salt
6 tablespoons (¾ stick) very cold
   unsalted butter, cut into small cubes
¾ cup cold buttermilk
Honey, for serving (optional)

LET'S COOK:

1. Preheat the oven to 400°F with a rack in the center position. Line a sheet pan with parchment paper.

2. Lay the strips of bacon side by side on the sheet pan. (No need to leave much space between them; the bacon will shrink as it cooks.) Bake the bacon until it starts to crisp at the edges, about 15 minutes.

3. While the bacon takes its first turn in the oven, make the biscuit dough: Whisk together the flour, baking

powder, baking soda, sugar, and salt in a medium-size bowl. Add the butter and use your fingertips or a pastry cutter to work it into the flour. Work quickly to avoid letting the butter become too warm. The mixture will look like pebbly sand; it's okay if the butter pieces run the gamut in size—you want a mix of oat-, lentil-, and pea-size pieces.

4. Pour the buttermilk over the flour mixture and use a fork to bring everything together in a shaggy

dough. Knead the dough in the bowl once or twice (try to avoid overmixing) to pick up the sandy pieces at the bottom of the bowl.

5. Lightly flour a work surface. Dump out the dough onto the surface and pat it with your hands into a ¾-inch-thick slab. Use a floured 2½-inch biscuit cutter to cut out as many biscuits as you can, gently

patting the dough back together when necessary; you should get 6 to 8 biscuits. Feel free to use a smaller cutter to get more biscuits; just reduce the baking time accordingly (check for doneness about 5 minutes earlier than normal).

6. Now back to the bacon: After it has baked for 15 minutes, carefully remove the pan from the oven and use kitchen tongs to flip over the strips. Arrange them evenly on the pan, leaving some empty space, wide enough for rows of biscuits, between them. Place the biscuits between the bacon strips (it's fine if they overlap the bacon), and use a pastry brush to pick up some of the bacon grease on the pan and brush it atop the biscuits.

7. Immediately return the pan to the oven—be careful, it will still be hot! Bake, rotating the pan halfway through, until the bacon is charred at the edges and the biscuits are fluffy, golden, and their bottoms are deeply browned, 20 minutes more.

8. Enjoy the biscuits and bacon warm, drizzled with some honey if you like.

TEACH ME HOW
TO MAKE THE BEST BISCUIT

The perfect biscuit—tall, flaky, and flavorful—seems like the Holy Grail of baking, but with a few simple tips in mind, pretty much anyone can achieve biscuit nirvana.

1. Aerate your flour before you scoop it into a measuring cup. This is done simply: Use a whisk to stir up the flour and ensure it's not so tightly packed before measuring.

2. Make sure your butter is really, really cold. Put it in the freezer for a few minutes, if you have to, and handle it as little as possible (the heat from your hands will cause it to soften and melt). The water in cold butter expands when exposed to the heat of the oven, and this expansion helps biscuits rise and also creates little "pockets" of buttery steam between the layers of dough.

3. Leave well enough alone! As I just said, handle the dough as little as possible. This will both prevent the cold butter flakes from melting and prevent the formation of gluten that, if overdeveloped, can cause biscuits to be dense and tough instead of light and flaky.

EGGS IN A HOLE IN A BREAD

SERVES 4 TO 6

I've heard these called "one-eyed Jacks" or "eggs in a window," and my sister Emily swears they're called "Emily eggs," but I've always just called them "eggs in a hole in a bread." A lot of prepositions, yes, but when you pull a hot pan of these from the oven on Saturday morning, I doubt anyone will care what you call them. For me, using a rich bread like challah is paramount, and I like to elevate the simple eggs-in-bread routine by tossing some fresh herbs and grated cheese on top. The best part is that using a sheet pan means not having to stand over the frying pan flipping runny eggs or fussing over multiple batches. Hot "eggs in a hole in a bread" for everyone!

8 tablespoons (1 stick) unsalted butter
1 loaf (about 20 ounces) challah bread
   (from the supermarket is fine), cut
   in ¾- to 1-inch-thick slices (8 to
   10 slices total)
8 to 10 large eggs

Kosher salt and freshly ground black
   pepper
¼ cup grated Parmesan cheese
2 tablespoons chopped fresh herbs
   such as parsley, chives, or cilantro

LET'S COOK:

1. Preheat the oven to 350°F with a rack in the center position.

2. Place the butter on a sheet pan and put the pan in the oven until the butter melts and begins to bubble, about 5 minutes.

3. While the butter is melting, use a 2-inch round cutter to cut a hole in the middle of each slice of challah. Save the holes!

4. Remove the pan from the oven; the pan will be very hot. Carefully dip the challah slices in the melted butter, turning each one to coat both sides. Arrange the bread in a single layer on the pan, leaving room for the holes. Do the same with the holes, placing them around the bigger pieces of challah.

5. Bake the challah until the bottoms are toasty, about 10 minutes.

Carefully remove the hot pan from the oven and use a spatula to flip each piece of bread and each hole so the toasted side is up.

6. Crack an egg into the hole in each slice of bread, and sprinkle the eggs with a good pinch each of salt and pepper, the grated Parmesan, and about half of the fresh herbs.

7. Return the pan to the oven and bake until the whites of the eggs have just set but the yolks are still runny, 10 to 12 minutes.

8. Serve hot from the oven, sprinkled with the remaining herbs, with the toasted challah holes, which are great for dipping into warm egg yolks, alongside.

BAKED APRICOT FRENCH TOAST

SERVES 8 TO 10

The ability to serve French toast for a brunch party without slaving at the stovetop for hours is a beautiful thing. And if we're feeling particularly on top of our game, we can even prep this thing the night before and store it, covered, in the fridge before baking.

I love the velvety texture, light sweetness, and color of apricot preserves in this custardy baked dish, but you could easily swap out for another flavor—strawberry-rhubarb or orange marmalade would be divine.

Butter or nonstick cooking spray, for greasing the pan
1 cup apricot preserves
1½ loaves (about 20 ounces each) challah bread (from the supermarket is fine), cut in 1-inch-thick slices (about 20 slices)
4 cups milk
4 large eggs

3 tablespoons granulated sugar
1 teaspoon kosher salt
1 tablespoon pure vanilla extract
2 tablespoons brandy (optional)
1 teaspoon freshly grated orange zest
2 tablespoons raw or turbinado sugar
Confectioners' sugar, fresh fruit, and/or pure maple syrup, for serving

---

LET'S COOK:

1. Generously grease a sheet pan with butter or mist it with cooking spray. If you're going to bake the French toast right away, preheat the oven to 400°F with a rack in the center position.

2. Spread some apricot preserves on one side of each slice of challah and place the bread, overlapping the slices, preserves side up, on the prepared pan.

3. Whisk the milk, eggs, granulated sugar, salt, vanilla, brandy (if using), and orange zest in a large measuring cup or bowl until well combined. Pour over the challah, thoroughly soaking each slice. There will be a bunch of liquid in the bottom of the pan. At this point, you can cover the pan with aluminum foil and refrigerate it overnight before baking.

4. If the French toast was refrigerated, preheat the oven to 400°F with a rack in the center position. Remove the foil from the pan.

5. Sprinkle the raw sugar evenly on top of the bread. Carefully slide the pan into the oven and bake until the French toast is very brown and puffed, 30 to 45 minutes.

6. Let the French toast cool slightly before serving with a dusting of confectioners' sugar, some fresh fruit, and/or drizzles of maple syrup.

WAIT, WHAT?

TURBINADO SUGAR

Also called raw sugar, turbinado sugar is a minimally processed form of sugar cane. You'll recognize the stuff by its large crystals, which are light brown. Turbinado is often used as a finishing touch atop baked goods like muffins and cookies; it endows the end product with a slightly sparkly sheen and satisfying crunch.

BANANA CINNAMON TOAST

SERVES 4 TO 6

Cinnamon swirl bread from the bakery (or even just the supermarket) is such a treat. Are you a raisin person? I like their sweetness but their absence isn't a deal breaker. I'd eat cinnamon swirl bread any way you give it to me. And if you give it to me dunked in melted butter, topped with bananas, and slathered with extra cinnamon sugar, all melted and gooey and warm, I'd say "Geez Louise" and ask you how you got a piece of toast to taste like a warm banana cinnamon roll. You'd say "Magic!" and I'd say "Genius!" and then we'd high-five. You're so good at brunch.

---

8 tablespoons (1 stick) salted butter
1 loaf cinnamon swirl bread, cut into
   1-inch-thick slices (about 8 slices)

½ cup sugar
2 tablespoons ground cinnamon
2 ripe bananas, thinly sliced

LET'S COOK:

1. Preheat the oven to 350°F with one rack about 4 inches from the broiler and another rack in the center position.

2. Place the butter on a sheet pan and put the pan on the center rack until the butter melts and begins to bubble, about 5 minutes.

3. Remove the pan from the oven and set it on a heatproof surface (the pan will be very hot). Carefully dip the bread slices in the melted butter, turning each one to coat both sides. Arrange the bread in a single layer on the pan.

4. Stir together the sugar and cinnamon in a small bowl to combine. Sprinkle the bread with ¼ cup of the cinnamon sugar, giving each slice a thin, even dusting. Bake the cinnamon bread on the center rack until crisp and toasty, about 10 minutes.

5. Remove the pan from the oven and turn the oven to broil. Using a spatula, flip the slices of bread. The cinnamon sugar layer will now be on the bottom. Place a layer of sliced banana on each piece of toast, then dust with the remaining cinnamon sugar.

6. Place the pan under the broiler. Watch it closely: You're looking for the toast to lightly char at the edges and the cinnamon sugar to bubble and caramelize atop the bananas (it will want to burn), 1 to 3 minutes.

7. Serve the banana cinnamon toast warm.

BIG DUTCH BABY WITH MEYER LEMON SUGAR

SERVES 8 GENEROUSLY, 16 FAIRLY

This is one BIG Dutch baby—it should make a lot of people happy. A Dutch baby, for those who are unfamiliar with the term, is basically an eggy, puffed-up, oven-baked pancake. (Also, Dutch babies aren't actually Dutch. They're thought to be German in origin but, somewhere along the way, "Deutsch" morphed into "Dutch" and here we are today.) A Dutch baby is sort of like a cross between a pancake and a popover, with a bit of soufflé thrown in for good measure. Needless to say, it's a dramatic and fantastic brunch option. We'll top ours with some berries and homemade Meyer lemon sugar for extra street cred; if you can't find Meyer lemons, though, regular lemons work just fine.

Make sure your brunch party is ready to eat as soon as the Dutch baby comes out of the oven, since it'll fall pretty quickly and the puff is part of the fun.

---

8 tablespoons (1 stick) unsalted butter
2 cups all-purpose flour
½ teaspoon kosher salt
¼ teaspoon ground nutmeg
8 large eggs

2 cups milk
1 teaspoon pure vanilla extract
½ cup sugar
2 teaspoons grated Meyer lemon zest
Fresh berries, for serving

LET'S COOK:

1. Preheat the oven to 425°F with a rack in the center position.

2. Place the butter on a sheet pan and put the pan in the oven until the butter melts and begins to bubble, about 5 minutes.

3. While the butter is melting, whisk together the flour, salt, and nutmeg in a medium-size bowl. Put the eggs in a blender or food processor and whirl on high speed for 1 minute. With the motor running, slowly pour in the milk and vanilla. Pour the egg mixture into a large bowl and whisk in the flour until combined. The batter will be quite thin.

4. Remove the pan with the butter from the oven; the pan will be very hot. Carefully tilt it to coat it with the melted butter, then pour in the batter. Return the pan to the oven and bake until the pancake is puffy and golden at the edges, about 20 minutes.

5. While the Dutch baby bakes, mash together the sugar and lemon zest in a small bowl (your fingertips or the back of a spoon work best) until the sugar is fragrant and yellow.

6. Remove the Dutch baby from the oven and immediately sprinkle the lemon sugar generously over it, reserving a bit for serving.

7. Slice into squares and serve immediately, with plenty of fresh berries and extra lemon sugar on the side.

WAIT, WHAT?

MEYER LEMONS

When I lived in California, I became obsessed with Meyer lemons. A cross between a lemon and a mandarin orange, the Meyer lemon is sweeter and more floral than a regular lemon. It has a thin, yolk-yellow peel and can be used in place of regular lemons in most applications. I love Meyer lemons for making lemon cakes and curds, brightening up salad dressings, and roasting with chicken and vegetables. Look for them between November and March.

BREAKFAST BERRY COBBLER

SERVES 10 TO 12

A colorful pan of roasted summer berries (you can use fresh or unthawed frozen) topped with golden cream biscuits: It's kind of the same thing as eating pie for breakfast, which, if you ask me, is always a good idea. And cobbler has the added benefit of being supremely simple to make, even in the bleary-eyed stupor of morning. Just grab a cup of coffee, slide this thing in the oven, and serve with dollops of plain or vanilla yogurt.

---

4 cups (about 2 pints) hulled, halved strawberries (if they're really big, you can quarter them)
1 cup (about ½ pint) blackberries
¼ cup plus 3 tablespoons sugar
Kosher salt
2 tablespoons freshly squeezed lime juice (about 1 lime)

2 cups all-purpose flour
2 teaspoons baking powder
¼ teaspoon baking soda
1½ cups heavy cream, plus extra for brushing the biscuits
Chilled plain or vanilla yogurt, for serving (optional)

LET'S COOK:

1. Preheat the oven to 400°F with a rack in the center position. Line a sheet pan with parchment paper.

2. Place the strawberries, blackberries, ¼ cup of the sugar, a pinch of salt, and the lime juice in a large bowl and toss them together to combine. Spread the berries evenly on the prepared pan with a rubber spatula. Roast until the berries just begin to soften and release some juice, 5 to 7 minutes (10 to 15 minutes if using frozen berries).

3. While the berries are roasting, make the biscuit dough: Whisk together the flour, remaining 3 tablespoons sugar, 1 teaspoon salt, the baking powder, and baking soda in a medium-size bowl. Add the heavy cream and stir to combine, just until a rough, shaggy dough comes together.

4. When the berries have finished their initial roast, carefully remove the pan from the oven. Use a 2-inch ice cream scoop to drop the biscuits on top of the berries, spacing the

biscuits evenly, 1 to 2 inches apart. You should get 10 to 12 biscuits.

golden brown and surrounded by soft, slumpy berries, 18 to 20 minutes.

5. Quickly brush the tops of the biscuits with cream. Return the pan to the oven and bake until the biscuits are

6. Serve the cobbler warm from the oven, with big scoops of vanilla yogurt, if you like.

APPLE DOUGHNUT COBBLER

SERVES ABOUT 8

This recipe replaces homemade biscuits with store-bought doughnuts for a brunchtime apple cobbler. It is equal parts ridiculous (I mean, we just throw boxed doughnuts on top of stuff now?!) and awesome (we throw boxed doughnuts on top of stuff now!). But really it's just soft, warm apples topped with soft, warm glazed doughnuts. Sweet and cakey over tart and fruity. Get outta town.

Butter or nonstick cooking spray, for greasing the pan
4 Granny Smith apples, peeled, cored, and cut into ¼-inch-thick slices
4 Golden Delicious apples, peeled, cored, and cut into ¼-inch-thick slices
1 teaspoon grated lemon zest
Juice of 1 lemon

½ cup sugar
1 teaspoon ground cinnamon
¼ teaspoon ground nutmeg
1 teaspoon pure vanilla extract
2 tablespoons all-purpose flour
4 tablespoons (½ stick) cold unsalted butter, cut into small cubes
8 glazed doughnuts (yeast or cake varieties both work)

LET'S COOK:

1. Preheat the oven to 375°F with a rack in the center position. Grease the bottom and sides of a sheet pan with butter or mist them with cooking spray.

2. Combine the apples, lemon zest, lemon juice, sugar, cinnamon, nutmeg, vanilla, and flour in a large bowl and toss gently to coat the apples. Spread them evenly over the prepared pan with a rubber spatula and dot with the cubed butter.

3. Bake until the apples are soft and starting to brown at the edges, 20 to 25 minutes.

4. Remove the pan from the oven and arrange the doughnuts on top of the apples, leaving a bit of space between the doughnuts. Return the pan to the oven and bake until the apples are bubbling at the edges and the doughnuts are warm and their glaze is slightly caramelized, another 20 minutes.

5. Let the cobbler cool for a few minutes before scooping up portions and serving warm.

RASPBERRY & WHITE CHOCOLATE SCONES

MAKES 8 TO 12 SCONES

The act of breaking open a warm, flaky scone, dabbing it with some soft butter, and washing it down with a swig of milky coffee or tea is a good one. Calming, in many ways. Sophisticated. But too often, scones are these big, hulking, sugary things, all carb and no class, you know? I mean sure, mine are stuffed with fresh raspberries and a handful of white chocolate, but cutting them on the smaller side helps keep them delicate and reasonable.

2½ cups all-purpose flour, plus extra for shaping the dough

3 tablespoons granulated sugar

1 tablespoon baking powder

1 teaspoon salt

8 tablespoons (1 stick) cold unsalted butter, cut into small cubes

⅓ cup white chocolate chips

1 cup cold half-and-half, plus extra for brushing the dough

1 teaspoon freshly squeezed lemon juice

1 large egg yolk

½ teaspoon pure vanilla extract

1 cup fresh or unthawed frozen raspberries

Turbinado sugar (see box, page 207), for sprinkling

Clotted cream (or whipped cream), butter, and jam, for serving (optional)

LET'S COOK:

1. Preheat the oven to 400°F with a rack in the center position. Line a sheet pan with parchment paper.

2. Whisk together the flour, sugar, baking powder, and salt in a large bowl. Add the butter and use your fingertips or a pastry cutter to work it into the flour until it feels moistened and the butter pieces look like small pebbles or peas. Gently stir in the white chocolate chips.

3. Whisk together the half-and-half, lemon juice, egg yolk, and vanilla in a small bowl and pour over the flour mixture. Stir with a fork just until everything comes together in a shaggy dough.

4. Generously flour the work surface. Dump out the dough onto the surface and pat it with your hands into a 12-by-14-inch and ½-inch-thick slab. Scatter the raspberries over the dough, fold the dough in

half over itself to trap the raspberries inside, and knead once. Shape the dough into a 10-inch circle about ¾-inch thick. Use a well-floured 2½-inch biscuit cutter to cut out 8 to 12 scones. You can gently reshape the dough once to get the maximum number of scones.

5. Gently place the scones spaced evenly apart on the prepared pan.

Brush the tops with half-and-half and sprinkle with the turbinado sugar. Bake the scones until craggy and golden brown, 15 to 20 minutes.

6. The scones are best served warm the day they are made, with clotted cream, butter, and jam for spreading, if you like.

COFFEE CRUMB CAKE

SERVES ABOUT 20

Have you ever tried one of those Entenmann's crumb coffee cakes? The ones in the white box, with the generous confectioners' sugar dusting? This is like that, only better. More flavor and fewer preservatives (read: none!)! A thin layer of bouncy, tender yellow cake peeks out beneath a heavy-handed avalanche of crumb topping, the whole thing smelling of subtle, warm spice. Serve with coffee for brunch perfection.

Nonstick cooking spray

FOR THE CRUMB TOPPING
½ pound (2 sticks) unsalted butter, melted
⅔ cup granulated sugar
⅔ cup packed light brown sugar
1½ teaspoons ground cinnamon
½ teaspoon kosher salt
2½ cups all-purpose flour

FOR THE CAKE
2¼ cups all-purpose flour
1 tablespoon baking powder
¾ teaspoon baking soda
1 teaspoon kosher salt
¼ teaspoon ground nutmeg
12 tablespoons (1½ sticks) unsalted butter, at room temperature
1¼ cups granulated sugar
4 large eggs
1½ cups sour cream
1 tablespoon pure vanilla extract

LET'S COOK:

1. Preheat the oven to 350°F with a rack in the center position. Mist a sheet pan with cooking spray, line it with parchment paper, then mist the parchment.

2. Make the crumb topping: Whisk together the melted butter, granulated sugar, brown sugar, cinnamon, and salt in a large bowl. Add the flour and stir with a wooden spoon to bring together a thick dough.

3. Make the cake: Whisk together the flour, baking powder, baking soda, salt, and nutmeg in a small bowl.

4. Cream the butter and sugar in a stand mixer fitted with the paddle, or in a large bowl with a handheld electric mixer, on high speed until light and fluffy, about 3 minutes. Beat in the eggs, one at a time, on medium-high speed until fully incorporated (the mixture may look curdled, but will smooth out as you add the rest of the ingredients). Add half of the flour and mix on low speed to incorporate, then gently mix in the sour cream and vanilla. Add the remaining flour and beat on low speed just until the batter is streak-free.

5. Dump the batter into the prepared pan and spread it evenly to the corners with a rubber spatula. Break up the crumb topping unevenly with your fingers and scatter the large and small pieces over the batter all the way to the edges.

6. Bake the cake until a skewer inserted into the middle comes out clean, 25 to 30 minutes.

7. Let the cake cool for at least 10 minutes before slicing it into squares and serving.

The cake will keep for up to 4 days, well wrapped in plastic or aluminum foil, in the refrigerator.

CINNAMON–BROWN SUGAR BREAKFAST TARTS

MAKES 8 TARTS

I had a thing for Pop-Tarts when I was younger. (Who didn't?) We had a toaster that would burn the oversweet rectangles every time, the cardboard-y edges and cinnamon glaze scorching in spots, but what did I care? I'd eat them cold if I had to. Anything for a brown sugar–cinnamon Pop-Tart (also anything for slap bracelets and Jonathan Taylor Thomas, but I digress).

It blew my mind when, years later, I figured out that I could make my own take on Pop-Tarts from scratch. And it's not even that difficult! A straightforward dough, a three-ingredient filling, a bit of bake time, and we've got breakfast tarts that blast the store-bought version out of the water. My inner child is (like, totally) freaking out.

---

2 cups plus 4 teaspoons all-purpose flour, plus extra for rolling out the dough
Kosher salt
1 tablespoon granulated sugar
3 ounces cold cream cheese, cut into roughly 1-inch cubes

12 tablespoons (1½ sticks) cold unsalted butter, cut into small cubes
2 large eggs
2 tablespoons milk
½ cup packed dark brown sugar
1½ teaspoons ground cinnamon
6 tablespoons confectioners' sugar
2 tablespoons pure maple syrup

LET'S COOK:

1. To make the dough, place 2 cups flour, 1 teaspoon salt, and the granulated sugar in a food processor and pulse to combine. Add the cream cheese and butter and pulse until the fats are incorporated but the mixture still looks rough and pebbly.

2. Whisk together 1 egg and the milk in a small bowl. Pour this down the feed tube of the food processor, then pulse just until the dough comes together in a big clump.

3. Generously flour the work surface. Dump out the dough onto the surface and form it with your hands into a rectangle about 8 by 6 inches. Wrap the dough tightly in plastic wrap and refrigerate it until firm, at least 1 hour, up to 1 day.

4. When you're ready to assemble the tarts, unwrap the dough (reserve the plastic) and cut it in half widthwise to form two rectangles of equal size. Rewrap one rectangle and refrigerate it while you work with the other.

5. Place a large piece of parchment paper on the work surface. Generously flour it and a rolling pin. Place the dough in the center of the parchment and roll it into a 12-by-9-inch rectangle about $1/8$-inch thick. Use a ruler and sharp knife to trim the dough if you need to. Transfer the dough, on its parchment, to the fridge to chill.

6. Roll out the second piece of dough in exactly the same way. You'll end up with two 12-by-9-inch sheets of dough. Chill both to firm up, at least 10 minutes.

7. Use a sharp knife to cut each sheet of dough in half lengthwise, then in quarters widthwise; you'll end up with eight 3-by-4$1/2$-inch rectangles per sheet (16 total). Return the rectangles of dough, still on their parchment sheets, to the refrigerator while you mix up the filling.

8. To make the filling, whisk the remaining 4 teaspoons flour, the brown sugar, and the cinnamon in a small bowl until well combined.

9. Flour a clean work surface and line up the chilled dough rectangles on it in two rows. Beat the remaining egg in a small bowl. Brush some over half the rectangles. These are the bottoms, and the egg will help the filling and tops to stick. Refrigerate the remaining egg, along with the brush.

10. Prick the other rectangles a few times with a fork. These will be the tops (pricking them will help vent the steam in the oven).

11. Spoon a heaping tablespoon of filling in the center of each bottom rectangle, leaving a $1/4$-inch border around the edges. Carefully place a top rectangle over each bottom and press the edges together with your finger to seal. Ensure an even seal by pressing the tines of a well-floured fork around the edges of each tart.

12. Line a sheet pan with parchment paper. Use a spatula to gently transfer the tarts to the prepared pan, spacing them evenly apart. Refrigerate the tarts, uncovered, one last time for 15 to 30 minutes.

13. While the tarts are chilling, preheat the oven to 350°F with a rack in the center position.

14. Brush the tops of the tarts lightly with the remaining beaten egg. Bake the tarts until deeply golden brown, 20 to 25 minutes.

15. While the tarts are baking, make the glaze: Whisk the confectioners' sugar, a pinch of salt, and the maple syrup in a small bowl until smooth.

16. Let the tarts cool slightly, then drizzle the maple glaze over them before serving.

Extra tarts can be wrapped tightly in plastic wrap and stored at room temperature for 2 to 3 days, or in the freezer for up to 3 months.

BLUEBERRY CORNMEAL MUFFIN TOPS

MAKES 16 MUFFIN TOPS

I n regular life, it's true: Nobody wants a muffin top. In breakfast life, though, everybody wants one. Breakfast life is the best. The writers of *Seinfeld* once shone a light on the merits of muffin tops (the breakfast kind; Elaine adamantly ate only the tops, prompting a storyline involving a muffin-top-only-bakery and a "stump removal" problem) and they were absolutely right. Almost everyone I know prefers the domed top of the muffin to the bottom. Tops are fluffier, crisper-edged, and, frankly, prettier to look at than bottoms.

These particular muffin tops aren't just a pretty face. Only faintly sweet, they're wonderfully textured with cornmeal and bursting with fresh blueberries. If you prefer a sweeter muffin, feel free to increase the sugar to ¾ cup or even 1 cup.

---

1 cup all-purpose flour
2 cups cornmeal (fine to medium grind)
1 teaspoon baking soda
½ teaspoon kosher salt
8 tablespoons (1 stick) unsalted butter, at room temperature, plus extra for serving
½ cup packed light brown sugar

1 cup sour cream
1 tablespoon freshly grated lemon zest
1 teaspoon pure vanilla extract
1 large egg
1 heaping cup fresh or unthawed frozen blueberries
A few pinches turbinado sugar (see box, page 207), for sprinkling

---

LET'S COOK:

1. Preheat the oven to 375°F with a rack in the center position. Line two sheet pans with parchment paper.

2. Whisk together the flour, cornmeal, baking soda, and salt in a medium-size bowl. Cream the butter and sugar in a stand mixer fitted with the paddle, or in a large bowl with a handheld electric mixer, on high speed until light and fluffy, about 3 minutes. Add the sour cream, lemon zest, vanilla, and egg and stir with a rubber spatula or wooden spoon to combine. Add the dry ingredients and stir gently, just until the batter comes together. It will be quite thick. Gently fold in the blueberries.

3. Use a large spoon or 2-inch ice cream scoop to dollop the batter onto the sheet pans, creating 16 tallish mounds of batter spaced about 1 inch apart. Sprinkle a bit of turbinado sugar atop each mound.

4. Bake the muffin tops until their tops are lightly golden and the blueberries begin to ooze juice, 15 to 18 minutes.

5. Cool on the sheet pan on a wire rack before enjoying warm with pats of soft butter.

These are best enjoyed the day they are made, but they will keep for up to 4 days, in an airtight container or zip-top bag, at room temperature. Lightly toast to re-crisp them.

LET'S TALK TOOLS

THE ICE CREAM SCOOP

Ice cream scoops are for more than just ice cream! I've got them in a number of different sizes and use them for everything from measuring out meatballs to scooping cookie dough—and muffin-top batter—quickly and efficiently. Ice cream scoops help keep muffin tops (and cookies, cupcakes, and meatballs) consistent in size so cook times are easier to navigate. Just be sure to wash them well after each use, so your muffin tops don't taste like meatballs and vice versa.

FRESH BRIOCHE CINNAMON ROLLS

MAKES 12 ROLLS

It's true, this recipe is . . . involved. There are a lot of steps written out here. But. These. Dang. Cinnamon. Rolls. They are so freaking good. It's rare that I'll pull out all the stops and make something that requires a fair amount of time and effort, but when I do, I make sure that thing is downright fantastic. And these? Well, they are. The secret is threefold: first, buttery brioche dough. Second, more butter and a hint of almond paste in the filling. And third: cinnamon–cream cheese glaze.

To minimize your stress level, I suggest making the brioche dough the day before you want to serve the rolls—in the morning you can mix up the filling, roll out the dough, and give the rolls a quick proof before baking and serving. Or you can bake the rolls a day in advance—that is, do everything up until the glazing step—and leave them, well wrapped in plastic, at room temperature overnight. Then all you need to do in the morning is rewarm them in a low oven and whip up the glaze! So really, it can be done. It should be done. Let's do this.

FOR THE DOUGH
3½ cups plus 2 tablespoons bread flour (see Notes), plus extra for rolling out the dough
½ cup granulated sugar
2 teaspoons kosher salt
5 large eggs
1 tablespoon plus 1 teaspoon active dry yeast (2 envelopes minus ½ teaspoon)
½ pound (2 sticks) plus 2 tablespoons cold unsalted butter, cut into small cubes
Nonstick cooking spray

FOR THE FILLING
3½ ounces (about ¾ cup) almond paste (see Notes)

8 tablespoons (1 stick) unsalted butter, at room temperature
1 cup packed dark brown sugar
2 teaspoons ground cinnamon
Pinch of ground nutmeg

FOR THE EGG WASH
1 large egg
1 tablespoon water or milk

FOR THE GLAZE
4 ounces cream cheese, at room temperature
4 tablespoons (½ stick) unsalted butter, at room temperature
½ cup confectioners' sugar
½ teaspoon ground cinnamon
½ teaspoon pure vanilla extract

LET'S COOK:

1. Make the dough: Mix together the flour, granulated sugar, and salt in a stand mixer fitted with the paddle, on low speed, until well combined. Add ¼ cup water, the eggs, and the yeast and beat on low speed until well combined and quite thick, 1 to 2 minutes.

2. Switch to the dough hook and mix on low speed to help develop the gluten, 6 to 8 minutes. The dough should be very elastic and stretch into a translucent square when pulled apart between your fingertips.

3. Continue mixing on low speed with the dough hook while you gradually but steadily add the butter cubes, crushing each between your fingers before dropping it into the dough.

4. After all of the butter has been incorporated, mix the dough on medium-low speed with the dough hook until it is smooth and satiny and completely pulls away from the side of the bowl, about 5 minutes.

5. Mist a large bowl with cooking spray and transfer the dough to it. Cover the dough with a clean kitchen towel and allow it to proof at room temperature until it rises and almost doubles in size, about 1 hour.

6. Punch down the dough and shape it into a large ball. Wrap the dough ball in 2 layers of plastic wrap and refrigerate it for at least 4 hours, up to 2 days.

7. When you're ready to assemble the cinnamon rolls, line a sheet pan with parchment paper.

8. Make the filling: Cream together the almond paste and butter in a stand mixer fitted with a paddle, or in a large bowl with a handheld electric mixer, on high speed. Add the brown sugar, cinnamon, and nutmeg and beat until smooth. Set aside.

9. Remove the dough from the refrigerator and place it on a well-floured work surface. Using plenty of flour to keep it from sticking, roll out the dough into a large rectangle, roughly 13 by 19 inches and ¼ inch thick.

10. Spread the filling evenly over the dough with a small knife or offset spatula, leaving a ½-inch border. Starting from one long side, carefully roll the dough tightly into a thick log. Place it seam side down on the work surface and use a sharp knife to slice the log into 12 slices, each roughly 1½ inches thick.

11. Place the rolls, cut side up, on the prepared pan, spacing them evenly apart. Mist one side of a sheet of plastic wrap with cooking spray, and place it sprayed side down over the rolls. Proof the rolls at room temperature until slightly puffed, about 1 hour.

12. When you're ready to bake, preheat the oven to 350°F with a rack in the center position.

13. Make the egg wash: Whisk together the egg and water in a small bowl. Uncover the rolls and brush them gently with the egg wash to coat.

14. Bake the rolls until well risen, deeply brown, and the filling is bubbly, 25 to 30 minutes.

15. While the rolls are baking, make the glaze: Beat together the cream cheese, butter, confectioners' sugar, cinnamon, and vanilla in a large bowl until completely smooth.

16. Let the cinnamon rolls cool for 5 minutes; they should still be quite warm. Slather the glaze on top. Serve the warm, gooey cinnamon rolls immediately.

NOTES: Using bread flour results in a chewier and more substantial cinnamon roll, but you can substitute all-purpose flour if you'd like.

Almond paste is a sweet, doughy mixture of ground almonds and sugar, usually sold in 7-ounce tubes. You can find it in small, rectangular boxes in the baking aisle of the grocery store. Since this recipe uses only half the tube, be sure to wrap the leftover paste tightly in plastic and store it in the refrigerator, where it will last for about a month. Bring the almond paste to room temperature before using it again.

TEACH ME HOW
TO DETERMINE WHEN TO STOP MIXING
Try the "windowpane test": Pull a small piece of the dough into a square with your fingers. If the square breaks easily when you stretch it, the gluten hasn't been developed enough and you need to keep mixing; if the dough seems quite elastic and doesn't break apart when you stretch it into an almost-transparent square, it's ready for the butter.

HAM & SWISS PASTRY BRAID

SERVES 6 GENEROUSLY, OR 10 TO 12 AS PART OF A SPREAD

Good news—you don't have to know how to braid to make a ham and cheese puff pastry braid! I'll walk you through some light dough folding and you'll have yourself a breakfast pastry.

A pastry braid can be sweet or savory, the former often filled with sweetened cream cheese and jam, the latter, in our case, with Dijon mustard, ham, and cheese. It's a four-ingredient stunner (okay, technically six, if you count the egg white and pepper) that's perfect alongside a simple bowl of fruit or a lightly dressed green salad.

Flour, for rolling out the pastry
1 box (14 ounces) frozen puff pastry
(Dufour brand), thawed according
to package directions
1 tablespoon Dijon mustard

5 ounces sliced Swiss cheese
5 ounces sliced ham
1 egg white, lightly beaten
Pinch of freshly ground black pepper

LET'S COOK:

1. Preheat the oven to 400°F with a rack in the center position.

2. Lightly flour a work surface and a rolling pin. Roll out the puff pastry to a 10-by-15-inch rectangle about ¼ inch thick. Place the pastry on a sheet of parchment paper so that one of the short sides is facing you.

3. Use a sharp knife to cut off the top corners of the rectangle at a 45-degree angle, leaving 4 inches of dough between them. Next cut out two triangular notches at the bottom of the rectangle, again leaving about 4 inches between the notches. The whole thing will kind of look like a short-stumped Christmas tree missing its pointy top. Finally make 8 diagonal slits, about 1 inch apart and parallel to the notches, along each side of the pastry, leaving a 4-inch-wide strip in the center intact. (The narrow flaps will get folded over to make the braid—see photos, page 230.)

4. Spread the Dijon mustard over the center strip of pastry (not on the side flaps) and layer the cheese and ham over the mustard, leaving a ¾-inch border at the top and bottom.

5. Fold the top and bottom edges of the pastry over the ham and cheese. Starting from the top and alternating sides, fold the diagonal flaps of pastry over the filling, crisscrossing them on top of one another, until all of the strips are interwoven and the filling is completely covered. Trim away any loose pieces of pastry at the bottom of the braid, lightly pinch the openings to seal it, and carefully transfer the parchment with the braid on it to a sheet pan.

6. Lightly brush the top and sides of the braid with beaten egg white and sprinkle it with the black pepper. Bake the braid until the pastry is deeply browned and the cheese is bubbling up through the slits, 25 to 30 minutes.

7. Let the braid cool slightly before cutting it into thick slices and enjoying warm.

CINNAMON SUGAR CRO-NOTS

MAKES ABOUT 9 CRO-NOTS

These are not what you think they are. First, they're made with puff pastry, not croissant dough. Second, they are baked, not fried. And third, you don't have to wait in line for four hours in New York City to enjoy one with your morning coffee. Hooray for cro-nots! Even if they're not a true croissant-doughnut hybrid, these little pastries are round and layered, sweet with cinnamon sugar and swathed in the simplest of vanilla glazes.

FOR THE PASTRIES
¼ cup granulated sugar
1 tablespoon ground cinnamon
1 box (14 or 17 ounces) puff pastry,
    thawed according to package
    directions
1 large egg, beaten

FOR THE GLAZE
1 cup confectioners' sugar
2 tablespoons milk
1 teaspoon pure vanilla extract

LET'S COOK:

1. Preheat the oven to 375°F with a rack in the center position. Line a sheet pan with parchment paper.

2. Make the pastries: Mix together the sugar and cinnamon in a small bowl until well combined. Sprinkle 1 tablespoon of the cinnamon sugar evenly over a clean work surface. Unfold the sheet of puff pastry onto the cinnamon sugar. Sprinkle another tablespoon of cinnamon sugar on top of the pastry. Use a rolling pin to roll the pastry into a large rectangle roughly 16 by 10 inches and ¼ inch thick. The cinnamon sugar will permeate the dough as you roll it out.

3. Fold the pastry in half, short edge to short edge. Lightly brush the top of the pastry with beaten egg. Sprinkle another tablespoon of cinnamon sugar over the pastry. Roll the pastry again into a rectangle about ¼ inch thick and 16 by 10 inches.

4. Again fold the pastry in half, short edge to short edge, and brush the top with egg. Sprinkle another tablespoon of cinnamon sugar evenly over the pastry. This time, roll it into an 8-by-8-inch square.

5. Sprinkle the remaining cinnamon sugar over the pastry. Use a 2½-inch round cutter to cut out about 9 cro-nots. Use a 1-inch round cutter to cut out the center of each cro-not, forming little puff pastry doughnuts.

6. Place the cro-nots on the prepared pan, spacing them evenly apart. Place the centers (cro-not holes) on the same pan, in the spaces between the cro-nots. Either discard the dough scraps or bake them on a separate sheet pan (they'll be misshapen but delicious). Bake until the cro-nots are puffy and their tops and sides are deeply golden brown, about 30 minutes. Place the pan on a wire rack and let cool slightly.

7. While the cro-nots are cooling, make the glaze: Whisk together the confectioners' sugar, milk, and vanilla in a small bowl until smooth.

8. Drizzle the glaze over the still-warm cro-nots before serving.
   Cro-nots are best enjoyed on the day they're made, but will keep for up to 3 days, tightly wrapped in plastic, at room temperature.

BROILED GRAPEFRUIT

SERVES 3 TO 6

My sister Emily likes to eat grapefruit with sugar. Or rather, she likes to eat sugar with a bit of grapefruit underneath. So I think she'd approve of this recipe, in which we positively caramelize our breakfast.

But really it's not so bad—a bit of brown sugar, a pinch of warm spice, and some large-flaked salt layer complex flavor notes over the tart and tangy grapefruit. It's a healthy, refreshing, and surprisingly satisfying breakfast or snack in the winter months, when grapefruit comes into season.

Look for unblemished grapefruits that feel very heavy for their size—this means they'll be full of juice and ready for eating.

---

3 Ruby Red grapefruits, halved
   horizontally
¼ cup packed dark brown sugar

½ teaspoon ground cardamom
1 teaspoon Maldon salt or other
   large-flake salt

LET'S COOK:

1. Preheat the broiler with a rack about 4 inches from the heat. Line a sheet pan with aluminum foil. (This isn't totally necessary—the grapefruit won't really stick to the pan—but it makes for the easiest cleanup.)

2. Place the grapefruit halves, cut side up, on the prepared sheet pan. Use a small paring knife or curved grapefruit knife to section the grapefruits, cutting around the outer membrane to separate it from the flesh, and between the individual sections.

3. Mix together the brown sugar and ground cardamom in a small bowl.

Sprinkle each grapefruit half with the sugar mixture, dividing it evenly. Sprinkle the salt atop the sugared grapefruit.

4. Broil the grapefruit, keeping a close eye on the pan and rotating it if needed, until the fruit is charred at the edges and caramel-y brown in the center, 3 to 5 minutes.

5. Let the grapefruit cool for 5 minutes before enjoying warm (I find a regular or grapefruit spoon the best tool to pop out the segments and catch all of the sweet juice while eating).

COCONUT-CASHEW GRANOLA WITH APRICOT & MANGO

MAKES ABOUT 10 CUPS

I learned from my Aunt Marie (who's always made her own) that granola doesn't have to come from a box. As it turns out, the homemade version is so much better because you can choose all of your favorite things to go into it (Marie likes dried cranberries, I go for apricots and mango) and leave out all of the weird preservatives and unpronounceable ingredients. And baking your own granola is the easiest—and probably healthiest—way to fill your home with the intoxicating smells of warm cinnamon, toasted coconut, and golden cashews.

I love the addition of ground flaxseed and wheat bran for their health benefits, including omega-3 fatty acids, fiber, and antioxidants. They can usually be found in the bulk or baking aisle of the grocery store, but if you have trouble finding them, it's okay to leave them out.

If you're hosting brunch with friends, serve this granola with milk or scattered over bowls of creamy yogurt and put some extra handfuls in simple jars for your guests to take home. Everyone will think you're so together, when really all you did was a bunch of mixing. Turns out you're popular *and* a genius!

Nonstick cooking spray (optional)
5 cups old-fashioned rolled oats (not quick-cooking)
½ cup ground flaxseed
½ cup wheat bran
1¼ cups unsweetened flaked coconut
1 cup raw cashews
½ cup slivered blanched almonds
1 tablespoon sesame seeds
½ cup melted coconut oil

½ cup creamy peanut butter (any kind will work)
¼ cup honey
1 tablespoon ground cinnamon
1 teaspoon ground ginger
¼ teaspoon fine sea salt
½ cup chopped dried apricots
½ cup chopped dried mango
¼ cup golden raisins

LET'S COOK:

1. Preheat the oven to 325°F with a rack in the center position. Lightly mist a sheet pan with cooking spray or line it with parchment paper.

2. Combine the rolled oats, flaxseed, wheat bran, coconut flakes, cashews, almonds, and sesame seeds on the sheet pan. Use your hands to toss and distribute all of the ingredients evenly.

3. Combine the coconut oil, peanut butter, honey, cinnamon, ginger, and salt in a small microwave-safe bowl. Microwave for 1 minute on high power until the coconut oil, peanut butter, and honey are warm and can be stirred easily with a spoon. (Alternatively, heat them in a small saucepan over low heat until the peanut butter has softened, about

5 minutes.) Stir together to blend completely.

4. Drizzle the coconut oil mixture evenly over the oat mixture, then use your hands to distribute it, tossing until the oats and nuts are finely coated and look slightly glossy. Spread out the granola into an even layer.

5. Bake, occasionally rotating the pan and using a spatula to mix everything, until the granola is completely dry and nicely toasted, about 30 minutes.

6. Remove the granola from the oven and let it cool completely on the sheet pan.

7. Add the apricots, mango, and raisins, and toss to combine.

8. Store the granola in airtight containers until you're ready to serve. It will keep for about 2 weeks at room temperature, or about 3 months in the freezer.

MAKE IT MINE
GRANOLA PAIRINGS

I love the semitropical vibe of flaked coconut, dried mango, and apricots in my granola, but there's definitely more where that came from, granola-toppings-wise. If you feel like mixing it up, try these winning combos.

- Toasted hazelnuts + cacao nibs

- Dried cherries + roasted, salted almonds

- Banana chips + dried blueberries

PEAR & ALMOND OVEN OATMEAL

SERVES 9 GENEROUSLY, OR 18 AS PART OF A SPREAD

This is an in-betweener of a recipe: not quite standard oatmeal, not quite breakfast pudding, not quite oat-y breakfast bars—it's an amalgamation of all three, actually. The idea behind this recipe originated with the venerable Heidi Swanson (she of the beautiful 101 Cookbooks blog), who bakes her oats with milk, egg, spices, and luscious berries in a buttered dish. The concept is a great one and I've riffed on it here, making a thinner sheet pan version, roasted pear-and-almond–forward, deep with autumn spice and subtle sweetness.

The oats and fruit are wonderful served warm, when everything is soft and yielding, but I've also had it cold, when it's sturdy enough to slice into neat squares and grab on the go. Either way you serve it, feel free to play around with your favorite fruits, nuts, spices, and sweeteners to customize this creative breakfast offering to your liking.

Nonstick cooking spray
4 cups old-fashioned rolled oats (not quick-cooking)
1½ cups sliced blanched almonds
2 teaspoons baking powder
1 tablespoon ground cinnamon
1 teaspoon ground ginger
½ teaspoon ground nutmeg
1 teaspoon kosher salt
4 cups unsweetened almond milk or other milk

½ cup pure maple syrup (plus optional extra, for serving)
2 large eggs
6 tablespoons (¾ stick) unsalted butter, melted and cooled slightly
1 teaspoon pure almond extract
3 pears (I like Bartlett), unpeeled, cut lengthwise through the fruit into ¼-inch-thick slices, any bits of stem and core removed
2 tablespoons dark brown sugar

LET'S COOK:

1. Preheat the oven to 375°F with a rack in the center position. Mist a sheet pan with cooking spray.

2. Stir together the oats, 1 cup of the almonds, the baking powder, 2½ teaspoons of the cinnamon, the ginger, nutmeg, and salt in a large bowl until well combined.

3. In another large bowl, whisk together the almond milk, maple syrup, eggs, half of the melted butter, and the almond extract until smooth. Pour this into the oats and stir until thoroughly combined.

4. Dump the oatmeal mixture into the prepared pan and spread it evenly to the corners with a rubber spatula. Arrange the pear slices evenly over the oatmeal. Sprinkle the pears with the brown sugar, the remaining ½ teaspoon cinnamon, and the remaining ½ cup almonds. Drizzle the rest of the melted butter evenly atop it all.

5. Bake until the pears are tender and the oatmeal has set and started to pull away from the sides of the pan, 35 to 40 minutes.

6. Serve the oatmeal warm, with extra drizzles of maple syrup if you like. (You can also chill it in the pan, covered with plastic wrap or aluminum foil, overnight or for up to 3 days. Slice it into neat squares; serve the squares toasted or at room temperature.)

Chapter 9

DESSERT
(THERE'S ALWAYS ROOM)

I don't want to call my sweet tooth major, but it's definitely major. Even if it's nothing more than a square of chocolate, I'm cranky if I can't nibble something sweet after dinner. My research* confirms that 97.6 percent of Americans have the same persistent craving. So we're all in good company!

This chapter culls from the theme of company and focuses on crowd-pleasing desserts, like the Stone Fruit Slab Pie (page 279) that serves 24 to 30 and Halloween Candy S'mores (page 271) for 12. Here you'll find a whole host of recipes meant to serve a bunch: everything from sheet cakes to cookies, from chocolate bark to roasted fruit treats (berries and fruits become rich and candy-like in the oven—try the Vanilla-Maple Roasted Pears, page 242, or the Broiled Plums with Meringue Hats, page 244—you'll flip), all meant to serve a bunch. Because after all, dessert is meant to be shared! So let's make enough that we won't mind sharing (much).

*I've done no research on this matter.

BUTTER-ROASTED APRICOTS WITH BOOZY WHIPPED MASCARPONE

SERVES 4 TO 6

I'm not usually one to eat fruit for dessert, so I understand that you may be looking at this page and thinking, *Apricots? Really? Where's the chocolate? This gal is a rube.* But take a closer look. See how it says "butter" and "boozy" up there? Those things count for something! Something good, I promise—even if, like me, you're the kind of person who likes to eat chocolate with your chocolate.

Here's how it goes: We're going to dab these little guys with butter and brown sugar, which will melt and caramelize and get positively saucy after a quick jaunt in the oven, and then we'll top them with soft mascarpone cheese, whipped to clouds with fresh vanilla bean, honey, and rum, and then, just for good measure, a sprinkling of chopped, toasty almonds. So we're getting rich, juicy summer fruit; subtly sweet, creamy cheese with hints (but really sometimes punches) of booze; and bites of salty crunch, too. It's fruit for dessert, and it's neither boring nor snooty nor sad. Who knew?

---

8 medium-size apricots, halved and pitted

½ teaspoon kosher salt

4 teaspoons unsalted butter, cut into very small cubes

4 teaspoons light brown sugar

1 tub (8 ounces) mascarpone cheese

Seeds scraped from ½ vanilla bean

1 tablespoon honey

1 tablespoon dark rum, brandy, or lemon juice

¼ cup chopped, roasted, salted almonds

LET'S COOK:

1. Preheat the oven to 400°F with a rack in the center position. Line a sheet pan with parchment paper.

2. Lay the apricot halves cut side up on the sheet pan, leaving about ½ inch of space between them. Sprinkle the salt evenly over the fruit. Dot each apricot half with about ¼ teaspoon butter and ¼ teaspoon brown sugar. Roast the apricots until they've begun to brown and release some juice, about 12 minutes.

3. While the apricots are roasting, whisk together the mascarpone cheese, vanilla bean seeds, honey, and rum in a medium-size bowl.

4. Let the apricots cool on the pan for 5 minutes. While they're still warm, place a few halves into each serving bowl, top with the whipped mascarpone and a sprinkling of almonds, and serve.

VANILLA-MAPLE ROASTED PEARS

SERVES 8

This is a perfect autumn dessert if I ever saw one. Firm and juicy pears are roasted with some fresh vanilla bean, pure maple syrup, warm spices, and sweet butter. The end result is tender fruit bathed in deep, spiced caramel. The whole thing is stunningly simple, yet perfectly harmonious, especially when finished with a scoop of ricotta cheese, crème fraîche, or ice cream.

Nonstick cooking spray
8 medium-size pears (I like Bartlett or Bosc), peeled, halved, and cored
¼ cup freshly squeezed lemon juice (about 1 lemon)
½ vanilla bean (a 2- or 3-inch piece)
½ cup pure maple syrup

½ teaspoon ground cardamom
Pinch of ground nutmeg
½ teaspoon kosher salt
3 tablespoons unsalted butter, cut into small cubes
Ricotta cheese, crème fraîche, or ice cream, for serving

LET'S COOK:

1. Preheat the oven to 375°F with a rack in the center position. Mist a sheet pan with cooking spray.

2. Arrange the pear halves cut side up on the prepared pan and pour the lemon juice evenly over them (this will keep them from browning).

3. Cut a lengthwise slit in the vanilla bean and use the back of a paring knife to scrape out the seeds; reserve them. Toss the scraped pod on top of the pears.

4. Whisk the vanilla bean seeds, maple syrup, cardamom, nutmeg, salt, and ¼ cup water in a medium-size bowl until smooth. Pour evenly over the pears. Dot the butter pieces on top.

5. Roast the pears, flipping them and basting with the syrupy sauce halfway through, until they are knife-tender and the sauce is deeply caramelized, about 50 minutes.

6. Serve the pears warm, drizzled with extra sauce and topped with scoops of ricotta, crème fraîche, or ice cream.

ROASTED BANANA SUNDAES

SERVES 4 TO 8

There's nothing wrong with a good, old-fashioned banana split (unless you run out of hot fudge—then you've got a problem), but roasting the bananas is a fun way to jazz up the classic. Banana peels turn black when roasted, but the fruit inside stays pale yellow and becomes pudding-y, tender, and sweet. I particularly like the juxtaposition of warm fruit and cold, creamy ice cream, smothered with all of my favorite toppings. The bonus is that toppings-wise, I can go wherever the mood takes me—rainbow sprinkles and maraschino cherries for nostalgia, or maybe cocoa nibs and pistachios for a more grown-up feel.

4 bananas, unpeeled, sliced in half lengthwise
¼ teaspoon ground cinnamon
1 to 2 pints good-quality ice cream

Your favorite sundae toppings such as hot fudge, whipped cream, chopped nuts, cocoa nibs, or maraschino cherries

LET'S COOK:

1. Preheat the oven to 400°F with a rack in the center position. Line a sheet pan with aluminum foil or parchment paper.

2. Lay the banana halves, still in their peels, cut side up on the prepared pan and sprinkle them evenly with the cinnamon.

3. Bake the bananas until the peels turn completely black, 12 to 15 minutes.

4. Gently transfer the bananas to banana split dishes or other long dessert dishes. Serve the bananas warm, in their peels (the fruit can be easily scooped out with a spoon), topped with big scoops of ice cream and plenty of sundae toppings.

BROILED PLUMS WITH MERINGUE HATS

SERVES 4 TO 6

A pan of plums under meringue sort of looks like a bunch of fruit wearing top hats, which I suppose is what I like most about this dish (aside from the taste, I mean). A cap of soft, golden meringue over gorgeous roasted stone fruit is a thing to behold; it is a light, sweet, unexpected end to any meal, whether fancy or casual.

Buying in-season plums makes this treat extra affordable (you could also use peaches or nectarines), and while the meringue caps look impressive, they're really so easy to do. Using an electric mixer makes homemade meringue such a snap. You'll see.

---

4 fresh plums, halved and pitted
  (larger varieties like black plums
  or red plums do well here)
¼ cup plus 1 teaspoon sugar

3 large egg whites, at room
  temperature
1 teaspoon pure vanilla extract

LET'S COOK:

1. Preheat the broiler with a rack about 4 inches from the heat and another rack in the center position. Line a sheet pan with aluminum foil.

2. Place the plums cut side up on the prepared pan. Sprinkle 1 teaspoon of the sugar evenly over the plums.

3. Broil the plums on the upper rack just until the sugar melts and the fruit starts to char at the edges, 2 to 3 minutes.

4. Remove the plums from the oven and set them aside to cool. Turn the oven to 350°F.

5. Whip the egg whites in a stand mixer fitted with the whisk, or in a large bowl with a handheld electric mixer, on medium-high speed until frothy. With the mixer running, add the remaining ¼ cup sugar in a slow and steady stream. Whip until medium peaks form, about 3 minutes. Add the vanilla and whip the whites to stiff peaks, another 3 minutes or so.

6. Use a spoon to scoop the meringue on top of the plums, piling it high. (Alternatively, you can use a piping bag with a large plain or star tip. Fit the bag with the tip, fill the bag with

meringue, and pipe the meringue onto the fruit.)

7. Bake the meringue-topped plums on the center rack until the fruit gently

softens and the meringue is deeply browned, 10 to 15 minutes. Serve warm.

ORANGE CARDAMOM POUND CAKE

SERVES 20 TO 24

The subtle sweetness of orange, the scent of cardamom—we're elevating our pound cake play, and we're feeding a crowd to boot. This sheet pan–baked cake is rich and moist, with a tight, springy crumb. It's perfect for topping with fresh berries and whipped cream and serving on a breezy patio. Or next to a roaring fire with a cup of tea. It'd also be great served on a blanket draped over a patch of warm summer grass. In any case, here's the recipe—I'll leave the rest to you.

Nonstick cooking spray
3 cups all-purpose flour
1½ teaspoons ground cardamom
1 teaspoon baking powder
½ teaspoon baking soda
½ teaspoon kosher salt
3 cups granulated sugar
2 tablespoons freshly grated orange zest (about 2 oranges)

¾ pound (3 sticks) unsalted butter, at room temperature
6 large eggs
1 cup plain Greek yogurt
¼ cup freshly squeezed orange juice (use 1 of the oranges you zested)
2 teaspoons pure vanilla extract
2 cups heavy cream
2 tablespoons confectioners' sugar
Fresh berries, for garnish

LET'S COOK:

1. Preheat the oven to 325°F with a rack in the center position. Mist a sheet pan with cooking spray, line it with parchment paper, and mist the parchment with cooking spray, too.

2. Whisk together the flour, cardamom, baking powder, baking soda, and salt in a large bowl.

3. Combine the granulated sugar and orange zest in the bowl of a stand mixer or in a large bowl if you'll be using a handheld electric mixer. Use your fingers to mash the sugar and zest together, rubbing vigorously until the zest is worked in and the sugar is a light shade of orange. If using a stand mixer, attach the paddle.

4. Add the butter to the orange sugar and cream on high speed until light and fluffy, about 3 minutes. Add the eggs one at a time, beating until fully incorporated. The mixture will lighten in color with the addition of each egg.

5. Whisk together the yogurt, orange juice, and vanilla in a small bowl.

6. Add one-third of the flour mixture to the butter mixture and beat on low speed to incorporate. Beat in half of the yogurt mixture. Beat in another third of the flour mixture, then the remaining yogurt mixture. Finish with the remaining flour mixture. Mix just until the batter comes together and is no longer streaky. Dump the batter into the prepared pan and spread it evenly to the corners with a rubber or offset spatula.

7. Bake the cake until the edges are golden and a skewer inserted into the center comes out clean, 35 to 40 minutes.

8. Place the pan on a wire rack and let the cake cool to room temperature.

9. While the cake cools, whip together the heavy cream and confectioners' sugar in a large bowl until medium-stiff peaks form, about 5 minutes.

10. Cut the cake into squares and serve warm or at room temperature, garnished with the whipped cream and fresh berries.

CANNOLI ROULADE

SERVES 8 TO 10

Depending on where you live, a sponge cake rolled up with filling is either called a roulade, a jelly roll, or a Swiss roll. I not-so-secretly wish I were French, so "roulade" it is. But it gets confusing when you give a French-sounding cake the attributes of a classic Italian pastry, so let's just call it dessert.

We'll give the traditional cannoli shell a day off, instead focusing on its partners in cannoli crime: chocolate chips and whipped ricotta. The result is a chocolate chip sponge cake rolled around a whipped ricotta–cream filling and slathered with a dark ganache. It looks and sounds like a fancy affair, but there are really just three major steps involved: baking and rolling the sheet cake, whipping up the simple filling, and whisking together a quick glaze. You can do it.

FOR THE CAKE
Nonstick cooking spray
½ cup cake flour
½ teaspoon ground cinnamon
¼ teaspoon kosher salt
¼ teaspoon baking powder
¼ teaspoon baking soda
4 large eggs
1 large egg yolk
½ cup granulated sugar
1 teaspoon pure vanilla extract
¼ cup mini chocolate chips

Confectioners' sugar, for rolling up the cake

FOR THE FILLING AND GANACHE
1 cup ricotta cheese
¾ cup confectioners' sugar
1 cup plus 2 tablespoons heavy cream
1 teaspoon pure vanilla extract
½ cup mini chocolate chips, plus extra for sprinkling

LET'S COOK:

1. Preheat the oven to 400°F with a rack in the center position. Mist a sheet pan with cooking spray, line it with parchment paper, and mist the paper, too.

2. Make the cake: Whisk together the flour, cinnamon, salt, baking powder, and baking soda in a small bowl.

3. Whip together the eggs, egg yolk, and granulated sugar in a stand mixer fitted with the whisk, or in a large bowl with a handheld electric mixer, on high speed until light yellow and doubled in volume, about 5 minutes. Whip in the vanilla extract. Add the flour mixture in two additions, whipping on low speed to

combine and scraping down the side of the bowl with a rubber spatula. Fold in the chocolate chips with the spatula. Pour the batter into the prepared pan and spread it evenly to the corners with the spatula.

4. Bake until the cake is golden and springs back when lightly poked, about 10 minutes.

5. While the cake is baking, lay a clean kitchen towel over a work surface. Fill a fine-mesh strainer with about ½ cup confectioners' sugar.

6. Remove the cake from the oven and immediately run a paring knife around the edges of the pan to loosen the cake. Working quickly, sift a thin layer of confectioners' sugar over the cake and while it is still warm, turn out the cake, sugared side down, onto the kitchen towel. Carefully remove the parchment from the cake, then sprinkle a layer of confectioners' sugar where the parchment used to be.

7. While the cake is still warm, gently roll up the towel and the cake, starting from the short side and rolling away from you. Let the cake cool completely in the towel.

8. While the cake is cooling, make the filling: Combine the ricotta and ¾ cup confectioners' sugar in a stand mixer fitted with the paddle, or in a large bowl with a handheld electric mixer, on high speed until fluffy and smooth, about 3 minutes.

9. If using a stand mixer, transfer the ricotta mixture to another bowl, clean and dry the mixer bowl, pour in 1 cup of the cream and the vanilla, and attach the whisk. If using a handheld mixer, clean and dry the beaters and pour 1 cup of the cream and the vanilla into another large bowl. Whip the cream and vanilla until stiff peaks form, about 5 minutes. Use a rubber spatula to fold the whipped cream into the ricotta until smooth and thoroughly combined.

10. When the cake is cool, unroll it onto the work surface. Spread the filling evenly over the cake, leaving a ½-inch border at the edges, and tightly but gently roll up the cake with the filling inside (this time leave the kitchen towel behind). If you like, use a sharp knife to trim the ends of the roulade to make neat edges. Transfer the cake to a platter.

11. Make the ganache: Melt the chocolate chips with the remaining 2 tablespoons cream in a small saucepan over low heat, whisking until shiny and smooth. Let the ganache cool slightly, then pour it over the roulade. Sprinkle the cake with extra chocolate chips.

12. Serve the cake in thick slices.
     The cake will keep, loosely covered with aluminum foil or plastic wrap, in the refrigerator for up to 3 days.

"GET YOUR OWN" FLOURLESS CHOCOLATE CAKES

SERVES 10

Every time I make these, I find myself hard-pressed not to dive headfirst into the pan before the cakes finish cooling on the rack—the smell of warm chocolate and butter is a hard one to resist, I think you'll agree. This is where the ramekins come in handy. I mean, who's to know if one little cake swiftly disappears before dinnertime? (No one, that's who.) Also, individual ramekins mean I don't have to share. I mean we. We don't have to share. Get your own!

These little cakes are intensely fudgy and rich, so they don't need much more than a sprinkling of confectioners' sugar on top. If you wanted to scoop some coffee ice cream over a warm cake, though, I wouldn't be the one to stop you.

½ pound (2 sticks) unsalted butter
8 ounces semisweet chocolate, chopped
1 teaspoon pure vanilla extract
1¼ cups granulated sugar
1 cup unsweetened Dutch-process cocoa powder (see box, page 252)
1 teaspoon espresso powder

½ teaspoon kosher salt
6 large eggs
Confectioners' sugar, for garnish (optional)
Ice cream (vanilla is good, coffee is even better) or heavy cream, for serving (optional)

LET'S COOK:

1. Preheat the oven to 350°F with a rack in the center position. Place 10 ramekins (roughly 3-inch diameter) on a sheet pan.

2. Melt the butter in a small saucepan over medium heat. Remove from the heat and stir in the semisweet chocolate. Stir until the chocolate is smooth and fully melted. Add the vanilla and stir to combine.

3. Whisk together the granulated sugar, cocoa powder, espresso powder, and salt in a large bowl. Add the eggs and whisk until smooth. Add the melted chocolate and whisk until well incorporated.

4. Divide the batter among the ramekins, filling each about three-quarters full. Bake until a skewer inserted into the center comes out with just a few moist crumbs, 30 to 40 minutes.

5. Let the cakes cool slightly—they will fall a bit in the center—before serving warm, dusted with confectioners' sugar, or topped with a scoop of ice cream or a glug of fresh cream, if you like.

The cakes will keep, wrapped in plastic, in the refrigerator for 3 to 4 days (you can eat leftovers cold from the fridge or rewarm them in a 350°F oven for about 15 minutes).

WAIT, WHAT?

DUTCH-PROCESS COCOA POWDER

Dutch-process cocoa powder is darker than natural cocoa powder, less acidic, and has a smoother, more complex flavor. In general, the two are not interchangeable, although you can use natural cocoa in this recipe if it's what you have on hand. Since it's not acidic, recipes that call for Dutch-process cocoa usually include an acid, such as baking powder or buttermilk, while natural cocoa (which is already acidic) is usually paired with alkaline baking soda. If you're not sure what kind of cocoa powder you've got, take a look at the ingredient label—if it says "cocoa processed with alkali," then it's Dutch-process.

PUMPKIN BRIOCHE PUDDINGS

SERVES 6 TO 8

These are warm-and-cozy individual puddings for a warm-and-cozy day. They're great around the holidays, when pumpkin-flavored treats seem to taste best. You can even prepare the puddings ahead of time, tucking the soaked bread into the ramekins, then refrigerating them for a few hours or overnight before baking them for company.

If you want to fancy these up a bit, feel free to fold a half-cup of raisins, nuts, or chocolate chips into the mix before baking. The puddings are wonderful served with fresh whipped cream, although a scoop of ice cream on top never hurt anyone, either.

I like using canned pumpkin for baking (I'm a fan of Libby's) because, unlike homemade versions, the puree is consistent in texture and flavor every time. You can certainly use homemade pumpkin puree for your puddings, but make sure to taste it and season it with some salt and drain it a bit if necessary, to ensure it's not weak or watery.

Butter or nonstick cooking spray, for
  greasing the ramekins
I can (15 ounces) pure pumpkin puree
2 cups half-and-half
1 cup packed dark brown sugar
2 large eggs
2 teaspoons ground cinnamon
1½ teaspoons pumpkin pie spice

1 tablespoon pure vanilla extract
½ teaspoon kosher salt
1 loaf brioche bread, cut into ¾-inch
  cubes (about 10 cups)
2 tablespoons cinnamon sugar
  (see Note)
Whipped cream or ice cream,
  for serving (optional)

LET'S COOK:

1. Preheat the oven to 350°F with a rack about 4 inches from the broiler and another rack in the center position. Arrange six to eight ramekins (4-to-6-inch-diameter) on a sheet pan, and grease them with butter or mist them with cooking spray.

2. Whisk the pumpkin, half-and-half, brown sugar, eggs, cinnamon, pumpkin pie spice, vanilla, and salt in a large bowl until smooth. Fold in the bread cubes with a rubber spatula until well coated. Allow the bread to sit until it has soaked up some of the custard, about 5 minutes.

Dessert (There's Always Room) • **253**

3. Distribute the soaked bread and any remaining custard among the ramekins. Sprinkle the cinnamon sugar evenly atop each.

4. Bake the puddings on the center rack until the tops look dry and a skewer inserted into the center comes out clean, about 30 minutes.

5. If you want to brown the tops of the puddings, turn the oven to broil and move the pan to the upper rack. Broil the puddings, watching them carefully to prevent burning, 1 to 2 minutes.

6. Serve the puddings warm, topped with whipped cream or ice cream, if you like.

NOTE: To make cinnamon sugar, combine ¼ cup sugar with 1 tablespoon ground cinnamon in an airtight container. Keep it on hand for this recipe, and for sprinkling on yogurt, roasted fruit, or buttered toast.

CARROT LAYER CAKE WITH CREAM CHEESE FROSTING

SERVES 20

When I was a kid, any cake that wasn't chocolate was dead to me. And cake with vegetables inside? Nice try, Grandma. It wasn't until pastry school that I finally recognized the greatness that is carrot cake. Or, at least, the greatness that carrot cake can be. For me, a truly great carrot cake is moist and bouncy, subtly spiced, and slathered with mounds of sweet-but-not-too-sweet cream cheese frosting. Extras like raisins, currants, or walnuts are negotiable—feel free to add or subtract them as you like.

Baking the cake on a sheet pan, then cutting it in half to form layers, sidesteps the need to grease and wash multiple pans, and also results in a pretty rectangular cake that serves a boatload of people.

FOR THE CAKE
Butter or nonstick cooking spray, for greasing the pan
2½ cups all-purpose flour
2 teaspoons baking powder
1 teaspoon baking soda
2 teaspoons ground cinnamon
1 teaspoon kosher salt
4 large eggs
2 cups granulated sugar
1½ cups canola oil
1 teaspoon pure vanilla extract
3 cups shredded carrots (about 2 large or 4 small carrots)

¾ cup chopped walnuts, plus extra for decorating (optional)

FOR THE FROSTING
2 blocks (8 ounces each) cream cheese, chilled
12 tablespoons (1½ sticks) unsalted butter, at room temperature
2½ cups confectioners' sugar
Freshly grated zest of ½ lemon
2 tablespoons sour cream
1 teaspoon pure vanilla extract

LET'S COOK:

1. Preheat the oven to 350°F with a rack in the center position. Grease a sheet pan with butter or mist it with cooking spray, line it with parchment paper, and grease or mist the parchment, too.

2. Make the cake: Whisk together the flour, baking powder, baking soda, cinnamon, and salt in a medium bowl.

3. Whip the eggs and granulated sugar in a stand mixer fitted with the whisk, or in a large bowl with a handheld electric mixer, on high speed, until pale yellow and thick, about 5 minutes.

4. Slowly drizzle in the oil while still whipping. When the oil is fully incorporated, whip in the vanilla. Add the flour mixture all at once and whip on low speed just until a smooth batter comes together. Use a rubber spatula to fold in the carrots and the walnuts (if using). The batter will be thick.

5. Dump the batter into the prepared pan and spread it evenly to the corners with an offset spatula.

6. Bake the cake until the sides pull away from the pan and it springs back when you gently poke it in the middle, 20 to 25 minutes.

7. Place the pan on a wire rack and let the cake cool completely.

8. Lay a large sheet of parchment paper on a work surface. Turn out the cooled cake onto the parchment and gently peel off the parchment from the pan. Use a sharp knife to cut the cake in half widthwise. Be careful; the cake will be delicate. Cut through the parchment underneath, too, so you can move each cake layer separately.

9. Make the frosting: Cream the cream cheese and butter in a stand mixer fitted with the paddle, or in a large bowl with a handheld electric mixer, on medium-high speed until smooth, about 3 minutes. Slowly add the confectioners' sugar a bit at a time, beating well until the frosting is light and fluffy, about 3 minutes. Add the lemon zest, sour cream, and vanilla and beat thoroughly to combine.

10. Gently place a big, flat plate or cutting board on top of one of the cake layers and very carefully invert everything so the cake sits on top. Remove the parchment paper. Scoop half of the frosting onto the cake with a rubber spatula and spread it evenly on top with an offset spatula, working from the center to the edges.

11. Carefully lift the second cake layer off its parchment (using two large spatulas helps) and place it on the frosted half, pressing down lightly to adhere. Frost the top of the cake in the same manner with the remaining frosting. Sprinkle a few walnuts (if using) on top to decorate.

12. If not serving right away, store the cake, uncovered (or covered with plastic wrap once the frosting hardens), in the refrigerator for up to 3 days. Take the cake out of the fridge about an hour before you want to serve it.

ITALIAN CHOCOLATE SHEET CAKE

SERVES 20 TO 24

This recipe makes a lush chocolate cake the size of Texas with a little Italian flair. And by "Italian flair" I mean Nutella (that revered chocolate hazelnut spread), and by "a little" I mean a lot. A mix of Nutella and creamy mascarpone cheese is literally the icing on this cake. It's rich and special, the perfect birthday cake for your favorite chocoholic, and it can be easily made ahead of time. In fact, it does well with a day in the refrigerator to let the flavors meld and mellow.

FOR THE CAKE
Nonstick cooking spray
½ pound (2 sticks) unsalted butter
1 teaspoon instant espresso powder
   (optional but recommended)
½ cup unsweetened natural cocoa
   powder (not Dutch-process)
2 cups all-purpose flour
1 cup granulated sugar
1 teaspoon salt
1 teaspoon baking soda
1 cup packed light brown sugar

2 large eggs
1 cup sour cream
1 teaspoon pure vanilla extract

**FOR THE FROSTING
AND FINISHING**
1 heaping cup Nutella or other
   chocolate hazelnut spread
1 tub (8 ounces) mascarpone cheese
1 cup toasted hazelnuts, roughly
   chopped

LET'S COOK:

1. Preheat the oven to 350°F with a rack in the center position. Mist a sheet pan with cooking spray, line it with parchment paper, and mist the paper, too.

2. Make the cake: Combine the butter with 1 cup water, the espresso powder (if using), and the cocoa powder in a small saucepan over medium heat. Stir until the butter melts. Bring to a boil and cook, stirring often, until smooth, about 3 minutes. Let cool until just warm to the touch.

3. Whisk together the flour, granulated sugar, salt, and baking soda in a medium-size bowl.

4. Whisk the brown sugar, eggs, sour cream, and vanilla in a large bowl

until smooth. Add the cocoa mixture and whisk to combine. Add the dry ingredients and stir with a rubber spatula just until the batter is smooth and streak-free.

5. Dump the batter into the prepared pan and spread it evenly to the corners with the spatula.

6. Bake until the sides of the cake pull away from the pan and the center springs back when lightly poked, 20 to 25 minutes.

7. Place the pan on a wire rack and let the cake cool completely before frosting.

8. Make the frosting: Beat the Nutella and mascarpone in a stand mixer fitted with the paddle, or in a large bowl with a handheld electric mixer, on medium-high speed, until light and silky, about 3 minutes.

9. Spread the frosting on top of the cooled cake (it will be a thick layer). Finish with a sprinkling of chopped hazelnuts.

10. Serve the cake right away or wait a day to let flavors deepen.
    The cake will keep, well wrapped in aluminum foil, in the refrigerator for up to 5 days.

THINNEST BROWNIES

SERVES 35 TO 40

Up until recently I was a thick-brownie type of girl. I wanted the biggest, fattest brownie at the bake sale. That was before I realized that thin brownies can be equally dense and fudgy as thick ones and, what's more, you can eat twice as many and still feel okay about yourself afterward. Logic.

These brownies have a deep chocolate flavor, a satisfyingly crackly top crust, and a moist-to-the-edges interior. Though great on their own, they'd do well as bookends to a scoop of your favorite ice cream for one amazing ice cream sandwich (see Variation).

Nonstick cooking spray
½ pound (2 sticks) unsalted butter
9 ounces bittersweet chocolate, finely chopped, or 1½ cups bittersweet or dark chocolate chips
1½ cups sugar

4 large eggs
1 tablespoon pure vanilla extract
1 tablespoon instant espresso powder (optional but recommended)
1 teaspoon kosher salt
1 cup all-purpose flour

LET'S COOK:

1. Preheat the oven to 325°F with a rack in the center position. Mist a sheet pan with cooking spray, line it with parchment paper, then mist the parchment, too.

2. Melt the butter in a small saucepan over low heat. (Alternatively, microwave it in a heatproof bowl on medium power in 30-second intervals until melted.)

3. While the butter is melting, place the chocolate in a large heatproof bowl. Immediately pour the hot butter over the chocolate. Let them sit until the chocolate melts a bit, about 1 minute,

then use a spoon or rubber spatula to stir them together until smooth.

4. Add the sugar to the chocolate mixture and whisk to combine (it will look a bit grainy). Whisk in the eggs one at a time, then the vanilla. Gently whisk in the espresso powder, if using. Gently whisk in the salt and flour until just incorporated.

5. Dump the batter into the prepared pan and spread it evenly to the corners with a butter knife or offset spatula.

6. Bake the brownies until the top looks light and crackly and a skewer inserted into the center comes out with just a few moist crumbs, about 18 minutes.

7. Let the brownies cool, then freeze for one hour before slicing and serving.

The brownies will keep, tightly wrapped in plastic or aluminum foil at room temperature, for 4 to 5 days (they'll last a few months if frozen).

VARIATION
BROWNIE ICE CREAM SANDWICHES

These can't be beat. Once you've sliced the brownies, make sandwiches with your favorite ice cream, then wrap them individually in parchment paper before storing them in heavy-duty zip-top bags in the freezer; they'll keep for a few months. Flavor-wise, it's really hard to go wrong, but here are some of my favorite combos:

- **Coffee ice cream.** I go Häagen-Dazs. Classy and adult.

- **Strawberry ice cream** (again Häagen-Dazs) is playful and sweet paired with the deep chocolate brownies.

- **Mint chocolate chip** is refreshing and cool. I love Three Twins's version.

- **Chocolate chip cookie dough** just makes everyone happy. For this, I've got to go with my friends Ben & Jerry.

TEACH ME HOW
TO MAKE THE PERFECT SLICE

Rich, fudgy brownies can be a mess to cut—the dense, moist crumbs love to stick to knives and hands and everything—but there's an easier way. The key lies in the freezer! Letting the brownies rest in the freezer for about an hour before cutting makes the whole thing a cinch. Cold brownies can easily be chopped into those perfectly clean-edged, camera-ready squares you see in the magazines (I'm looking at you, Martha Stewart). And the bonus? This little trick opened my eyes to the complete satisfaction that is a cold-from-the-freezer brownie. I may never eat one warm again (that's probably a lie, but I'm making a point here).

OATMEAL CHOCOLATE CHIP COOKIES

MAKES ABOUT 25 COOKIES

This is a tweaked version of a recipe I got from my friend Jen King, who co-owns Liddabit Sweets, an artisanal confectionery in Brooklyn. They don't do anything just plain ordinary at Liddabit (hand-dipped candy bars and caramels with beer and pretzels inside, hello) so needless to say, this is one good cookie.

I prefer oatmeal cookies with plentiful chocolate chips, but feel free to substitute raisins if you're that guy—no judgments. Well, a few judgments. I hope we can still be friends.

1½ cups all-purpose flour
2 teaspoons baking soda
1 tablespoon plus 1 teaspoon ground cinnamon
1 teaspoon salt
2¼ cups old-fashioned rolled oats
9 tablespoons (1 stick plus 1 tablespoon) unsalted butter, at room temperature

1 cup plus 2 tablespoons packed light brown sugar
½ cup plus 1 tablespoon granulated sugar
1 teaspoon pure vanilla extract
2 large eggs
1 heaping cup chocolate chips (I like bittersweet, but any kind will do)

LET'S COOK:

1. Preheat the oven to 325°F with racks in the upper and lower thirds. Line two sheet pans with parchment paper.

2. Whisk together the flour, baking soda, cinnamon, salt, and oats in a medium-size bowl.

3. Beat the butter, brown sugar, and granulated sugar in a stand mixer fitted with the paddle, or in a large bowl with a handheld electric mixer, on high speed, until light and fluffy,

about 3 minutes. Add the vanilla, then beat in the eggs, one at a time, until smooth.

4. Add the flour mixture and stir gently with a wooden spoon to combine. Fold in the chocolate chips.

5. Scoop the dough by the heaping tablespoonful onto the pans, leaving about an inch of space between cookies. Flatten each cookie slightly with the palm of your hand (see Note).

6. Bake the cookies until they are slightly puffed and golden brown, 12 to 15 minutes.

7. Let the cookies cool slightly before enjoying warm.

The cookies will keep, in an airtight container at room temperature, for about 1 week.

NOTE: After you flatten the cookies in Step 4, they may be frozen until solid on the sheet pan, about 30 minutes. Transfer them to a heavy-duty zip-top bag for storage. Bake them right from frozen when you want some; they may take an extra few minutes.

PEANUT BUTTER COOKIES

MAKES ABOUT 20 COOKIES

The chocolate chip cookie gets all the glory, but there's something sublime about a peanut butter cookie done right.

I've found that the secret to moist, chewy, truly peanut buttery cookies is threefold: first, processed (not "natural") peanut butter; second, lots of brown sugar; and third, a shorter-than-seems-right bake time. If you like a crunchier cookie, leave your pan in the oven for a few extra minutes.

---

1 cup all-purpose flour
½ teaspoon kosher salt
½ teaspoon baking soda
8 tablespoons (1 stick) unsalted butter, at room temperature

½ cup creamy peanut butter
1 cup packed dark brown sugar
1 large egg
½ teaspoon pure vanilla extract

LET'S COOK:

1. Preheat the oven to 350°F with a rack in the center position. Line a sheet pan with parchment paper.

2. Whisk together the flour, salt, and baking soda in a small bowl.

3. Beat the butter and peanut butter in a stand mixer fitted with the paddle, or in a large bowl with a handheld electric mixer, on high speed, until smooth, about 2 minutes.

4. Add the brown sugar and continue to beat until the mixture is light and fluffy, about 2 minutes more. Add the egg and vanilla and beat to combine.

5. Add the flour mixture all at once and mix on low speed until the dough just comes together. If it is very soft, refrigerate it to firm up, about 1 hour.

6. Scoop the dough onto the prepared pan in 1¾-inch mounds (I like to use an ice cream scoop), spacing them evenly apart. Use a well-floured fork to gently press a crosshatch pattern into each cookie.

7. Bake the cookies until they have spread and browned at the edges, but are still quite soft, exactly 12 minutes. Let the cookies cool slightly on the pan before enjoying.

The cookies will keep, in an airtight container at room temperature, for about 1 week. (Alternatively, you can freeze them, tightly wrapped in plastic or a freezer-safe zip-top bag, for a few months.)

COCONUTTY GANACHE THUMBPRINTS

MAKES ABOUT 45 SMALL COOKIES

Coconut seems to be an ingredient that people either adore or despise. I fall squarely into the adoration camp. To me, the combination of chocolate and coconut feels deliciously decadent—like some sort of tropical love affair. An island romance . . . with a cookie. This one's got a buttery base, a toasty coconut overcoat, and a rich, smooth, coconut ganache center.

The bonus here is that if you've got any ganache filling leftover at the end of the cookie parade, you can store it in a glass jar with a lid (it'll last a few weeks in the fridge) and rewarm the stuff before pouring it over a bowl of ice cream—instant homemade Magic Shell!

---

3 cups all-purpose flour, plus extra
    for working the dough
1 teaspoon kosher salt
¾ pound (3 sticks) unsalted butter,
    at room temperature
1 cup sugar
2 teaspoons pure vanilla extract
2 large eggs

1 cup sweetened, shredded coconut
¾ cup semisweet chocolate chips
3 tablespoons solid coconut oil
    (see Note)
Flaky sea salt (such as Maldon,
    see box on page 234),
    for sprinkling

LET'S COOK:

1. Preheat the oven to 350°F with a rack in the center position. Line a sheet pan with parchment paper.

2. Whisk together the flour and salt in a medium-size bowl.

3. Cream the butter and sugar in a stand mixer fitted with the paddle, or in a large bowl with a handheld electric mixer, on high speed, until light and fluffy, about 3 minutes. Add the vanilla and beat to combine.

4. Add the flour to the butter mixture in three additions, mixing on low speed just until the dough starts to come together.

5. Lightly flour a work surface. Dump out the dough onto the surface and gather it into a ball. Use a 1¼-inch ice cream scoop to portion the dough into balls, and place them on a large plate or piece of parchment.

6. Beat the eggs in a small bowl until smooth. Place the shredded coconut on a plate. One at a time, roll the dough balls first in the eggs, coating them thoroughly, then in the coconut. Place the dough balls on the prepared pan, spacing them about an inch apart.

7. Use the handle end of a wooden spoon, dipped in flour, to create a uniform "thumbprint" indentation in the center of each cookie.

8. Refrigerate the cookies before baking, 20 to 30 minutes. This will ensure they keep their shape in the oven.

9. Bake the cookies for 10 minutes. Remove the pan from the oven and re-press the indentations with the spoon handle. Return the pan to the oven and bake until the cookies are golden brown, another 10 minutes. Let cool completely on the pan.

10. While the cookies are cooling, make the ganache: Pour water to a depth of 2 inches into a saucepan, and bring to a boil over medium-high heat. Place the chocolate chips and coconut oil in a heatproof bowl and set it over the pan so the bottom of the bowl rests just above the surface of the water. Whisk the chocolate mixture until it is smooth. Let the ganache cool slightly (it shouldn't feel hot to the touch) before drizzling it into the cookie thumbprints.

11. Top the cookies with a sprinkle of sea salt, and enjoy immediately, while the chocolate centers are still warm and gooey, or after about 20 minutes, when the centers have hardened and set.

   The cookies will keep, in an airtight container at room temperature, for 3 to 4 days.

NOTE: Solid coconut oil is available at most natural foods supermarkets, such as Whole Foods.

ESPRESSO BISCOTTI

MAKES ABOUT 36 BISCOTTI

I like cookies dunked in my coffee, so it stands to reason that coffee in my cookies is something I can get behind. These biscotti are crisp-edged and tender-centered, shot through with both espresso powder and chocolate-covered espresso beans. As cookies go, these little lovelies are on the adult end of the spectrum, meant to be dipped artfully in a hot cup of coffee or tea for a good morning jolt or a sweet and crumbly afternoon pick-me-up.

3¼ cups all-purpose flour, plus extra for shaping the dough
1 tablespoon baking powder
1 teaspoon kosher salt
1½ cups sugar
10 tablespoons (1¼ sticks) unsalted butter, melted and cooled
3 large eggs

2 tablespoons instant espresso powder
1 tablespoon coffee liqueur, such as Kahlúa, or 1 teaspoon pure coffee extract
1 tablespoon pure vanilla extract
1 cup chopped chocolate-covered espresso beans
1 large egg white

LET'S COOK:

1. Preheat the oven to 350°F with a rack in the center position. Line a sheet pan with parchment paper.

2. Whisk together the flour, baking powder, and salt in a medium-size bowl.

3. Whisk the sugar, butter, eggs, espresso powder, liqueur, and vanilla in a large bowl until smooth. Add the flour mixture and stir with a rubber spatula until the dough is well combined. Stir in the espresso beans.

4. Generously flour a work surface and your hands. Divide the dough in half and shape each piece into a 2½-by-15-inch rectangular log about 1½ inches thick. Place the logs on the prepared pan, spacing them evenly apart.

5. Beat the egg white in a small bowl until frothy. Brush the logs gently with the egg white. Bake them until golden brown (they will begin to smell fantastic), about 30 minutes.

6. Remove the pan from the oven but leave the oven on. Let the logs cool completely on the pan.

7. Transfer the cooled logs to a cutting board. Use a serrated knife to slice them, on a slight diagonal, into roughly ½-inch-thick biscotti. Lay the biscotti cut side down on the sheet pan still lined with parchment.

8. Bake the biscotti again, carefully flipping them halfway through, until golden on both sides, an additional 20 minutes.

9. Let the biscotti cool completely on the pan.

    The biscotti will keep, in an airtight container at room temperature, for up to 2 weeks.

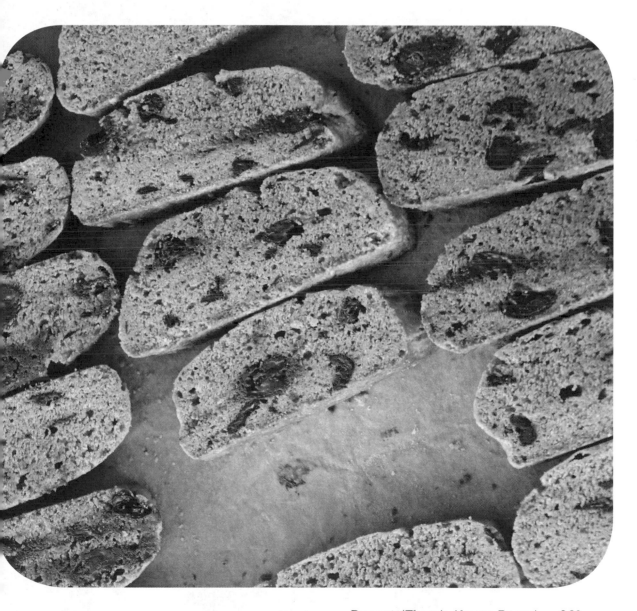

HALLOWEEN CANDY S'MORES

SERVES 12

S'mores meet Halloween! Purists may scoff, but that's cool because more for us. Besides, it's hard to argue when your mouth is full of sweet, salty, peanut-butter-cup–marshmallow-graham gooeyness. I just love how the broiler steps up to let us have this classic summertime staple even in the colder months, or when we need to please a s'more-hungry crowd.

You can use your favorite chocolate candy for this special treat—"fun-size" Halloween candy definitely fits the bill (I'm into mini Kit Kats and Almond Joys, or regular-size Reese's cups), but luckily, leftover candy from Easter, Valentine's Day, and Christmas make it possible for us to have creative holiday-themed s'mores year round.

---

12 graham crackers, broken into 24 squares

12 pieces "fun-size" chocolate candy
12 marshmallows

LET'S COOK:

1. Preheat the broiler with a rack about 4 inches from the heat. Line a sheet pan with aluminum foil (not essential but it makes cleanup easier).

2. Lay half of the graham cracker squares on the prepared pan and top each with a piece of candy. Place a marshmallow on top of each piece of candy.

3. Place the pan on the rack under the broiler. Watch carefully for the marshmallows to brown on top— it can take as little as 20 seconds, depending on your oven.

4. Remove the pan from the oven and carefully use a pair of kitchen tongs to flip each marshmallow over so the uncooked side now faces up. Broil the s'mores, again watching carefully, until the second side of each marshmallow is good and toasty, another 20 seconds or so.

5. Remove the pan from the oven and top each of the marshmallows with one of the remaining graham crackers, smushing them together gently. Enjoy immediately!

CHOCOLATE CANDY BARK

MAKES ABOUT 4 CUPS BARK

This fun and creative treat makes a wonderful holiday or hostess gift (it keeps well) and is an absolute snap to make. The chocolate melts right on the pan itself—all you have to do is spread it out and scatter tasty treats atop.

You can use this as a base recipe. It's extremely customizable—you make the bark using any kind of chocolate you please (or multiple kinds, all at once) and the toppings are pretty much limitless (see box for more ideas).

3 cups chocolate chips (dark, milk, and/or white, depending on your preference)

About 2 cups toppings such as crushed Oreo cookies, peppermint candies, or English toffee; coarsely broken pretzels or potato chips; coarsely chopped Reese's Pieces or M&M's

LET'S COOK:

1. Preheat the oven to 325°F with a rack in the center position. Line a sheet pan with parchment paper.

2. Spread out the chocolate chips in an even layer in the center of the sheet pan; leave the edges bare.

3. Bake the chocolate chips until they've started to melt but still hold their shape, 5 to 7 minutes.

4. Remove the pan from the oven and use a small offset or rubber spatula to spread the melting chocolate evenly around the pan. If you're using more than one type of chocolate and don't want them to mix, wipe the spatula between spreadings.

5. Immediately sprinkle the topping(s) evenly over the melted chocolate, gently pressing them down so they'll adhere. Refrigerate the bark, uncovered, until the chocolate is firm and the toppings have set, about 1 hour.

6. Use your hands to gently break the bark into 2- or 3-inch pieces, working quickly so the chocolate doesn't melt.

The bark will keep, in an airtight container in the refrigerator, for up to 5 days with absorbent toppings like chips, cookies, and pretzels; up to 2 weeks with hard candies, nuts, and dried fruit.

SALTED ROSEMARY TOFFEE CRUNCH

SERVES 15 TO 20

Crunchity crack. With a side of sea salt. I've seen versions of this recipe that use matzoh or saltine crackers as the base for the buttery toffee on top, but I love the complexity of flavor and slight sophistication that using rosemary crackers brings. I also love the look and flavor of sea salt, but you can feel free to toss other toppings over the melted chocolate layer—roasted pistachios, chopped dried apricots, or cocoa nibs would all be great choices.

---

2 boxes (5 ounces each) rosemary crackers (I like Carr's or La Panzanella)
½ pound (2 sticks) unsalted butter
1 cup packed light brown sugar

1 teaspoon kosher salt
2 bags (10 to 11 ounces each) dark or bittersweet chocolate chips
1 tablespoon coarse sea salt

LET'S COOK:

1. Preheat the oven to 375°F with a rack in the center position. Line a sheet pan with aluminum foil or parchment paper.

2. Arrange the crackers in a single layer on the prepared pan. Don't worry if they overlap a little bit.

3. Melt the butter in a small saucepan over medium-low heat. (Alternatively, microwave it in a heatproof bowl on medium power in 30-second intervals until melted.) Add the brown sugar and kosher salt and whisk until dissolved and smooth. Pour evenly over the crackers.

4. Bake until the toffee topping is bubbly and looks sticky, about 7 minutes.

5. Remove the pan from the oven and sprinkle the chocolate chips in an even layer atop the crackers and toffee. Return the pan to the oven and bake until the chocolate melts, 1 minute. Remove the pan from the oven again and use a small heatproof spatula to spread the melted chocolate over the crackers until evenly coated. Sprinkle the sea salt on top.

6. Refrigerate until the toffee has cooled completely and the chocolate is firm, about 30 minutes. Break the toffee crunch into bite-size pieces and enjoy!

The toffee crunch will keep, in an airtight container in the refrigerator, for a few weeks.

IN-AN-APPLE CRISP

SERVES 8

I ndividual apple crisps are a fun mash-up of baked apples and apple crisp, where the apples serve as single-serving bowls for the oaty-crisp bits. Cute and clever as they are, these heat-slouched, oat-filled apples are surprisingly versatile—serve them with thick Greek yogurt instead of vanilla ice cream, and you could absolutely call this brunch.

8 medium-size baking apples
    (I like Honeycrisp or Pink Lady),
    unpeeled
1 lemon
¾ cup old-fashioned rolled oats (not
    quick-cooking)
¼ cup packed dark brown sugar

3 tablespoons cold unsalted butter,
    cut in ¼-inch cubes
½ teaspoon ground cinnamon
¼ teaspoon ground nutmeg
¼ teaspoon ground ginger
½ teaspoon kosher salt
¼ cup coarsely chopped walnuts
Vanilla ice cream, for serving

LET'S COOK:

1. Preheat the oven to 350°F with a rack in the center position. Line a sheet pan with parchment paper.

2. Core the apples and use a spoon to gently hollow out the centers, leaving at least a ½-inch border around the edge. Arrange the apples scooped side up on the prepared pan, spacing them evenly apart.

3. Cut the lemon in half and squeeze its juice into the hollow of each apple. (This will both flavor the apples and prevent their flesh from turning brown.)

4. Stir together the oats, brown sugar, butter, cinnamon, nutmeg, ginger, salt, and walnuts in a small bowl.

Generously spoon the oat mixture into the apple hollows, mounding it on top and sprinkling a bit around each apple as well.

5. Bake the apples until they have slumped and puckered, are knife-tender, and the crumbly tops are brown and crisp, 45 minutes to 1 hour.

6. Let the apples cool slightly before serving, topped with ice cream and the brittle-like mixture that has caramelized on the pan.

    The apples will keep, in an airtight container in the refrigerator, for 2 to 3 days. To reheat them, microwave them individually, in heatproof bowls, for 1 minute.

ALMOND-CHERRY JAM CROSTATA

SERVES 10 TO 15

In truth, this treat is less like a crostata (a kind of Italian free-form pie) and more like a giant butter cookie. Personally, I don't mind in the slightest. It assembles like a crostata—sweet cherry jam and slivered almonds (a pretty and complementarily flavored pair) are wrapped up informally in a soft, buttery disk of dough—but the whole thing slumps into itself in the oven, blurring the lines of dough and filling to create the giant-cookie effect. It's crisp at the edges and sticky with jam in the center, and the toasted almonds give it a good final crunch. Sliced into imperfect squares, it makes an excellent afternoon pick-me-up with some cold milk or hot tea.

½ pound (2 sticks) unsalted butter, at room temperature
½ cup plus 2 tablespoons sugar
1 teaspoon pure vanilla extract
½ teaspoon pure almond extract

1¾ cups plus 2 tablespoons all-purpose flour, plus extra for rolling out the dough
⅔ cup cherry jam or preserves
⅓ cup sliced blanched almonds

LET'S COOK:

1. Preheat the oven to 350°F with a rack in the center position.

2. Cream the butter and sugar in a stand mixer fitted with the paddle, or in a large bowl with a handheld electric mixer, on high speed until light and fluffy, about 3 minutes. Add the vanilla and almond extracts and mix well on medium speed to combine. Add the flour all at once and mix on low speed until a crumbly dough comes together.

3. Scoop out ½ cup of the dough, wrap it in plastic, and refrigerate it.

4. Lightly flour a rolling pin and a piece of parchment paper large enough to line a sheet pan. Gather the remaining dough into a disk about 1 inch thick, and place it on the parchment. Roll out the dough to a large oval about 14 inches long, 10 inches wide, and ¼ inch thick. The dough will be quite soft, so work quickly. Transfer the dough, still on the parchment, to a sheet pan.

5. Spread the jam thickly over the dough, leaving a 1-inch border all around. Sprinkle the almonds over the jam, then gently fold the bare edges of the dough toward the center, pleating it as necessary, to create a free-form crust. Use your fingers to crumble the refrigerated dough into small pieces, sprinkling it over the almonds and jam.

6. Bake the crostata until the edges are deeply brown and the jam is bubbling, 35 to 40 minutes.

7. Let the crostata cool slightly and firm up before slicing it into squares. Serve warm or at room temperature. The crostata will keep, in an airtight container at room temperature, for 4 to 5 days.

STONE FRUIT SLAB PIE
SERVES 24 TO 30

Sweet and flaky summer fruit pie for a crowd—what could be better? The concept of slab pie is pretty genius; you get all of the perks of traditional pie (juicy fruit, brown and buttery crust, and a sweet, fragrant glaze), plus the added bonuses of volume and portability. The square slices are easily picked up and eaten out of hand, no utensils necessary (unless you want to serve it with ice cream, of course). It's a perfect dessert for that big family get-together by the beach on July 4th, or perhaps a summer block party in the neighborhood. Pie for all!

If you make this with thin-skinned fruits like nectarines, plums, or apricots, there's no need to peel them first. However you'll want to blanch and peel fuzzy-skinned peaches—see the box on page 281 for instructions.

---

5 cups all-purpose flour, plus extra for rolling out the dough
3 tablespoons granulated sugar
2½ teaspoons kosher salt
1 pound (4 sticks) very cold butter, cut into small cubes
About 1 cup ice-cold water

10 cups sliced stone fruit, peeled if necessary (about 4 pounds)
¼ cup freshly squeezed lemon juice (from about 1 lemon)
¾ cup packed dark brown sugar
¼ cup plus 2 tablespoons cornstarch
1 large egg
1 cup confectioners' sugar

LET'S COOK:

1. Whisk together the flour, granulated sugar, and 2 teaspoons of the salt in a large bowl. Add the butter and use your fingertips or a pastry cutter to work it into the flour. Work quickly to avoid letting the butter become too warm. When you're done, you'll have butter pieces the size of small lentils and large pebbles.

2. Add the cold water ½ cup at a time, working it in with a wooden spoon. Once the dough starts to come together, ditch the spoon and use your hands to gather the dough into a large, cohesive ball. If it's too dry and crumbly, add more water until it really comes together, but try not to overwork the dough—no kneading here.

3. Divide the dough into two equal pieces and wrap each one tightly with plastic wrap. Refrigerate them for at least 1 hour, up to 2 days.

4. While the dough chills, prepare the fruit filling: Place the fruit in a large bowl, add the lemon juice, brown sugar, cornstarch, and the remaining ½ teaspoon salt and toss gently to combine and coat the fruit thoroughly. Transfer the fruit filling to a large colander set over another bowl and allow the fruit to drain until ¼ cup juice has collected in the bowl, about 20 minutes.

5. When you're ready to bake, preheat the oven to 350°F with a rack in the center position.

6. Generously flour a work surface and a rolling pin. Unwrap one piece of dough. Roll out the dough to an 18-by-12-inch rectangle about ¼ inch thick. Work quickly so the dough doesn't get too warm and become difficult to work with. If it does, transfer the dough to a parchment-lined sheet pan and pop it back in the refrigerator or into the freezer for a few minutes to firm up.

7. Flour your hands and carefully transfer the rolled-out pie crust to a sheet pan: Gently fold the dough in half like a book, set it over the pan with the folded edge over the center of the pan, and unfold it once it's there safely. Gently press and lift the dough up and over the edges of the pan on all sides; the crust should hang over by about ½ inch.

8. Using a slotted spoon, transfer the fruit to the crust, spreading it in an even layer. Reserve any juice that has collected in the bowl. Set the pie aside, ideally in the refrigerator (if you have room), while you roll out the top crust.

9. Roll out the second piece of dough in the same manner as the first, this time ending up with an 18-by-13-inch rectangle. Use your favorite 2-inch cookie cutter to cut a steam vent or two from the center of the top crust, or use a sharp knife to make a few thin slits (if you use a cookie cutter, either discard the cutouts or place them decoratively

over the top crust once the pie is assembled). Carefully drape the top crust over the filling, using the same folded-book technique as in Step 7. Use kitchen shears to trim any dough that hangs more than ½ inch over the edges of the pan.

10. Use well-floured hands to pinch the top and bottom crusts together gently. Fold the overhanging dough under itself toward the edges of the pan and tuck it inside the pan. Use a fork to crimp the edges of the crust all the way around.

11. Whisk the egg and 1 teaspoon water in a small bowl to combine. Brush the top of the pie with the egg wash.

12. Bake the pie on the center rack, rotating the pan halfway through, until the crust is deeply golden brown and the filling is bubbling, 60 to 70 minutes.

13. Place the pan on a wire rack to cool until the pie is just warm to the touch.

14. While the pie cools, whisk together the confectioners' sugar and 5 tablespoons of the reserved fruit juice in a small bowl until smooth. Drizzle the glaze on top of the warm pie with a spoon or whisk; it will harden as the pie cools.

15. Cut the pie into squares and serve warm (with delicious runny glaze) or at room temperature (with delicious hardened glaze).

The pie will keep, well wrapped in aluminum foil or plastic, in the refrigerator for 3 to 4 days.

TEACH ME HOW

TO PEEL A PEACH

With the right technique, it's easy to peel peaches—all you need is a paring knife, a big pot of boiling water, a slotted spoon, and a large bowl filled with lots of ice cubes and water (called an "ice bath" in professional kitchens). Here's how it's done:

1. Use the paring knife to cut a small × in the bottom of each peach, opposite the stem end.

2. Drop the peaches into the boiling water and leave them there for 30 seconds.

3. Use the slotted spoon to transfer the peaches from the boiling water to the ice bath. Let them sit in the ice bath for 30 seconds.

4. Use your fingers to peel the skin off the blanched peaches, starting from the little X you cut earlier. It should slip right off!

APPLE GALETTE

SERVES 8

In college I majored in French, so I can say with some authority that *galette* is just a fancy French word for "lazy man's pie." Then again, it's been kind of a while since I graduated and my memory is *pas très bien* . . .

So maybe I need to brush up on my French vocabulary, but I've been pretty fluent in French pastry for a while, and I can confidently say that whatever its literal meaning, a galette is, in fact, a lazy man's pie—it's got all the makings of a pie (crust and filling), just without the pie dish, precision, or fuss. A galette is forgiving. Messy is fine. We can call it "rustic" and serve it for company. Tender crust, warm apples with sugar and spice, all topped with a pile of melting ice cream—how could you say *non*?

---

2 cups all-purpose flour, plus extra
    for rolling out the dough
½ teaspoon kosher salt
⅓ cup plus 1 tablespoon sugar
12 tablespoons (1½ sticks) cold
    unsalted butter, cut into small cubes
½ cup ice-cold water
4 large apples (I like Granny Smith,
    Golden Delicious, or a mix of both)
Juice of 1 lemon

½ teaspoon ground cinnamon
Pinch of ground nutmeg
2 tablespoons salted butter, cut into
    very small cubes
1 egg, beaten, or ½ cup heavy cream
    (for brushing the crust)
½ cup apricot jam
Vanilla or salted caramel ice cream,
    for serving (optional)

LET'S COOK:

1. To make the dough, place the flour, salt, and 1 tablespoon of the sugar in a food processor. Pulse for about 5 seconds to combine. Add the unsalted butter and pulse about 10 times, until the butter has been processed into bits of various sizes. Pour the cold water down the feed tube, then pulse the mixture until the dough starts to come together.

2. Lightly flour a work surface. Dump out the dough onto the surface. Flour your hands and gather the dough into a flat disk; it will be a bit wet and sticky. Wrap it tightly in plastic wrap and refrigerate it until firm, at least 1 hour, up to 1 day. (Alternatively, chill it in the freezer for about 30 minutes.)

3. Preheat the oven to 400°F with a rack in the center position. Line a sheet pan with parchment paper.

4. Clean and generously flour the work surface and rolling pin. Unwrap the dough, set it on the surface, and roll it out to a 15-by-12-inch rectangle, about ¼ inch thick. Carefully transfer the dough to the prepared pan, handling it gently. Place the pan, uncovered, in the refrigerator or freezer, to firm up the dough while you prepare the apple filling, about 10 minutes.

5. Peel, core, and slice the apples into ¼-inch-thick slices. Place the slices in a large bowl, drizzle the lemon juice over them, and toss very gently to coat. Mix together the cinnamon, nutmeg, and the remaining ⅓ cup sugar in a small bowl.

6. Remove the dough from the refrigerator or freezer. Arrange the apple slices in tight, overlapping rows down the middle of the rectangle, leaving a 1-inch border on all sides. Generously sprinkle the apples with the sugar mixture and dot them with the salted butter. Fold the dough border over the apples, overlapping it where necessary, to create a free-form crust.

7. Brush the exposed crust with the beaten egg. Bake the galette until both the crust and apple edges are deeply brown, 45 to 60 minutes. Let the galette cool for 5 minutes.

8. While the galette is cooling, combine the apricot jam with 2 tablespoons of water in a small saucepan over medium heat and whisk until smooth. Brush the apples with the apricot glaze. Allow the glaze to set until no longer runny, about 10 minutes.

9. Slice the galette into big squares and serve it warm with generous scoops of ice cream. The galette also does well at room temperature alongside some coffee or tea.

   The galette will keep, well wrapped in plastic or aluminum foil, in the refrigerator for 4 to 5 days.

CONVERSION TABLES

Please note that all conversions are approximate but close enough to be useful when converting from one system to another.

OVEN TEMPERATURES

FAHRENHEIT	GAS MARK	CELSIUS
250	½	120
275	1	140
300	2	150
325	3	160
350	4	180
375	5	190
400	6	200
425	7	220
450	8	230
475	9	240
500	10	260

NOTE: Reduce the temperature by 20°C (68°F) for fan-assisted ovens.

APPROXIMATE EQUIVALENTS

1 stick butter = 8 tbs = 4 oz = ½ cup = 115 g

1 cup all-purpose presifted flour = 4.7 oz

1 cup granulated sugar = 8 oz = 220 g

1 cup (firmly packed) brown sugar = 6 oz = 220 g to 230 g

1 cup confectioners' sugar = 4½ oz = 115 g

1 cup honey or syrup = 12 oz

1 cup grated cheese = 4 oz

1 cup dried beans = 6 oz

1 large egg = about 2 oz or about 3 tbs

1 egg yolk = about 1 tbs

1 egg white = about 2 tbs

LIQUID CONVERSIONS

U.S.	IMPERIAL	METRIC
2 tbs	1 fl oz	30 ml
3 tbs	1½ fl oz	45 ml
¼ cup	2 fl oz	60 ml
⅓ cup	2½ fl oz	75 ml
⅓ cup + 1 tbs	3 fl oz	90 ml
⅓ cup + 2 tbs	3½ fl oz	100 ml
½ cup	4 fl oz	125 ml
⅔ cup	5 fl oz	150 ml
¾ cup	6 fl oz	175 ml
¾ cup + 2 tbs	7 fl oz	200 ml
1 cup	8 fl oz	250 ml
1 cup + 2 tbs	9 fl oz	275 ml
1¼ cups	10 fl oz	300 ml
1⅓ cups	11 fl oz	325 ml
1½ cups	12 fl oz	350 ml
1⅔ cups	13 fl oz	375 ml
1¾ cups	14 fl oz	400 ml
1¾ cups + 2 tbs	15 fl oz	450 ml
2 cups (1 pint)	16 fl oz	500 ml
2½ cups	20 fl oz (1 pint)	600 ml
3¾ cups	1½ pints	900 ml
4 cups	1¾ pints	1 liter

WEIGHT CONVERSIONS

U.S./U.K.	METRIC	U.S./U.K.	METRIC
½ oz	15 g	7 oz	200 g
1 oz	30 g	8 oz	250 g
1½ oz	45 g	9 oz	275 g
2 oz	60 g	10 oz	300 g
2½ oz	75 g	11 oz	325 g
3 oz	90 g	12 oz	350 g
3½ oz	100 g	13 oz	375 g
4 oz	125 g	14 oz	400 g
5 oz	150 g	15 oz	450 g
6 oz	175 g	1 lb	500 g

INDEX

C

Cabbage-apple slaw, warm, thick-cut pork chops with, 125–26

Caesar salad dressing, buying, 161

Caesar salad garlic bread, 160–61, *161*

Cakes:
  cannoli roulade, 248–50, *249*
  carrot layer, with cream cheese frosting, 255–57, *256*
  chocolate sheet, Italian, 258–59, *259*
  coffee crumb, 218–19, *219*
  flourless chocolate, "get your own," 251–52, *252*
  orange cardamom pound, 246–47, *247*

Cannoli roulade, 248–50, *249*

Caprese turkey burgers & sweet potato wedge fries, 42–44, *43*

Carrot(s):
  buttered, & herby breadcrumbs, rack of lamb with, 137–39, *138*
  layer cake with cream cheese frosting, 255–57, *256*

Cashew(s):
  -coconut granola with apricot & mango, 235–36
  spicy brown sugar–rosemary, 38, *39*

Cauliflower, curried chicken with apricots & olives, 54–55, *55*

Cheese:
  apple, prosciutto & radicchio pizza, 140–42, *141*
  baked Brie & strawberries, 8, *9*
  baked feta & chunky mango chutney, 10–11, *11*

bbq chicken nachos, 18–19, *19*

biscuits, Nana's spicy, 30–31, *31*

blue, dressing, DIY, 64

broiled steak & asparagus with feta cream sauce, 117–18, *118*

butter-roasted apricots with boozy whipped mascarpone, 240–41, *241*

Caesar salad garlic bread, 160–61, *161*

cannoli roulade, 248–50, *249*

caprese turkey burgers & sweet potato wedge fries, 42–44, *43*

cheeseburgers with bacon & charred onion, 121–22

cheesy baked polenta with mixed herbs, 192

cheesy herb focaccia, *188*, 189–90

chicken Parmesan, 58–59, *59*

cream, frosting, carrot layer cake with, 255–57, *256*

crispy mushroom & burrata crostini, 28–29, *29*

fancy tuna melts, 104–5, *105*

goat, hearty ratatouille with, *152*, 153–54

goat, herbed, & zucchini tart, 14–15, *15*

Greek stuffed roly-poly squash, 166–67, *167*

grilled, smoked Cheddar & apple, 177–78, *178*

ham & Swiss pastry braid, 229–30, *230*

Italian chocolate sheet cake, 258–59, *259*

& Italian meat stromboli, 143–44, *144*

lasagna'd Hasselback potatoes, 145–46, *146*

pepperoni French bread pizza, 147–48, *148*

pesto sauce, 44

portabella cap pizzas with garlic knots, 179–80, *180*

roasted beet & orange salad with pistachios & feta, 155–57, *156*

roasted fennel panzanella, 158, *159*

roasted figs with Gorgonzola & honey, 12

roasted sausage & red grapes with polenta & Gorgonzola, 133

spaghetti squash "noodle" bowls, 162–63, *163*

spanakopita with yogurt sauce, 24–25

sun-dried tomato–stuffed chicken & chard, 56–57

Cheeseburger, variations, 122

Cheeseburgers with bacon & charred onion, 121–22

Cherry jam–almond crostata, 277–79, *278*

Chicken:
  & baby broccoli, quick, with spicy peanut sauce, 52–53, *53*
  bbq, nachos, 18–19, *19*
  & black bean enchiladas, 65–66
  curried, with cauliflower, apricots & olives, 54–55, *55*
  & chard, sun-dried tomato–stuffed, 56–57
  drumsticks, Buffalo, & charred romaine, *62*, 63–64
  Jerome, 51
  legs with fennel & orange, 60–61
  Parmesan, 58–59, *59*

MOLLY GILBERT, a graduate of Amherst College and the French Culinary Institute, is a cooking instructor, food blogger (dunkandcrumble.com), former private chef, and recipe tester in the kitchen of *Saveur*. She lives in Seattle with her husband, Ben.